CW00551754

GRACEWING

PUBLISHING

REVIEW COPY

We enclose, for review, a copy of

God's Wild Flowers
Saints with Disabilities

Price: £12.99.

Date:

Please send us a voucher copy of any
review you publish.

Gracewing Ltd · Gracewing House
2 Southern Avenue · Leominster · Herefordshire · HR6 0QF · England
Tel: 01568 616835 · Fax: 01568 613289 · E-mail: gracewingx@aol.com
Web site: www.gracewing.co.uk

GOD'S WILD FLOWERS

For Bev and Elizabeth

He set before me the book of nature; I understood that all the flowers He has created are beautiful, how the splendour of the rose and the whiteness of the lily do not take away the perfume of the little violet or the delightful simplicity of the daisy. I understood that if all flowers wanted to be roses, nature would lose her springtime beauty, and the fields would no longer be decked out with little wild flowers. And so it is in the world of souls, Jesus' garden. He willed to create great souls comparable to lilies and roses, but He has created smaller ones and these must be content to be daisies or violets destined to give joy to God's glances when He looks down at His feet. Perfection consists in doing His will, in being what He wills us to be.

Saint Thérèse of Lisieux, *The Story of a Soul*, Chapter I

GOD'S WILD FLOWERS
SAINTS WITH DISABILITIES

PIA MATTHEWS

GRACEWING

First published in 2016
by
Gracewing
2 Southern Avenue
Leominster
Herefordshire HR6 0QF
United Kingdom
www.gracewing.co.uk

ISBN 978 085244 881 6

Typeset by Gracewing

Cover design by Bernardita Peña Hurtado

CONTENTS

5 Slow learners, fools for God, the simple and the pure in heart..107

6 Bearing the weight of the world...................................125

7 Belonging to Jesus to the end: cancer, tuberculosis and terminal diseases

PREFACE

I DO NOT OFTEN tell people that we have a disabled daughter. This has nothing to do with an attitude to disability or concern about what others might think. Rather, when strangers out of small talk ask me about our children I begin with the eldest and, by the time I get to Paula, the fifth child of eight, most of these polite inquirers have already lost interest. If attention is retained as far as Paula the common reaction, combined with pity for Paula's condition, Rett Syndrome, is that we were extraordinarily brave or perhaps reckless to go on to have three further children after Paula. If it then becomes known that I write and teach on moral theology, bioethics and healthcare, two things are commonly assumed: firstly, that our daughter's disability is the rationale for my choice of academic subjects and secondly, that at some point, I must have been very angry with, but am now presumably reconciled to God. In fact, I completed further studies in bioethics and healthcare after my theology degree because, having studied in a Catholic seminary and being female, I had no plans to continue studies with my fellow male students, who were all seminarians. Their further year involved training for the priesthood. An MA in bioethics and then a PhD was for me a door that opened at the opportune moment. And I have never been angry with God.

I was recently asked to write a paper with the title
'God, why me?' for a conference concerned with
disability and the family. I suspect that I would not
have been able to say what I did if I did not 'have' a
child with disabilities. That gives some kind of licence,
a privileged view that is, at least to a certain extent,
immune from criticism. I am what is known as a
'primary source'. Certainly I cannot censure anyone
for questioning or being angry with God. After all, look
at Job, King David when his son fell gravely ill, the
disciples seeking to apportion blame for the man born
blind as recounted in Saint John's Gospel. Instead, in
essence, in my paper, I pointed out that if their child
is bright or talented or good looking, parents tend not
to refer to God but to a good genetic inheritance or
successful parenting, a good upbringing. The 'why me'
question is raised when a child is 'not quite what was
expected', when the 'normal' run of things—growing
up, developing sense, wisdom, practical skills, leaving
home, forming relationships—is not going to happen
in the anticipated way. Perhaps not unsurprisingly,
parents would rather a physical disability than an
intellectual one. The 'why me' is at times questioning
whether *I* can cope, whether *I* can deal with the
inevitable extra healthcare needs or shortened life,
whether *I* can overcome the grief of a perceived lost
'normal' future for my child, whether *I* can manage
the stares or discriminatory comments. Certainly these
are real and difficult questions for many parents and
they require new strategies, sometimes involvement
from teams of professionals, understanding and help
from relatives and friends. A 'thick skin'. Often a fight
for services, help, access to what other people take for
granted. Sometimes, even a period of mourning what

could have been. However, I think we need to look harder at the 'God, why me?' question.

So, God, why *me?* Each child is unique. Of course, some people object to the use of the word 'unique' and, in particular to the word 'special' to describe children with disabilities. After all, they say, we are all unique and special and so therefore the words are meaningless: no one is special if we are all special. Nevertheless, I would say that this is not the common experience of parents. Each child is special, whether disabled or abled. 'Specialness' does not reduce children to the same. And in Catholic thinking, not only is every human being unique, every human being is also a gift. So, for me, the 'God, why me' question raises a much more interesting issue: not why did God pick on me to be the parent of a disabled child, but rather, from the perspective of the person with disabilities, why *me, me* as this gift. Then, unpicking the question further, not why was I born this way but what is it that you, God, have in mind for me? Catholic teaching has always set great store by the idea of vocation and co-operation: in the Gospels, Jesus personally calls people and they respond. Sometimes the vocation is not expected. Saint Mark writes of the cure of the Gerasene demoniac. After his cure the man begs to be allowed to stay with Jesus but he is sent back home, though also charged with proclaiming what the Lord has done for him. Sometimes the response is unexpected. Saint Matthew tells of the rich young man who has loved God and loved his neighbour and is being personally addressed by Jesus, eye to eye as it were, but he cannot bring himself to give up his possessions and follow the Lord. We do not know what became of the young man. The 'God, why me' question is really about God—what have you chosen *me* for. Whatever my abilities, capacities, whether disabled or abled, the question is, 'what is my unique call and vocation and how am I going to respond?'

And this raises interesting questions about those with profound disabilities. I would like to explain about profound disability. This is from our daughter Paula's point of view, though it has to be said that this is pure speculation on my behalf. Paula cannot tell me how she sees the world. Rett Syndrome is a rare and pervasive developmental disorder that leads to profound, multiple and complex disabilities. Disabilities are physical and intellectual/mental. The person with Rett Syndrome is totally dependent and requires twenty-four hour care. The condition slowly becomes apparent over the first year and a half of life as the child fails to develop 'normally' (if there is such a thing) and begins, in the destructive phase of the disorder, to lose what little skills she has gained in the first few months of life. There is no cure, the symptoms are often difficult to manage, life span is often shortened. It is a genetic disorder, meaning there is an abnormality on one of the genes, but more often than not it is a spontaneous mutation. It can happen to anyone. It really is pure gift. When I watch our four month old grand-daughter engage with the world around her, with her parents, reaching out to grasp books, copy and communicate by a smile in return for a smile I notice just how Paula is stuck. At twenty two, at twelve, at two, Paula was outstripped by any three to four month old infant.

Imagine you are curled up in bed. You cannot move position unless you find yourself rolling over because you cannot work out the strategies for moving one leg and then the other, or one arm and then the next. Sitting up or getting out of the bed are simply beyond your thinking abilities. So you are stuck where you find yourself. You have opened your eyes but you do not know if it is day or night, time to get up or go to sleep, and anyway, these are all meaningless without someone there to get you up or tuck in the blankets or arrange what you are to do. Either you wait to drift back to sleep again or shout a bit and see what happens. You sing a little to yourself, waiting to see if anyone comes. No one comes, and after a while, you fall asleep again. You do not know that Daddy is there listening as he does every night. Waiting to see if you need anything, if you will go back to sleep. Experience has told him that, if he goes in to see you, then you are happy to see him. It is nice to see him, worth keeping yourself awake, however tired you are. It could be play time. But it is past midnight and you should be asleep.

People come in to see if you are awake and say 'good morning', they break into your consciousness for a brief moment, they come and go. At this point, it is necessary to say that although you can see and hear, you find the processing part a bit difficult and you have a huge time delay. It takes literally minutes for you to realise something is happening and then to make sense of what that thing is. Fortunately, it is the same people who come and go, so it is much easier to grasp who it is: it has become instinct. The advantage of lots of brothers and sisters who take time with you. So when they go, you can laugh to yourself because you know who was there with you. There was a time when you could walk by yourself and go after them, but not anymore. Then there is being got up, washed, pad changed, dressed, given breakfast, teeth and hair brushed, made ready for the day. The day is whatever other people decide is to happen.

Imagine someone has just called your name. 'Paula'. You think about it and. 'Paula'. You hear it again and just as you. Someone says 'Paula' again. Then again, 'Paula'. An object appears as you are trying to think of your name. Hard juice mug hits your closed teeth or a spoon arrives. You were not ready. 'So', the voice says, 'Paula you're not hungry, you don't want a drink?' and the food and drink disappear. And you are so close to working it all out but stuck on that 'Paula' again. Imagine someone calls your name. There is someone reaching out to you, and you love people. You want to reach out too, but your time delay means you do not react straight away. Moreover you cannot do two things at once: you cannot look at the person and reach out at the same time. So you look away and a few minutes later, when you have worked out what to do, you turn to look and reach but the person has gone, turned away, without waiting. Imagine you have noticed something interesting. You stare at it. You cannot reach it or say anything, but you can look hard at a person who is also there then look hard again at the thing in the hopes that the person realises you are eye pointing, trying to communicate. The person does not see. This is quite a tiring exercise. Maybe it is not worth doing it again in the future.

You have perceptual difficulties. Imagine that you cannot work out if lines on the floor are marks or steps or insurmountable barriers. When the floor pattern changes you do not know if you are going to step from something solid to something spongy. When the floor pattern changes you do not know if you are going to step from something solid to something spongy. When the floor pattern changes you do not know if you are going to step from something solid to something spongy. No this is not a typing mistake: it happens time and time again in exactly the same situation, the same place. Like Ground Hog Day. And you can see feet, sometimes more than two which may or may not be yours. By the way, you tend to look downwards because of scoliosis, curvature of the spine, and the spinal jacket, like a suit of armour, that you wear to stop your internal organs from being squashed, can only to a limited extent help you stand upright. Standing itself is quite a tricky business, never mind walking. It is a question of balance, which you do not have, and so you need to hold on to someone or something very tightly. Whatever it is, you do not let go. The person objects. You are holding too tightly, you are pinching. But you are scared. If you fall, you cannot save yourself or put your arms out to break the impact. If it is a good day, the walking goes relatively smoothly; if it is a bad day, you become anxious, clammy and shaky. Worst is when you are being hurried. Anything too fast disrupts your way of trying to make sense of what is going on, it makes you fearful. Moreover you have odd patterns of breathing, some-times breath swallowing, holding breath, simply forgetting how to breathe. This means that doing things quickly not only is disorientating, it also makes you feel dizzy. And then there are the epiform moments when your brain fizzes and your arm moves erratically, your leg jerks, you go vacant. It lasts only a few seconds but long enough to make you so very tired. It gives you a headache. And people pull you up to walk again.

You feel uncomfortable. It may be hunger or cold or heat or pain but you do not know what it is and you cannot cry out or point to where it hurts. This goes on every day in every place even the most familiar. Routine helps you because you do not have to think so hard about every little thing... If you, the reader, have got this far without losing interest, or even despite a feeling of claustrophobia, a feeling of fear at living with such anxiety, then do not worry. In reality (or a reality) this is perhaps how it is and yet, it is still alright.

You also feel happy. These fears and anxieties can be dealt with if people know how it is. There are always people around, from family to people at your part time college placement where you go for the therapies that keep you going. Each day is something different: you are taken horse riding, you go swimming (hydrotherapy), trampolining (rebound therapy), tricycling. Everyday is also walking therapy. New, inventive and creative ways are offered for you to see, touch, taste, smell, hear things. A sensory approach to experiences to help you make sense of the world. You are with other people who also find life hard going, who also enjoy exploring the world of senses, a world of the experiences of colour, music, texture, hot and cold, sugar and spice. In this world, people stop and take time with you. They go at your pace, they know what you like, they have studied your facial expressions, your little gestures, your smiles and frowns. They know what reduces your anxiety, what makes you comfortable. They work at finding out what works for you. At home, there are always hugs and smiles. In reality, helping you to flourish as a person is easy because once people understand what you need, they are more than willing to put themselves out, to think in new ways, to go the extra mile. And soon it becomes a way of doing things, with no extra miles. The way it should be. Simply put, you are in the world as a witness to the great things that God has done, you remind people to stop and look, listen, touch and taste. And, in the same way that everyone is here to help others, you give people the opportunity to love and to show love, without self interest or personal gain, to be creative, to think outside the box, to achieve something that really makes a difference in someone's life. While many people think it is hard to help people with profound disabilities, in fact it is much, much more difficult the other way round, to help people who think they are totally self-sufficient, autonomous, proud of themselves and their achievements, people who do not need anyone or anything, the inwardly unperceptive, the spiritually stunted, people with such a deep and profound lack.

Each Sunday, you go to Church and follow the same pattern. Being walked in, smiling at the man who is always at the door (though it took a long time to educate him into waiting for a smile), negotiating the sitting down and getting balanced without too much increased anxiety, listening and rocking a little to the organ and the singing, reaching out to the lady next to you or the man behind. You never notice the stares. Then being walked up to Communion, and each time you look at the priest and open your mouth—without much of a delay. At this point Mummy could be accused of sentimentalism, but in the everyday way of things for you, this is, she thinks, remarkable.

Paula lives with us at home. We would not have it any other way and we are fortunate because, even with all of Paula's difficulties, this works. It works because there are lots of us. There are many other families where it simply is not a possibility that their child lives with them. Perhaps the child's needs are too complex, or the support required is too intensive. Then they have to make the very painful decision to live apart. Paula's bedroom is downstairs, since she cannot do staircases any more. She is near all the other rooms so she is a part of what is going on. Needless to say, at various times, there is one of her brothers or sisters in her room. After all, who better to go and chat to than someone who does not judge, who will never divulge a secret, who will gently pat your hand and laugh with you, whatever you say, who will look you in the eye with pure acceptance for who you are, and no pretences.

For us, Paula's family, is it hard? Yes. For Paula, is it hard? I suspect yes. But so are expectations, disappointments, complex relationships, exams, job prospects, paying bills, work-life balances. Paula does not worry about any of these because what is truly important—relationships with God and with other people— are actually rather simple.

To return to vocation and our response. Every Wednesday morning, I used to take Paula to visit two of her friends Bev and Elizabeth. Bev and Elizabeth were in what Elizabeth called the 'autumn years' of life. Bev joked that it was more like winter. Bev was ninety, had severe arthritis, eating and swallowing difficulties, and was pretty much confined to the house, reliant on carers and on Elizabeth. Bev's friend and daily visitor, Elizabeth, was in her eighties. Both, they told me, were noticing more and more the downside of being elderly, where everything ached, familiar words evaporated, steps got higher, pathways grew steeper, friends became ill and died.

When Paula and I went to visit our friends on a Wednesday, it was not just a social call, though coffee, juice and biscuits were always provided. Paula and I, and our two friends Bev and Elizabeth were all on the same path: the path to holiness. As a Eucharistic Minister, Elizabeth brought Holy Communion to Bev, who could no longer get to Mass. Each one of us felt immensely privileged: Bev, that the Church community came out especially to her, Elizabeth that she had been commissioned for a ministry that stretches back to the New Testament, me that I had been invited to join in such an intimate and sacred moment. And Paula? We do not know what she thinks or feels. But she watched intently when the candle was lit, she listened when the prayers began, she waited with apparent anticipation for her turn to receive Holy Communion. Bev and Elizabeth chided me for writing this. They said this made Paula look too passive, as if she had nothing to contribute. They insisted that I write how Paula made such a difference, how they got to know her ways, how they appreciated her silence and her smiles. Elizabeth said how Paula 'hallowed' our time together. And they were of course right. Moreover, as Jesus said, where two or three meet in my name, I am there among them. Jesus could have added and when we meet, there will be laughter, joy and companionship. So indeed, 'God, why me?'

During our short service, we prayed for those facing trouble in the world. We prayed for our sick friends and our well friends and for those who had died. Inevitably, perhaps, for this generation, we called upon the community of saints in our prayers. Then, we added some less well known saints to our litany, saints who seem to have had something in common with people we knew. To discover, as we had done, that there are saints who had arthritis, dementia, found life difficult to cope with, were bed ridden, had cancer or tuberculosis, had lost limbs or were paralysed, or found learning difficult, is not merely an addition to our knowledge about the real and concrete lives of the saints. Certainly it challenges us if we think of the saints simply as perfect physical and intellectual specimens of the human race in purely human terms. However, it also reminds us that people do not set out on the path to holiness *in spite of* what some may see as difficulties or disabilities. People come as they are and God helps them to move on. Saints are real people, but people who are examples of holiness. And people with disabilities are also saints. Bev, Elizabeth, Paula and I are, we hope, and with the aid of grace, saints in the making.

At the age of ninety, Bev died, peacefully, at home, after watching her favourite television programme, and after a good cup of tea. She just slipped away. She was not alone: Elizabeth was with her. Bev spent the last years of her life with severe disabilities, but also with patient endurance. She was frustrated at herself for not being as able as she would have liked, yet she faced her difficulties with admirable cheerfulness and humility—humility because she had to ask for help and she accepted her dependence on others. Bev was once a responsible and effective nurse, caring for and in charge of others. It was difficult for her to let go of that sense of control. In her last years, being house bound, she was always there for other people who would call to offer help, but instead received personal attention. Just like the Magi who came to visit Jesus with gifts and seemed to leave with nothing, people always left with more. Bev entrusted the care of herself to others. That entrusting of herself became a gift of herself to us. As Saint Paul writes to the Philippians, 'I thank my God whenever I think of you, and every time I pray for you all, I always pray with joy.'[1]

Notes

1   Ph 1:3–4.

INTRODUCTION

T HE PARABLE OF the Sower is perhaps one of the best known and loved parables of the New Testament. Jesus tells his disciples that the seed is the Word. Sometimes the Word is sown on the edge of the path, in people who forget it immediately; sometimes it is sown on rocks, in people who welcome it at first, but because they do not let it root in them, it does not last; sometimes it is sown in thorns where the worries or distractions of the world choke the Word in them, and so it produces nothing. And sometimes it is 'sown in rich soil; they hear the Word and accept it and yield a harvest, thirty and sixty and a hundred-fold.'[1] This book is about a particular harvest: saints with disabilities, God's wild flowers. You find wild flowers on the margins, in the least likely of places. They are everywhere. Wild flowers often challenge those with notions about ordered, tidy and apparently normal gardens. Wild flowers can be hardy or fragile, knotted and twisted or simple. But they are always beautiful in their own way. One of the insights given to Saint Thérèse of Lisieux is that we are all different, and we have all been given different gifts and voca-tions: in the garden of Jesus there are some great souls 'comparable to lilies and roses,' and there are some smaller ones 'and these must be content to be daisies or violets.' If all flowers wanted to be roses, then 'the fields would no longer be decked out with little wild flowers.'[2] God creates and rejoices in diversity. He calls

xxviii*God's Wild Flowers*

us all, whatever our condition or situation, to grow in perfection, to co-operate with Him, and become what He wills us to be.[3]

Why are there so many saints, and why do we need yet another book on another collection of people who have been canonised or beatified? And why people with disabilities? These are important questions for everyone, whether religiously minded or not. Notably, none of the saints or blessed written about in this book were cured of their disabilities, and this book is not about those who have been cured through saintly intercession. But it is a book about people who lived with disability. Disability under the UK Equality Act 2010 involves a physical or mental impairment that has a substantial and long term negative effect on the ability to do normal daily activities. For those interested in hearing about saints, asking such questions is a reminder that sainthood is about the call to holiness, and holiness is a path for all human beings whatever their capacities or abilities. For those who feel excluded by stories of apparent perfection, it can be empowering to hear about saints and the blessed who had learning difficulties, or who ended their days in care homes, or who lived with and embraced impairment. For those who are sceptical not only about God, but also about finding meaning in human existence, it can be liberating to read about people who found graced meaning in their own personal situations. For those who inhabit a world that has lost a sense of the mystery of being, and forgotten that every human being has a part to play in history, it can be eye-opening to discover that the most unlikely of people, the disabled, are also, in the words of Pope Saint John Paul II, 'workers in God's vineyard'.[4] For a world that knows only the secular story, a story that sees only function, usefulness, speed and efficiency as the markers of human beings, the Church reminds the world of a different story. This different story is told in the Church's love of the saints and the blessed. In particular this story unfolds in the lives of people with disabilities, and especially disabled saints and the blessed, because disabled people remind everyone that power, strength and control are not the most important values to be pursued in this life. The lives of the saints demonstrate the power of following Christ. The lives of disabled saints and the blessed show that, as Saint Augustine put it, grace blows where God chooses, and grace 'does not pass over any kind of capacity'.[5]

Why saints?

Although Pope Francis is rapidly catching him up, Pope Saint John Paul II is well known as the pope who canonised and beatified more people than all his predecessors together since 1588, the year the Congregation for the Causes of Saints was founded.[6] The task of this congregation or dicastery is to prepare everything for the Pope to be able to put forward new examples of holiness. And by canonising and beatifying so many Servants of God, Pope Saint John Paul was perhaps onto something. Long before he became pope, he astutely realised the significance of not only role models, but also of personal stories. After all, in the secular world this move to telling my story is powerful: the media demonstrates this in reality TV and in documentaries; campaigners realise this when they offer personal stories, particularly of celebrities, to forward their agenda, and recently this has been especially noticeable in campaigns to promote assisted suicide. The use of role models, again of celebrities or sports personalities, is accepted practice in initiatives that seek to turn around the lives of those who have failed or become lost in society. However, Pope Saint John Paul was not simply responding to the signs of the times and the secular use of role models by playing the game of countering one apparent role model or story with another. Rather, by canonising and beatifying people who had shown heroic virtue and true holiness in their lives, Pope Saint John Paul was demonstrating gospel teaching in practice.

Before he became Pope, as professor of ethics in Lublin University, Karol Wojtyła became interested in the work of the German philosopher Max Scheler. Max Scheler thought that following a role model, whether that model was a parent or a national hero, was the central point about the moral life. To a certain extent Karol Wojtyła agreed, but with one proviso: the only model to follow is Jesus Christ. The call to discipleship, to follow Christ, is clearly the gospel call. As Saint Matthew's Gospel recounts, with Jesus as the way to the Father, our ultimate vocation is to be perfect as our heavenly Father is perfect. For Karol Wojtyła, this call to holiness is a religious ideal because perfection is linked to the Father and to the Son through the Holy Spirit. It is also a reality since this perfection is already found in Jesus. Notably, it is also practical since holiness can be realised in acts which the person can do: it is following Jesus. Significantly, Karol Wojtyła saw the call to holiness as the primary message of the Second Vatican Council and, as Pope he saw that the implementation of the message of the Council was his primary task.

Pope Saint John Paul clarified the call to holiness in his Apostolic Letter *Novo Millennio Ineunte* at the close of the Great Jubilee Year 2000 and the beginning of the new millennium:

> As the Council itself explained, this ideal of perfection must not be misunderstood as if it involved some kind of extraordinary existence, possible only for a few "uncommon heroes" of holiness. The ways of holiness are many, according to the vocation of each individual. I thank the Lord that in these years he has enabled me to beatify and canonise a large number of Christians, and among them many lay people who attained holiness in the most ordinary circumstances of life. The time *has come to re-propose wholeheartedly to everyone this high standard of ordinary Christian living:* the whole life of the Christian community and of Christian families must lead in this direction.[7]

If this 'high standard' of living is for all human beings, then it does not exclude those who live lives of difficulty and impairment, or of disability, whether or not disability is seen in a negative light or simply as a fact. Indeed, given the large number of people with disabilities, it should come as no surprise that there are more than a few saints among them. The perfection of holiness is not physical or even mental perfection in terms of a perfect and attainable norm, the so called perfect person. The way of holiness is unique for each person, it is to be the person that God wants each one of us to be, and conformed in our own special way to the likeness of His Son. For Pope Saint John Paul, then, 'holiness, a message that convinces without the need for words, is the living reflection of the face of Christ'.[8]

Nevertheless, as Pope Saint John Paul pointed out, holiness is not purely an individual affair. Holiness is for the 'whole life of the Christian community'. Each person is called to the perfection of love, thus helping others to grow in holiness.[9] By looking to the saints and blessed we are inspired to build up the Kingdom of God on earth and we are reminded that the saints and blessed show us their brotherly and sisterly concern.[10] As we on earth are brought closer to Jesus through love for one another, so too does our communion with the saints brings us closer to Him.[11] And through fellowship with the communion of saints, we join in praising the Most Holy Trinity.[12]

Why disabled saints?

There are many and varied approaches to disability, and the saints and blessed in this book show some of these different approaches in the way they live their lives. There are saints and blessed who see their disability as an impairment that initially stands in the way of what they think is their vocation, until God shows them otherwise. There are saints and blessed who suffer because of the attitude of others to their disability, rather than suffering the disability itself. There are saints and blessed for whom their disability becomes a path for empathy with others. There are saints and blessed who see disability and suffering as a sign of God's will and love, requiring obedience and submission. There are saints and blessed who simply do not regard their disability as anything other than another aspect of who they are as human beings. There are saints and blessed who are tempted to despair, but in the end find peace and hope. However, in all cases the saints and blessed show in their lives a special and enduring love of God and of others, a life of heroic virtues and perseverance, in the vocation entrusted to them.

In his *Message for the First Annual World Day of the Sick*, Pope Saint John Paul II called people who are sick or who have disabilities the 'main actors'.[13] To a world that values independence and autonomy, they are main actors because they witness to the full dignity of every human being no matter what their situations or conditions, a dignity that can never be lost and a dignity that does not depend on levels of rationality or ability. Moreover, through their physical or mental dependence, they can demonstrate in the daily living out of their lives the dependence that all human beings have on God. In his *Address to the Sick and Disabled* given in Santiago de Compostela during the Fourth World Youth Day, Pope Saint John Paul II said that people with disabilities are on the 'front line' of the new evangelisation, 'exceptional spreaders of the Gospel,' and so are, with all human beings, 'labourers in the vineyard'.[14] In particular, people with disabilities call attention to what the Pope regarded as a vital but much neglected principle that can counter today's insistence on individualism and autonomy: the principle of solidarity and the 'fundamental need for solicitude' by every human being for every other human being, especially for the vulnerable and those in most need.[15] Paradoxically perhaps, because of the illusion of strength and self-sufficiency, it is not those who have disabilities who are often in most need.

Pope Saint John Paul II himself became one of these main actors, perhaps most specifically when he was suffering from Parkinson's disease. Pope Saint John

Paul II continued as Pope with his disabilities. The different ways in which Pope Saint John Paul II and Pope Benedict XVI followed their vocations illustrates that there are different paths to holiness. Pope Saint John Paul II carried on as Pope whereas Pope Benedict XVI resigned. However, these different ways are not a comment on each other. It is not as if one way is right and the other way wrong. Pope Benedict XVI faced different challenges in his life, and so dealt with them in a different way. In Pope Saint John Paul's case, it was important for him to show that God does not pass over any ability or disability. In the reality of his own life, Pope Saint John Paul lived out his own challenge to what he called the 'culture of death', a culture concerned principally with function, speed and efficiency, that considers any life that requires 'greater acceptance, love and care' as 'useless', 'an intolerable burden', redundant and to be rejected or eliminated.[16]

A life of holiness is a call to live a life of faith and allow 'grace to take us by the hand'.[17] The pilgrim Church follows the footsteps of the saints because the saints in their 'lived theology' show Christ to her, and it is the Church's task 'to reflect the light of Christ in every historical period'.[18] We may add with Pope Saint John Paul II that the face of Christ can be seen in every human being, especially the sick and disabled.[19] The saints and the blessed in this book are identified as having had a disability or impairment that was lasting. It was not cured, though some asked for a cure, it was not a sudden illness like the plague or fever. Stories include those of people who were amputees, epileptics, diabetics, who were paralysed, who were cancer sufferers, people who were deaf and blind, people with restricted growth (dwarfism), or who were crippled, people who had depression, people who were considered to be slow learners, elderly people with chronic ailments, people with mental frailty or memory loss. For some there is not sufficient evidence to say what the disability was, and at times a reading between the lines may suggest the presence of, for instance, a learning disability. In some cases, the disability was merely a factor in the person's life, in other cases it meant that a person had to re-evaluate completely his or her life as he or she was, for instance, refused admission into a longed for religious institution on the grounds of disability. In some cases, the saint had lived in a particularly simple way that many would associate with intellectual disability. Most though not all were canonised or beatified by Pope Saint John Paul II and Pope Saint John Paul's own story is placed alongside the stories of other people with disabilities.

The object is not to single a person out as having a particular disability as if that provides a complete answer to someone with a similar disability, after all there are no stories of saints with profound intellectual disability. Moreover, it is certainly not the case that these people became saints *in spite of* their disability. It is not possible to give more than a flavour of the life and path to holiness of each person. Nevertheless, in highlighting the person's disability the intention is not to define the person by a disability. Rather, it indicates the possibility of demonstrating that this aspect of the person's life is a tangible aspect of a life of heroic virtue. The object is to demonstrate that all human beings, whatever their situation, need God's grace to grow in holiness, and the saints and blessed are witnesses to this activity of grace. Furthermore, it is to show that as Pope Saint John Paul II said, 'for disabled

people, as for any other human being, it is not important that they do what others do but that they do what
is truly good for them, increasingly making the most
of their talents and responding faithfully to their own
human and supernatural vocation'.[20] These saints and
blessed with disabilities, and this includes Pope Saint
John Paul II himself, show the possibility of responding to their God-given personal vocation with heroic
virtue. They show that God is at the centre of their
lives.

Saints and Blessed: process and procedure

Although the causes of the saints and blessed follow
a meticulous process of examination, certain aspects
of people's lives, notably if they have a disability, are
not always clear from the evidence, or receive only a
brief mention. This is perhaps because disability or
impairment, like any other human aspect, is subordi-
nate to the evidence that God's power is acting in the
lives of the saints and blessed. Often this action of
grace becomes obvious in the reaction of people after
the person has died when his or her life is recalled and
re-evaluated. Certain illnesses, intellectual disabilities,
depression or eccentricity are difficult to attribute
definitively to some people for a variety of reasons. In
previous centuries when most people were illiterate,
a learning difficulty would not stand out; the notion
of a dark night of the soul was often used to describe
both a spiritual experience and what some today
would see as depression, though depression need not
be associated with the spiritual experience. Medical
advances mean that we can now put names to some
illnesses that in the past were simply called a poor

constitution or poor health. An overview of the process
for sainthood may help at this stage to contextualise a
conversation about saints and the blessed with disabilities, especially since sainthood is often associated with
perfection. It explains perhaps why some of the blessed
do not have feast days, unless they are observed within
a particular religious institution, or in a particular
place; why in the case of early and medieval saints
information may be sparse, and indeed that evidence
comes from the reactions of the people to their deaths.
Perhaps the clearest argument against the belief that
saints have to be perfect specimens of humanity comes
in the fact that none of the saints and blessed included
in this book were cured of their disability or poor
health: like many other people they died from illness,
disease, cancers, tuberculosis or the ravages of age.
And if it is still thought that sainthood is to do with
some ideal perfect person, simply look at the often
imperfect though abled Saint Peter.

The cult of the saints did not grow out of the pagan
practice of honouring ancestors or emperors by declaring them divine or at least semi-divine: saints are not
gods. Saint Augustine explained the nature of sainthood in his treatise against Faustus who, as a teacher
of Manichaeism, thought that everything in the material world was produced by an evil deity, and that only
the elite had within them sparks of the divine: only the
perfect would do. Faustus charged the Catholics of
turning the flesh and bone martyrs into the equivalent
of pagan idols. Saint Augustine replied that worship
or adoration, *latria*, is only given to God; humble
reverence, *dulia*, is given to the saints in recognition of
the gifts granted to them by God.[21] Higher reverence,
but still *dulia*, is owed to Mary the Mother of God. In

his Apostolic Constitution to the Congregation for the Causes of the Saints, *Divinus Perfectionis Magister*, issued on 25 January 1983, Pope Saint John Paul II repeated the Church's perennial teaching that Jesus, together with the Father and the Holy Spirit are 'alone holy', and that the Holy Spirit is sent to inspire all human beings to imitate this holiness. To emphasise that holiness is primarily the work of God, the Pope referred to the Second Vatican Council's document on the Church, *Lumen Gentium*: 'the followers of Christ, called and justified in the Lord Jesus not according to their works but according to His own purpose and grace, through baptism sought in faith truly become sons of God and sharers in the divine nature, and thus truly holy'. This imitation is in co-operating with God, and God chooses 'from many' people who, by following Christ closely, give 'outstanding testimony to the Kingdom of heaven by shedding their blood or by the heroic practice of virtues'. From their witness we in turn are further inspired and drawn to reach the Kingdom.

Pope Saint John Paul II noted the tradition of remembering those who were closest to Christ at the beginning of Christianity, the Apostles and martyrs, as well as those who imitated Christ in their lives. In the early days of Christianity, especially during the sporadic persecutions, the witness of the martyrs sent such a powerful message that relics and bones were collected, and the birthday, that is the day of death, of the martyr was celebrated to strengthen the faith of those following on. Indeed, Saint Augustine said that the pagan authorities began to outlaw the collection of relics and burnt the bodies of martyrs to try and stop this practice as well as to attempt to thwart the Christian belief in the resurrection of the body.[22]

Moreover, the idea that private individuals could determine public honour was not recognised. In the first one thousand years of Christianity a bishop or synod of bishops would authorise a particular cult by translating relics to a suitable church, but only after strict examination proved the person was worthy. As cases of martyrdom grew less, the focus moved from the martyrs to the confessors, those who with heroic virtue confessed faith in Christianity in the face of torture, and later those who lived a holy life. By the eleventh century, veneration of a saint could only become universal with the authority of the Bishop of Rome and this became the norm under Pope Gregory IX in 1234. In the fourteenth century it was recognised that certain causes had yet to be initiated or had not been concluded, so the Holy See limited some cults to specific places or people until examination had been concluded, hence the origin of the process of beatification. The distinction between saints and blessed was made definitive by Pope Sixtus IV in 1483. Pope Sixtus V established the Congregation for Rites in 1588 to look into the causes of saints and to consider the sacred liturgy. One of the officials was the Promoter of the Faith, known as the devil's advocate, whose job it still is to raise objections against canonisations and beatifications. In 1634 Pope Urban VIII forbade the setting up of a public cult unless either the martyrdom or heroic virtue of the person had been formally recognised by the Congregation of Rites. For anyone already regarded as a saint whose cause had not been through the process, it had to be proven that there had been public veneration for at least one hundred years before

the publication of the decree. In 1969 Blessed Pope Paul
VI divided the Congregation of Rites into two separate
offices, the Congregation of the Causes of Saints, which
has sole jurisdiction over the beatification and canonisation processes, and Congregation for the Divine
Worship. Pope Saint John Paul II changed the title of
the Congregation to read 'for the Causes of Saints' and
he issued *Divinus Perfectionis Magister* to make the
procedure for canonisation more streamline as well as
to retain its thorough research. In particular, in the
light of historical studies and especially the field of
historical criticism, accurate information is to be
sought, any writings of the 'servant of God' are to be
scrutinised, witnesses are to be examined. Any inquiry
into alleged miracles is to be conducted separately
from the inquiry into virtues or martyrdom, and any
evidence of healings is to be examined by a board of
medical experts. Moreover, in the light of collegiality,
the local bishop is involved in these processes, a
reminder perhaps of the original practice and of the
significance of the impact a person's life has on his or
her community.

The process of gathering and documenting evidence
does not begin until five years after the death of the
person in question, though this can be waived by the
Pope, and has been done in two recent cases, that of
Mother Teresa of Calcutta and Pope Saint John Paul
II. A waiting time of five years gives an indication of
whether or not the person's reputation for sanctity is
lasting. The bishop of the diocese in which the person
has died then petitions the Holy See and this initiates
a cause for beatification and canonisation. There is an
opportunity for any of the departments or dicasteries
of the Church to object, and if there is none then the

bishop is told *nil obstat*, nothing stands in the way of beginning the process. From this point onwards, the person is known as a 'servant of God'. The diocese organises the gathering of evidence about the person's life and virtues, and it examines any writings whether public or private. The diocese then sets up a tribunal, with the final word going to the bishop, to decide whether or not the evidence has demonstrated heroic virtue of the servant of God. This conclusion is sent to the Congregation for the Causes of the Saints along with the *Acta,* a bound volume of all the documentation. The Congregation appoints a Relator, who, with a theological commission, supervises the cause of the servant of God and ensures that the documentation is properly prepared before the commission either affirms or negates the cause. Their recommendation is passed onto members of the congregation who are cardinals, archbishops and bishops, and they then vote. If the vote is affirmative, a recommendation of a Decree of Heroic Virtues is sent to the Pope whose judgment is final. If the Pope recognises the person's heroic virtue then the person becomes Venerable.

Evidence of a miracle is considered to be the clearest sign that the servant of God is now united with God. A miracle must have occurred as a result of the intercessory power of this particular servant of God, it must have no natural explanation following strict scientific criteria, and a theological commission must rule that it is the work of God. This is done in the diocese where the miracle took place, and the decision is sent to the Congregation in Rome. The Congregation's judgment on the miracle is communicated to the Pope. If the Pope agrees to a Decree of Miracle, then the servant of God can be beatified. In the case of martyrdom, the requirement for a miracle can be waived, and once the Congregation affirms that the martyrdom is true martyrdom, a recommendation is made to the Pope who can then decide to issue a Decree of Martyrdom. The servant of God is declared Blessed with a beatification rite. Pope Benedict XVI encouraged the practice that the Prefect of the Congregation conducts the beatification rite as an indication that the servant of God was not yet declared a saint by the Church, and so was due only limited veneration, usually at the local level or in the person's religious institute. In an exception, Pope Benedict conducted the beatification rite for Pope Saint John Paul II.

To proceed to canonisation, a second miracle is required under the same criteria as before. It is possible for the Pope to authorize veneration of a person as a saint without going through this rigorous process. In some situations it may be difficult to collect all the evidence, yet it may also be clear that there is strong devotion to the person and so evidence of a universal cult. The Pope then can declare a person a saint by equipollent (equal in force or effect) or equivalent canonisation. By canonisation the Pope does not 'make' the person a saint. He does however declare that the servant of God is with God, and that the person has been an example of a follower of Christ, the kind of example to be imitated.

Reading these letters written by the Spirit

> You are a letter, known and read by all men,
> written on your hearts. Clearly you are a letter
> of Christ which I have delivered, a letter written
> not with ink but by the Spirit of the living God,

> not on tablets of stone but on tablets of flesh in
> the heart. 2 Corinthians 3:1–3

In his second letter to the Christians at Corinth, Saint Paul speaks about the authentic discipleship of the community he founded there, authentic because it has for its authority not letters of recommendation from other people but rather it stems from 'the Spirit of the living God'.[23]When we read about the saints and blessed, we are given an insight into the lives of people who have been so completely caught by Christ that He has become central to their way of life. This way of life might have been in a religious institute, in the family, in society or in solitude. But wherever it was, the servant of God demonstrated a unique and personal way of living out the gift of his or her vocation in a way that also allows us to glimpse God's action at work. The cases of saints and the blessed with disabilities are no different in that respect from the cases of other saints and blessed, in the same way as people with disabilities are no different from those who are otherwise abled. Moreover, the stories of saints and the blessed are relevant to all of us, abled and disabled, because in their many different ways their situation helps us and inspires us in our own journey.

Sometimes the vocation that a person chooses is not one that God gifts to them and especially disability may prevent that person from following a particular path: Chapter 1 looks at the servants of God who God made into living Gospels in their new path. Sometimes the saints and blessed with disabilities surprise the abled with their originality and vitality: Chapter 2 looks at servants of God through whom God showed the Church to be alive and active in living out the Church's social teaching where all, whatever their

capacities or abilities are workers in God's vineyard.
Sometimes persecution gives just cause for finding
refuge elsewhere: Chapter 3 reminds us that saints and
the blessed with disabilities also had the courage to
stay and minister to their flock in spite of personal risk.
Sometimes suffering seems overwhelming and without meaning: Chapter 4 considers the perplexing and
at times disturbing situation of victim souls who lived
both in pain yet always full of joy in the Passion of
Christ, and those who united their sufferings with
Christ's. Sometimes what most people highly prize,
intellectual ability, is in short supply and people are
mocked for their apparent lack of mental prowess:
Chapter 5 speaks of saints and blessed who were called
slow learners or who had intellectual disabilities, yet
who offered in purity, simplicity and in a love free
from affectation a new way of looking through the eyes
of God at what matters in human life.

   Sometimes sensitivity leads to the feeling of having
to bear the whole weight of the world: Chapter 6 tells
of those who were anxious, depressed, possessed by
their own demons, who nevertheless showed resolute
perseverance and trust that God rescues and preserves
us. Sometimes people are scourged with terminal
illnesses like tuberculosis and cancer: Chapter 7
presents people who lived in patience, in kindness,
entrusting themselves to God and to others. Sometimes
a person's disabilities seem to obscure or hide not only
who that person is but also what contribution he or
she can make: Chapter 8 introduces people who were
deformed, stunted, crippled, amputees, blind or deaf
who appeared to have nothing to give but who
brought great riches through their lives of faith. Sometimes in old age all that a person has done seems to

fade away and there is nothing left but waiting for the end: Chapter 9 takes servants of God who had considerable, yet not unusual, disabilities at the end of their lives and shows how a life conformed to Christ transforms life even at its very end. The final Chapter 10 reflects on the lived theology of disability and suffering that has been presented through the lives and voices of the saints and blessed, with an after word for carers. To quote Saint Paul's second letter to the Corinthians:

> In everything we prove ourselves authentic servants of God: by resolute perseverance in times of hardships, difficulties and distress; when we are flogged or sent to prison or mobbed; labouring, sleepless, starving; in purity in knowledge, in patience, in kindness; in the Holy Spirit, in a love free of affectation; in the word of truth and in the power of God; by using the weapons of uprightness for attacks and for defence; in times of honour or disgrace, blame or praise; taken for imposters and yet we are genuine; unknown and yet we are acknowledged; dying, and yet here we are, alive; scourged but not executed; in pain yet always full of joy; poor and yet making many people rich; having nothing, and yet owning everything. (2 Corinthians 6:4–10)

Notes

1   Mk 4:1–20.

2   Saint Thérèse of Lisieux, *Story of a Soul, the Autobiography of St. Thérèse of Lisieux*, translated by J. Clarke (Washington: ICS Publications, 1996), p. 14.

3   Second Vatican Council, *Lumen Gentium*, 39–41.

4   Pope Saint John Paul II, *Christifideles laici*, 53.

5   Saint Augustine, *On the Merits and Remission of Sins*, I, 32.

6   Pope Saint John Paul II gave the dicastery this new name in 1988.

7   Pope Saint John Paul II, *Novo Millennio Ineunte*, 31.

8   *Ibid.*, 7.

9   Second Vatican Council, *Lumen Gentium*, 39.

10   *Ibid.*, 50.

11   *Ibid.*

12   *Ibid.*, 51.

13   Pope Saint John Paul II, *Message for the First Annual World Day of the Sick* (21 October 1992), 5.

14   Pope Saint John Paul II, *Address to the Sick and Disabled* (19 August 1989), 3.

15   Pope Saint John Paul II, *Redemptor hominis*, 15.

16   Pope Saint John Paul II, *Evangelium Vitae*, 12.

17   Pope Saint John Paul II, *Novo Millennio Ineunte*, 19, 20.

18   *Ibid.*, 8, 16, 27.

19   Pope Saint John Paul II, *Address to the Sick and Disabled* (19 August 1989), 5.

20   Pope Saint John Paul II, *On the Occasion of the International Symposium on the Dignity and Rights of the Mentally Disabled Person* (5 January 2004), 4.

21   Saint Augustine, *Against Faustus*, XX, 21.

22   Saint Augustine, *City of God*, I.12.

23   2 Co 3:1–3.

1

Becoming Living Gospels when Disability Seems to Close the Door

Anyone who enters through me will be safe.

John 10:9

Introduction

ISABILITY IS PERPLEXING. Nevertheless, it is now becoming a topic in its own right, a subject to be studied with its own journals, academic papers and books. In part this is due to disability rights movements and the recognition that disability can no longer be simply spoken about in exclusively negative terms. In particular, much academic interest has gone into examining what are called 'models' of disability. These models provide a framework for thinking about how people experience disability. This can be the experience of people who are said to be disabled, people who are carers, family, professionals, and even the experience of society. Different models have been identified and each has its strengths and weaknesses. There is the medical model that focuses on what a person cannot do, on impairment, restriction, limitation, lack of ability. The 'problem' of disability lies in the person who is in need of curing or fixing, and the object of this model is to work out strategies to help the disabled person overcome his or her limitations. The newer social model of disability challenges the medical model. According to the social model, the 'problem' of disability does not rest with the person. Rather, disability arises from social discriminatory structures, barriers and especially attitudes that prevent people from having equal access and from participating in society. Disability under this model becomes a failure of society, and people with disabilities are an oppressed minority. Although the medical and the social model predominate, there are other models. The charity or tragic model for instance casts disabled people in the role of victims to be pitied or to be rescued by handouts; the infant model sees people, notably the intellectually disabled, as childlike and in need of coddling.

Whichever model is applied, there is no doubt that there is discrimination but there is also no doubt that impairment actually is a factor in the lives of some people. However, what happens when disability plays a decisive role in a person's life, when it seems to close the door to a longed for hope or aspiration? All religious life is a call from God and not merely a human desire. In a particular religious community there may be a number of elements that have to be judged and evaluated. Does the person have not only the mental but also the physical aptitude for this life, maybe a life of solitude, asceticism or work and prayer ethic? Courage and maturity may be necessary, but so too is the physical strength to bear the burdens of the order or institute. In many cases of the saints and blessed, the person has been frustrated in what he or she believed to be his or her calling. The person may have been refused permission to enter an order or the priesthood, on the face of it denied an opportunity for holiness. However, in many cases the person has followed a different but perhaps more significant vocation. When the person's disability seems to have caused a door to shut another door has opened, and one that has led the person towards what God has wanted.

In his homily on the beatification of six servants of God including Blessed, now Saint, Maria Cristina Brando, a young woman who was refused entry to the convent of her choice and so was led on another path to holiness, Pope John Paul II explained that the Good News is 'personally addressed to each one and asks to be expressed in his life style'. Pope John Paul II called Christians 'living Gospels' when they are transformed into 'eloquent signs' of God's mercy. When this happens, their witness can touch hearts more easily. Moreover, the Pope added, 'as docile instruments in the hands of divine Providence, they have a profound effect on history'.[1]

This personal call is demonstrated in those whose disability has prevented them from following a course of their own choosing. In walking through a different door, they have shown that they are doing God's work that has been uniquely entrusted to them, and in persevering despite setbacks they have shown heroic virtues. Of course, some may have been safer in a religious order after all some of these doors led to martyrdom. And Blessed Hyacinthe was able to make his final vows specifically because of his disability.

Saint Alonso de Orozco

1500–1591
Arthritis
Feast Day 19 September

Alonso was born on 17 October 1500 in Oropesa near
Toledo in Spain where his father was the governor of
the local castle. Alonso began his schooling in Talavera
de la Reina, one of the principal cities in the district,
and he was also a choirboy at Toledo Cathedral. At the
age of fourteen he went to study law at the University
of Salamanca. In 1520 Alonso heard Saint Thomas of
Villanova preach the Lenten sermons. This so affected
the young man that he left the law and entered the
Friary of St Augustine and he was ordained a priest in
1527. Alonso developed not only a clear understanding
of his faith but also a deep spirituality, and his superiors decided to appoint him to a ministry of preaching
because of his ability to proclaim the Gospel. In this
vocation of a travelling preacher, Alonso set his heart
on martyrdom and in 1549 he started for the missions
in Mexico. On the way to the Canary Islands, Alonso
suffered a severe bout of arthritis and his doctors
forbade him to continue. Now unable to realise his
goal, he was forced to return to Spain and in 1554 he
was appointed royal preacher at the court of Emperor
Charles V. This meant that Alonso had to move with
the emperor and in 1561, when the new King, Philip
II moved his capital to Madrid, Alonso reluctantly
moved with him. Although his position of royal
preacher afforded the opportunity for many privileges,
Alonso wanted only to live a life of austerity and
poverty so he lived in the local monastery. Devoted to

his Augustinian calling, he attended daily prayer, he visited the sick and prisoners, helped the poor, and he wrote several works to aid in pastoral ministry and to foster vocations to the Augustinian way of life. His spiritual works were widely read. Famously, he only slept for three hours a night. In 1591 he fell ill from fever, though this did not prevent him from celebrating daily Mass. In the month before he died, Alonso was visited by many notable people, including King Philip II, Princess Isabel and the Archbishop of Toledo. He was held in such regard by people of all states of life that his death was greeted with great sadness and the people of Madrid filed past the chapel of rest in his honour. Alonso was beatified by Pope Leo XIII in 1882 and canonised by Pope John Paul II in 2002.

Blessed Amadeus IX of Savoy

1435–1472

Epilepsy

Feast Day 30 March

Amadeus was born in Thonon Savoy in 1435, son of Duke Louis I of Savoy. In a political move, as an infant Amadeus was betrothed to Yolande, daughter of Charles VII of France, in the hope that there would be lasting peace between Savoy and France. The couple married in 1451 when Amadeus was sixteen and they lived faithfully and happily together. Amadeus suffered from severe attacks of epilepsy and general ill health. Nevertheless, he led an austere life and he began each day by hearing Mass. When Amadeus inherited the dukedom after the death of Louis, he did not pursue political power nor did he seek to increase the Savoy kingdom, and at the time this lack of ambition was put down to his disabilities. Instead, Amadeus proved to be a wise ruler. He discharged the debts of the dukedom, he became reconciled with Savoy's national enemies, and he forgave his brothers when they rebelled against him. He became renowned for his clemency and readiness to pardon all offences. Above all, he sought to root out any oppression of the poor, and he set out to promote the happiness and welfare of his subjects. Gradually, he became best known and loved for his benevolence. Amadeus was given the name blessed in his life time because of his virtue, his piety, his sense of justice and his concern for the welfare of his people. He was also noted for his spiritual life and frequent reception of the sacraments. Apparently, when asked by a foreign minister if he kept hounds he told the minister he would show them to him the next day at noon. Amadeus took the minister to a window overlooking a large square and pointed to the number of poor people sitting and eating at his tables. He told the minister 'those are my hounds with whom I go in chase of heaven'. By 1470 his seizures were so incapacitating that Amadeus gave control of the dukedom to his wife. On his deathbed at the age of thirty seven he reminded his sons and noblemen to 'be just, love the poor and the Lord will give peace to your lands'. Amadeus died in 1472 and was beatified by Pope Innocent XI in 1677.

Saint Angela of the Cross (Angelita Guerrero y González)

1846–1932
Poor health
Feast Day 2 March

Angelita, was born on 30 January 1846 in Seville in Spain to a poor working family. Her father worked as a cook and her mother as a laundress in a local convent. When Angelita was still young her father died so she had to leave her education and help support the family. She found work as a cobbler in a workshop owned by Antonia Maldonado who was keen to foster the spirituality of her employees. Antonia Maldonado encouraged the whole workforce to pray the rosary together and to read about the lives of the saints. In spite of her own poverty, Angelita was always aware of those who were less fortunate than herself. She gave her Friday meal to the poor and encouraged other employees in the workshop to contribute a little to others. Antonia Maldonado recognised the piety of the young Angelita and found her a spiritual director so that she could grow further in her spirituality. At the age of nineteen Angelita sought permission to enter the Discalced Carmelites in the Santa Cruz district of Seville. However, the superiors of the order were concerned that Angelita's poor health would make it too difficult for her to cope with their strict regime and so she was not accepted. In 1868, after a period of caring for cholera victims during an epidemic in Seville, Angelita applied to another order in Seville, the Daughters of Charity. Although the nuns were aware that Angelita's health was still frail, they agreed to admit her provisionally. However, when her health did not improve after time spent in Cuenca and Valencia the nuns decided that she would have to leave and Angelita returned to work in the shoe workshop. Under instruction from her spiritual director she began to write a spiritual diary and in it she expressed her thoughts about what might be her vocation. Having heard about wealthy people who were happy to donate to charities but who thought the poor should be content with their lot, Angelita discerned that her vocation lay with being poor with the poor in order to bring them to Christ. In 1875 she and three friends began a community life together in a room they rented in Seville and they gave assistance day and night to the poor and sick who would otherwise have been abandoned. They called themselves the Sisters of the Company of the Cross, and when they were not ministering to the poor they led a contemplative life of prayer and silence. More women came to join them and they had to find larger premises, always with the understanding that these communities had to remain poor. Over twenty three further convents were established before Angela died in 1932. Known as the Mother of the Poor, Angela was beatified by Pope John Paul II in 1982 and canonised in 2003.

Blessed Angela Salawa

1881–1922
Multiple sclerosis, stomach problems
Feast Day 12 March

Angela was born on 9 September 1881 at Siepraw, a village south of Krakow in Poland. Although Angela's father worked hard as a blacksmith, the family lived in poverty. Nevertheless, her parents brought up their twelve children in a pious and devout household. Angela was the eleventh child and she was known to be unruly and capricious. She had little education and by the age of fifteen she had a job helping a neighbouring family run their farm. She resisted the suggestion of her parents that she married and instead she went to join her sisters in Krakow where they worked as maids. At this stage of her life, Angela made the most of her relative freedom, and outside work her main interest was in clothes and enjoying herself. Then suddenly one of her sisters died. Angela's whole life changed and she began to attend church as often as she could, she embroidered cloths for the services and she joined the Association of Saint Zita, a religious group for maids. Angela felt called to a more formal religious life. However, her hopes of joining a congregation of cloistered nuns were dashed. Angela was not able to provide the required dowry to the convent, but more seriously, she suffered from ill health, possibly the early symptoms of multiple sclerosis, and stomach problems. Still wishing to lead a religious life, she began a novitiate for the Third Order of St Francis in 1912. During the First World War Angela made it her vocation to visit wounded soldiers. She brought them food and she also took it upon herself to speak to them about faith in Christ. She shared whatever food she had with the poor as well. Finally, in 1917 her health collapsed completely and she had to give up her work. It appears that she developed multiple sclerosis alongside her stomach ailments. Angela spent the next five years in a rented room under the care of the Association of Saint Zita. Angela died in 1922 and she was beatified by Pope John Paul II in 1991.

Blessed Anita Cantieri

1910–1942

Intestinal fever, peritonitis, stomach problems, tumours, rheumatism, heart problems

Anita was born on 30 March 1910 in Lucca in Italy. She was known as a quiet and thoughtful child who loved her lessons. Anita was still very young when she felt called to the religious life and as a teenager she encouraged her friends to contribute to charities for the poor. She allowed her confessor to make the choice of which order she should join, and he thought that the contemplative life of the Carmelites would be most suitable. Anita joined the Carmelites, however her health began to deteriorate and the doctors diagnosed intestinal fever, then called Maltese fever. After only fifteen months of life in the convent, the sisters felt obliged to send Anita home. They hoped that she would recover and return to them. Although disappointed, Anita accepted this as the will of God and resolved to give herself wholly to God no matter where she found herself. Throughout her illness Anita designed for herself daily observances, offering her trials of the day to God in the morning, reciting the rosary, engaging in daily meditation, and praying for the conversion and salvation of sinners. Eventually Anita came to realise that she could not become a Carmelite nun and so instead she entered the Third Order Carmelites in 1935. Two years later she enrolled in Catholic Action and among other charitable work she helped with catechesis. Anita's health grew worse and increasing fevers and peritonitis caused her to become confined to bed where she was cared for by her mother and sisters. To begin with, Anita worried that she was a burden to her family, but she then began to see her illnesses also as part of the will of God. Many people came to visit her and ask both for her prayers and for consolation in their own difficulties. She suffered stomach and further tumours, and had problems with her heart and trachea, as well as with rheumatism. Anita's greatest concern was that she would still be able to receive the Eucharist and that she would make a good death, and so in hope she abandoned herself to the mercy of God. She died the day after she received the Last Sacraments and after she asked her sister to arrange her hands in an attitude of prayer since she could no longer move them herself. Anita was beatified by Pope John Paul II in 1991.

Saint Camillus de Lellis

1550–1614
Leg ulcers, chronic illness, stomach problems
Feast Day 14 July

Camillus was born on 25 May 1550 in Bocchianico in the province of Naples in Italy. His father was a soldier and so was often away from home. By all accounts, his father had a fiery temper and Camillus seems to have inherited this particular characteristic. Camillus was unruly, he often played truant, and his mother found him hard to control. Camillus was only twelve when his mother died in 1562 and he was taken in by relations who did not concern themselves much with their young charge. Camillus decided to follow in his father's footsteps and at nineteen he became a soldier. He fought against the Turks at Lepanto then he joined in further campaigns in Dalmatia and Africa. It is likely that he suffered some kind of injury at this time which resulted in his legs becoming ulcerated and diseased. He had also become addicted to gambling and was known for his aggressive behaviour. When his unit was disbanded, Camillus found work as a builder at a Capuchin monastery. He became interested in the religious life, but each order to which he applied rejected him. Although this was possibly due to his lack of education, his health was also a contributory factor especially since doctors had judged that his diseased legs were incurable. Camillus was taken in by the Hospital for the Incurables in Rome where he was treated for his ulcers. In the hospital Camillus became acutely aware that sick people were often neglected and at times abused so he decided to develop his own ministry to them. However, his ingrained aggression surfaced once again and he was asked to leave the hospital after engaging once more in gambling and unruly behaviour. Camillus started to regret his lack of education and, in an act both of humility and courage, he began studies with the Benedictines, enduring the ridicule of his much younger fellow pupils. He then returned to the hospital where he eventually became its director and introduced significant reforms in patient care. Camillus became a priest and in 1584 he founded the Order of the Ministers of the Sick, the Camillians, who had a particular ministry to plague victims. This proved to be an important ministry given the number of boats quarantined in Rome's harbour due to plague. In 1591 the Order provided the first medical field unit to soldiers fighting in Hungary and Croatia. Camillus suffered from various debilitating and chronic conditions and at times was unable to walk. He died in 1614. Camillus was beatified in 1742 by Pope Benedict XIV and was canonised in 1746.

Blessed Carlos Manuel Rodriguez

1918–1963
Ulcerative colitis, general poor health, cancer
Feast Day 13 July

Carlos was born on 22 November 1918 in Caguas in Puerto Rico. His family had a strong Christian faith and this helped them to bear significant economic hardship when a fire destroyed their small business and the family home. Carlos was a keen student as well as a devout child. From the age of thirteen he began to suffer from ulcerative colitis, a disability that severely affected him for the rest of his life. His illness meant that he could not pursue his studies at the high school. He took some work in Caguas, eventually working as an office clerk until 1946. He then tried for a bachelor's degree at the University of Puerto Rico but despite good grades, his health once again failed him and so he had to leave before completing his second year. Nevertheless, he continued to read and study on his own in many fields from religion and science to philosophy and music. He also learnt to play the piano and organ for church services. Carlos spent most of his salary encouraging others to grow in the love and knowledge of Christ. In particular, he was interested in the liturgy and he translated articles on spirituality and liturgical subjects. He also produced two publications, *Liturgy* and *Christian Culture* and he organised a liturgy circle and choir. Carlos had both a brother and sister in the university faculty and so he organised another liturgy circle for students and lecturers at the Catholic University Centre. He also produced a publication on liturgical seasons, *Christian Life Days*, for the students. He organised and partici- pated in various panels and discussion groups to promote the liturgy and especially its focus on the Paschal Mystery. He taught catechism and provided the materials himself. He promoted the active partici- pation of the laity in church life. His health slowly declined and in 1963 he was diagnosed with advanced terminal rectal cancer. Radical surgery left him with a colostomy and to begin with Carlos felt a great sense of loss of dignity that grew into a feeling of abandon- ment by God. His doctors then discovered that the cancer had spread to his liver. Carlos continued to receive the Eucharist every day and he rediscovered a deep sense of God before he died. Carlos died in 1963 and he was beatified by Pope John Paul II in 2001.

Blessed Dolores Rodriguez Sopena

1848–1918
Poor eyesight

Dolores was born on 30 December 1848 in Velez Rubio, Spain. At the age of eight Dolores required an eye operation that left her with very poor eyesight. In 1866 her father was appointed judge in Almeria and conse- quently the seventeen year old Dolores was introduced into society life. However, Dolores preferred a different kind of life, and without the knowledge of her parents she cared for two people suffering from typhoid and a person with leprosy. She also accompanied her mother in visits to the poor. Her father was sent to Puerto Rico and before the family joined him there in 1872, Dolores taught catechesis in a women's prison, in hospitals and at Sunday school. In Puerto Rico Dolores took a Jesuit as her spiritual advisor and under the Jesuit influence she founded the Association of the Sodality of the Virgin Mary as well as schools for disadvantaged children. Next, her father was appointed as State Attorney in Santiago in Cuba, then still a Spanish colony, and so the family moved there. At first, due to political difficulties, Dolores restricted her activities to visiting the sick in the military hospital but soon she was able to offer help in the form of education and healthcare to poor and marginalised people. Dolores felt that she was being called to religious life and she applied to join the Sisters of Charity. However, she was refused admission because of her very poor eyesight. Her mother died in Cuba, and in 1877 her father decided to retire to Spain so the family moved back to Madrid where Dolores resumed her outreach to the poor. She opened what she called a Social House where people could come and resolve their difficulties and she started up a project to visit deprived families in the slum areas. With the support of her bishop, Dolores founded a lay association to extend social activities to other parts of Spain. She began a religious community to continue her work with the poor, and, acutely aware of the political climate, she also ensured it had a civil arm so that it could operate even in an anti-clerical climate. Moreover, the community did not wear habits because Dolores wished to reach even those who felt alienated from the Church. Dolores took the view that the foundation of all her work was in the intrinsic dignity of all people as brothers and sisters in Christ. Dolores died in 1918 and she was beatified by Pope John Paul II in 2002.

Blessed Edmund Bojanowski

1814–1871
Tuberculosis
Feast Day 7 August

Edmund was born on 14 November 1814 in the village
of Grabonog, in Poland, into a family of Polish nobility
who were deeply Christian. At the age of four Edmund
became ill and appeared to be close to dying. He
recovered and his mother attributed his cure to her
prayers to Our Lady of Sorrows. Although Edmund's
medical condition was no longer life-threatening, he
continued to suffer ill health and had to be educated
at home. By twenty he developed tuberculosis. In spite
of his illness he began university studies at Wroclaw
and then at Berlin. However, his ill health prevented
him from pursuing studies for the priesthood.
Edmund's love of country people led him to collect
and publish songs, stories and sayings from the rural
communities. This love developed into an interest in
culture and education and it led him to provide books
for schools, and to set up libraries and orphanages.
Edmund was also especially active in caring for the
sick during the cholera epidemic of 1848–1849. He
founded a hospital and then an order of nuns to serve
the poor. He began studying for the priesthood but
died in 1871 before being ordained. Edmund was
beatified by Pope John Paul II in 1999.

Blessed Hyacinthe Marie Cormier (Henri Cormier)

1832–1916
Haemorrhages
Feast Day 21 May

Louis Stanislas Henri Cormier was born on 8 December 1832 in Orleans in France. His father was from a family of successful merchants but he died when Henri was young. At first Henri studied at home and later he was taught by the Christian Brothers. In 1846 at the age of thirteen, Henri entered the junior seminary in Orleans where he showed particular aptitude in music. He joined the major seminary in Orleans and while he was a seminarian, he was admitted into the Third Order of St Dominic. Although he was under the canonical age, Henri was granted a dispensation and was ordained in 1856. He felt called to join the Dominican Order that had been re-established in France in 1850 after its suppression, and having acquired the necessary permission from his bishop, he entered the novitiate taking the name Hyacinthe Marie. Although he excelled academically, his health prevented him from making his religious profession: he frequently coughed up blood and had internal haemorrhages perhaps associated with tuberculosis. A decision was made to send him home. Fortunately, the Master of the Order who happened to be visiting at the time was impressed by Hyacinthe's dedication and he was willing to make a case to the Holy See for special dispensation for Hyacinthe to be professed. Hyacinthe was moved to the convent of Santa Sabina on the Aventine Hill to join the international novitiate there.

Pope Pius IX agreed that Hyacinthe could make his profession provided that he stayed clear of haemorrhage for one month. Hyacinthe repeatedly failed, the most he managed was twenty nine days. Then in 1859 he fell profoundly ill and he was given the Last Rites. He was allowed to make his solemn profession on what appeared to be his death bed. However, Hyacinthe recovered. He was made sub-master of novices at Santa Sabina and in 1863 he was elected prior to a convent in Corsica. Two years later he became Prior Provincial at Toulouse, a post he remained in for nearly ten years. He then became prior in Marseilles, then Prior Provincial once more. In 1891 he was elected definitor for the General Chapter in Lyons. Called to Rome, Hyacinthe was appointed Procurator of the Order and then in 1904 he was elected Master of the Order, a post he held until 1916. As Master of the Order he was instrumental in reorganising the Angelicum, the College of Saint Thomas in Rome. Hyacinthe developed studies based on the teachings of Saint Thomas and this became the standard not only for the Dominicans but also for secular clergy. He retired to the Basilica of San Clemente in Rome and died after a short illness in 1916. Hyacinthe was beatified by Pope John Paul II in 1994.

Saint Jaime Hilario Barbel (Manuel Barbel)

1898–1937
Hearing problems
Feast Day 18 January

Manuel Barbel Cosan was born on 2 January 1898 in the small town of Enviny in northern Spain. He was a serious, academic boy and he entered the junior seminary of the diocese of Urgel. However, when he developed hearing problems he was sent home. In 1917 at the age of nineteen he entered the novitiate for the La Salle Christian Brothers at Irun and he took the name Jaime Hilario. He soon became a gifted teacher himself but his hearing problems forced him to retire from teaching and instead he worked in the gardens at the La Salle house at San Jose at Tarragona. In 1936 civil war broke out in Spain and while he was on his way to visit his family he was recognised as a Christian Brother arrested and imprisoned. In 1937, after a summary trial he was convicted for belonging to the religious order and shot by firing squad. The first round of bullets did not kill him and he was then shot at point blank range. Brother Jaime was beatified by Pope John Paul II in 1990 and canonised in 1999.

Saint Marciano José (Filomeno López y López)

1900–1934
Deaf, general ill health
Feast Day 9 October

Marciano was born on 17 November 1900 in El Pedregel in the Castile La Mancha region of Spain. His family were ordinary working people and Marciano grew up to be a kind and obedient young man with a deep devotion to Our Lady. Just before he turned twelve, Marciano joined the La Salle Christian Brothers in Burgos for his religious formation and he had hopes to one day become a teacher with the Brothers. However, an ear infection caused him to become deaf and he was forced to return home where he looked after a small flock of sheep. Marciano was persistent and he persuaded the Brothers to allow him to return even if it meant that he could only do manual work cleaning, taking care of the church and doing repairs. Despite the fact that he was deaf and in poor health, Marciano was able to make his final profession in 1925. At a time of intense anti-clericalism in the region, Marciano was sent to help the Brothers in the mining town of Turon in north-east Spain. The chef of the community had been too afraid to accompany the Brothers, so Marciano offered to take his place. On 5 October 1934 a group of rebels forced their way into the school and the eight Brothers, together with a Passionist priest, were arrested and imprisoned. Initially Marciano was considered to be merely an employee and so he could have been released. However, he explained that he was a member of the community. Brother Marciano and his companions were martyred by firing squad in 1934. Brother Marciano was beatified by Pope John Paul II in 1990 and canonised in 1999.

Saint Maria Cristina Brando (Adelaida Brando)

1856–1906
Bronchitis, general poor health, heart problems
Feast Day 20 January

Adelaida was born on 1 May 1856 in Naples in Italy to wealthy parents, though soon after Adelaida was born her mother died. From an early age Adelaida showed an interest in the religious life and at about the age of twelve she made her own profession to God. As a teenager she tried to enter the Monastery of the Sacramentine nuns in Naples but her father prevented her. Then at last with her father's permission she twice tried to enter the Poor Clare convent of the Fiorentine but had to withdraw because of illness and each time she returned home to be nursed back to health. She suffered from chronic acute bronchitis and she found that she could get some, albeit little, relief from her condition by sleeping upright in a chair. This disability remained with her for the rest of her life. At the age of twenty in 1876 she was well enough to enter the Monastery of the Sacramentine nuns. When she took the habit she took the name Maria Christina. However, once again she had to withdraw on account of her health. This time there was no possibility of returning to convent life. Her half sister also had to leave the Poor Clares, so in 1878 the two joined other young women at the newly founded Teresian Sisters house in Torre del Greco near Naples. The new congregation grew quickly and it moved to Casoria, becoming known as the Pious Institute of the Perpetual Adoration of the Blessed Sacrament, with Maria as its first superior. The new congregation wished to be both practical and spiritual so alongside its devotion to the perpetual adoration of the Eucharist, it took as its mission the education of young girls. By 1892 the expanding congregation required larger premises and they moved to a more spacious house near a church. In order to be near the tabernacle, Maria had a cell built next to the church where every night, whether awake or asleep, she sat in a chair since she was still suffering from bronchitis and now had additional heart problems. The congregation continued to increase and more houses were set up. Maria professed her temporary vows in 1897 and made her final profession in 1902. Maria died in 1906 and was beatified by Pope John Paul II in 2003 and canonised by Pope Francis in 2015.

Blessed María del Transito de Jesus Sacramentado (Maria Cabanillas)

1821–1885
Poor health
Feast Day 25 August

Maria was born on 15 August 1821 to a wealthy family on an estate called Santa Leocadia. The estate later became the town of Carlos Paz near Cordoba in Argentina. Maria attended school in Cordoba and in 1840, while still studying she looked after her younger brother who was preparing for the priesthood. When her father died in 1850, Maria set up a new home with her family, including her mother, her brother now a priest, her sisters and her five orphaned cousins. Maria was well known for her life of prayer, devotion to the Eucharist, her catechetical work and care of the sick. After the death of her mother in 1858, Maria entered the secular Third Order of Franciscans and she made her profession with a vow of perpetual virginity in 1859. At this stage of her life she knew she wanted to serve God and she saw her mission as the instruction of poor abandoned children, though as yet she did not know how to put that vocation into action. In 1867 a cholera epidemic struck Cordoba, and Maria worked tirelessly with the sick. In 1873 she entered the newly built Carmelite monastery in Buenos-Aires. However she was forced to leave the following year when she fell ill. Later in 1874, thinking herself recovered, she entered the convent of the Sisters of the Visitation in Montevideo but once again due to ill health she had to leave. Resigned to the fact that ill health had prevented her from life in a convent, Maria made a conscious decision to abandon herself to Divine Providence and she returned to her inspiration of founding an order to educate and assist orphans and poor children. With the help of the Franciscans, she and two friends began the Congregation of the Third Order Franciscan Missionaries of Argentina. The three sisters made their profession in 1879. The congregation flourished and three new schools were set up in San Vicente, Rio Cuarto and Villa Nueva. Maria herself grew progressively weaker physically and she died in 1885. Maria was beatified by Pope John Paul II in 2002.

Blessed Marie Rivier

1768–1838
Rickets, stunted growth, frail health
Feast Day 3 February

Marie was born on 19 December 1768 in the little community of Mountpezat in Ardeche in France. When she was only sixteen months old she fell out of bed and damaged her hip and ankle so badly that she was crippled and could not walk, though at the age of nine she was cured through the intercession of Mary. However, Marie suffered from rickets and this contributed to her stunted growth and left her in frail health. In spite of her ill health and even though she was still only a teenager, Marie took it upon herself to gather a group of girls and instruct them in the faith as well as to look after poor children. She and her sister attended the boarding school of the Sisters of Notre Dame in Pradelles in the Upper Loire region of France where she was very much influenced by the holiness of the nuns. Feeling called to religious life, Marie asked to enter the convent but was refused because of her poor and apparently failing health. Instead, in 1786 at the age of eighteen Marie set up a school where the children were instructed not only in academic subjects but also in the faith and in the love of God. She became a Dominican and Franciscan tertiary and her particular vocation was in helping the unemployed young people of the town as well as the sick. The advent of the French Revolution had put great pressure on religious orders, nevertheless in 1796, when all the other convents were being closed Marie gathered together four companions and they started an attic school as the beginnings of a new congregation, the Sisters of the Presentation of Mary. Marie made her religious profession in 1797. She also held secret Sunday services when a priest was not available. The community opened its first novitiate in 1803 and it steadily grew so that by 1810 there were forty six houses dedicated to prayer, education and pastoral work. The order continued to spread throughout France and abroad. Marie died in 1838 and she was beatified by Pope John Paul II in 1982.

Blessed Paolo Manna

1872–1952
Tuberculosis
Feast Day 15 September

Paolo was born on 16 January 1872 in Avellino in Italy. He studied philosophy at the Gregorian University in Rome and then, feeling that his vocation lay in missionary work, he decided to enter the Theology Seminary of the Institute for Foreign Missions in Milan. He was ordained in 1894. In 1895 he left for Eastern Burma and the mission of Toungoo where he worked for ten years. However, he suffered from tuberculosis and his illness forced him to return to Italy. Unable to continue missionary work in person, he devoted the rest of his life to the missionary cause. With the aim of including all Catholics in the missionary apostolate, Paolo founded the Missionary Union of the Clergy in 1916. This was given the title Pontifical in 1956. He published information about missionary work and established a seminary for foreign missions as well as a society for missionary sisters. Paolo died in Naples in 1952 and he was beatified by Pope John Paul II in 2001.

Blessed Pina Suriano

1915–1950

Despair, arthritis, heart condition

Giuseppina, known as Pina, was born on 18 February 1915 in Partinico in Sicily. After she had made her First Communion and received Confirmation, Pina became a member of the local Catholic Action group, even though she was only seven years old. By the age of twelve she was active in parish and diocesan life, and she became increasingly involved in the activities of Catholic Action. The motto of Catholic Action was prayer, action and sacrifice and Pina dedicated herself to the Mass, daily meditation and following the teachings of the Church. Pina felt called to the religious life however her parents were bitterly opposed. As they told her, 'better to have a dead daughter than a daughter who is a nun'. Her mother in particular ostracised her because of her religious activity. As an obedient daughter Pina found this conflict hard to bear. She experienced both isolation and a sense of despair to the point of feeling abandoned even by God. Despite these difficulties, with the permission of her spiritual director she made a vow of chastity in 1932 and she renewed this vow every month. Finally in 1940 her parents relented and she was accepted by the Institute of the Daughters of St Anne in Palermo. However only eight days later a medical examination revealed a heart problem and Pina was forced to leave. Throughout her life, and despite her disappointment at not being able to follow what she believed to be her vocation, Pina was active in Catholic Action. From 1939 to 1948 she was secretary of Catholic Action and president of the youth section from 1945 to 1948. In 1948 she and three of her friends dedicated their lives for the sanctification of priests. Soon after Pina began to suffer from a violent form of rheumatic arthritis and in 1950, as she was preparing to go to Mass, Pina suffered a fatal heart attack. Pina was beatified by Pope John Paul II in 2004.

Saint Rafael Arnáiz Barón

1911–1938
Ill health, diabetes
Feast Day 26 April

Rafael was born on 9 April 1911 in Burgos in Spain into a family that was comfortably well off. His father was a forestry engineer and the family owned a number of estates. Although his education was interrupted by episodes of pleurisy and fever, Rafael enjoyed school. He was diligent, well behaved, and especially keen on spiritual studies and art. He took up architectural studies in Madrid in 1930 and although he was called up for military service he was pronounced unfit for duty. In 1934 at the age of twenty three, and feeling called to a life of contemplation and prayer, Rafael entered the Trappist Monastery of San Isidoro de Dueñas. However, only four months later he developed a severe form of diabetes and was forced to return home. He spent the next few years going between the monastery and home. Rafael was not able to take his final vows because the Canon Law of the time did not permit anyone of poor health to do so. Rafael came to accept that he could want only what God willed for him and nothing more. Finally, Rafael was made an oblate and he lived on the fringes of the community. In 1938 at the age of twenty seven Rafael died in the monastery infirmary after falling into a diabetic coma. Rafael was beatified by Pope John Paul II in 1992 and canonised by Pope Benedict XVI in 2009.

Saint René Goupil

1608–1642
Deaf, ill health
Feast Day 26 September

René was born on 13 May 1608 in the village of St Martin near Anjou in France. In 1639 René joined the Jesuit novitiate in Paris. The novitiate record describes him as an educated surgeon who could read and write. However, René had to leave the order after only a few months because of what the record called bodily indispositions, moreover, he was very hard of hearing. His health began to improve and in 1640 René travelled to New France in North America as an unpaid volunteer to the Jesuit mission. For two years he worked with particular skill and care as a surgeon for the Indians at a hospital run by Augustine nuns near Quebec where, it was noted, he saw Jesus in each of his patients. René was asked to go and take care of

Indians living in Huronia, south of Ontario. On the
journey René and his companions, the Jesuit priest
Father Isaac Jogues and Guillaume Couture, were
captured by Mohawk warriors. They were taken to the
Iroquois territories near present day New York where
they were savagely tortured. In captivity René used
his medical skills for the benefit of his companions and
for wounded Mohawks. Still eager to become a Jesuit,
René asked Father Jogues to accept his vows as a Jesuit
Brother. A few days later, René was seen marking a
small child with the sign of the cross. This was inter-
preted as a sign of a curse and René was clubbed to
death with a tomahawk. René was beatified by Pope
Pius XI in 1925 and canonised in 1930.

Notes

[1]   Pope Saint John Paul II, *Homily* (27 April 2003).

2

ALL ARE WORKERS IN THE VINEYARD
DISABLED PEOPLE AND THE SOCIAL TEACHING OF THE CHURCH

I am the vine, you are the branches. Whoever remains in me, with me in him, bears fruit in plenty.

John 15:5

Introduction

SOME DISABILITY GROUPS believe that the Church has been neglectful of people with disabilities. In particular, they note that the Church's social encyclicals do not deal specifically with disability issues. Moreover, there is the perception that the Church, concerned as it is with holiness and therefore, it is presumed, with perfection, naturally sees the disabled as somehow deficient. However, it is clear that the Church's social teaching does not single out people with disabilities and this is precisely because they are like all human beings, and like all human beings they are subjects of the Church's care. Moreover, the principles of the Church's social teaching apply equally to the

disabled as to the abled. The principles include the
option for the poor, participation, the common good,
subsidiarity, solidarity and justice.

Still, one of those principles, the option for the poor
and marginalised, applies in particular to people with
disabilities. Certainly, disabled people more often than
not live in poverty from the simple fact that opportunities for suitable work are not always available.
Nevertheless, the option for the poor does not simply
recognise this fact, and it is definitely not a principle
that seeks only to give the rich a chance to do something for the poor or the strong to do something for
the weak. Rather, the option for the poor reminds
everyone that those who are little in the world's eyes
are the ones who are especially loved by God, and
Jesus identifies himself with these little ones. One of
the foundations of Church social teaching is the principle that every human being, no matter what his or
her situation or condition, has full human dignity, a
dignity that is not conferred on the person by others
nor can it be taken away. This dignity belongs to every
person because every human being is made in the
image and likeness of God. One way in which human
dignity is conveyed is in the possibility of participation
in family and social life. Being enabled to participate
is a recognition of the two principles of subsidiarity
and solidarity: through subsidiarity, the principle that
recognises that each person has a part to play and
requires the freedom to do this without interference,
each person has a unique contribution to make to
building up the community; through solidarity, the
principle that reminds us that we are all responsible
for each other, the community becomes a family of
people united in brother and sisterhood.

The roots of the Church's teaching can be found in scripture and in the earliest of Church tradition. Christians were well known in the pagan world of antiquity for their care of the poor, the marginalised and those in need, and for the rescue of the abandoned and of infants. After all, they were following the call of Jesus: whatever you do to the least, you do to me. As Saint Augustine explained we do not complain that we were born in a time when we can no longer see God in the flesh because God is among us in those who are hungry, thirsty, poor and in need.[1] Third Orders were frequently attached to a religious order so that those who were 'in the world', and indeed those who were not accepted into a religious order on account of their disabilities, could live by a rule of life inspired by the spirit of the order. Thus, for instance there is a Third Order of St Francis, of St Dominic and of St Teresa. These third orders were especially appealing for those whose health was too precarious to enter the order fully.

In this scriptural and historical tradition of care for those in need, the encyclical of Pope Leo XIII, issued in 1891, marked the beginning of a new movement of social action and it immediately became highly influential for people, especially young adults, who were looking to do God's work in the world. Industrialisation, urbanisation, political revolutions and new political social movements brought with them new problems. To try and solve some of these problems Pope Leo called for the setting up of associations to help individuals. These associations were dedicated to addressing the needs of people and also to enabling people to participate more fully in society. Then the experience of the First World War brought to the fore the requirements of justice and peace. Charity came to be seen not as handouts but as a matter of justice, and the opportunity to work came to be regarded as not merely a way of earning a living but as part of living a fulfilling human life.

However, people with disabilities are not merely the recipients of the Church's care. Nor are they seen simply as those who qualify under the option for the poor and marginalised. People with disabilities are also main actors in the area of social justice. In the spirit of solidarity many people with disabilities have also helped to build up the community by seeking out those in need. In *Christifideles laici*, Pope John Paul II's encyclical on the mission and vocation of the faithful, the Pope said that 'even the sick are sent forth as labourers into the Lord's vineyard'.[2] This work of the labourer is work that leads to the person's fulfilment and their holiness, and so it is work that both the abled and disabled are called to do. As Pope John Paul II explained in his homily on the beatification of seven servants of God, among them Blessed Anna Eugenio Picco, in a 'vital synthesis between contemplation and action' faith is translated into the 'extraordinary experience of love for God and service to neighbour' through social action.[3] Disabled saints and the blessed, working in the field of social action, witness to a true solidarity and so demonstrate heroic virtues when they answer the needs of all human beings whether abled or disabled.

Blessed Angela Truszkowska (Sophia Camille Truszkowska)

1825–1899

Respiratory disease, tuberculosis, deafness, headaches, stomach cancer

Feast Day 10 October

Sophia Camille was born on 16 May 1825 in Kalisz in Poland. Her parents were from a noble Polish family and Sophia, the eldest of their seven children, was born prematurely and suffered from poor health and hearing problems. She was well educated but at the age of sixteen, because of her frail health, respiratory problems and early onset of tuberculosis, it was decided that she should move to Switzerland with her tutor. During her time abroad she felt she had a conversion experience and hoped to join a religious order. However, her parents did not give their permission since they had great hopes for their bright daughter. Later when she accompanied her father to Germany for treatment for his failing condition, Sophia began to discern that her mission was to go beyond cloistered life. Sophia's father had worked as a lawyer with troubled young people and Sophia recognised the consequences of social deprivation and family breakdown. In particular she became more aware of the requirements of social justice, and she began to see her mission in terms of addressing the need for religious instruction and charity among the Polish people. She joined the Society of St Vincent de Paul and set about improving the lives of the poor through her practice and her prayer. She rented an apartment in Warsaw where she and her cousin looked after homeless children, educated them and gave them the opportunity to hear Mass and pray at the shrine of St Felix of Cantalice at a nearby Capuchin church. In 1855, under the spiritual direction of the Capuchin fathers, Sophia began her novitiate in the Third Order of St Francis taking the name Sister Angela and her motto for her way of life became 'Praise Him as much as you can'. The numbers of women volunteering to help her grew, and in the same year she set up the Congregation of the Sisters of St Felix of Cantalice, the Felician Sisters, who devoted themselves to the care of the poor, sick and elderly. As the Congregation grew, one branch concentrated more on the contemplative life, the other branch on active mission, including setting up makeshift hospitals to care for wounded soldiers, both Polish and Russian, during the Polish rebellion against Russian rule in 1863–1864. The Congregation continued to grow from strength to strength. The sisters opened day care centres and retreat centres and a new branch was created in the United States. Throughout her life Mother Angela suffered from hearing problems, headaches and stomach problems. At the age of forty four Angela became completely deaf and her stomach problems increased. Her disabilities caused her to resign from active leadership of the community and she was diagnosed with stomach cancer. Mother Angela died in 1899 and she was beatified by Pope John Paul II in 1993.

Blessed Anna Eugenia Picco

1867–1921
Degenerative bone condition, amputee
Feast Day 7 September

Anna Eugenia Picco was born on 8 November 1867 in Crescenzago in the district of Milan in Italy. Her parents were famous musicians who were often on tour and so initially she was brought up by her grandparents, and her parents visited only occasionally. Later, Eugenia's mother returned alone giving Eugenia the impression that her father was dead. Her mother had decided to take over the care of her daughter and Eugenia was brought up in an environment that by all accounts was morally bankrupt. In particular, Eugenia's mother avoided religion since presumably that would conflict with her rather degenerate life-style. Despite the fact that Eugenia did not have any religious input in her upbringing, Eugenia felt called to the religious life and in 1887, at the age of twenty, she ran away from home to join the Congregation of the Little Daughters of the Sacred Hearts of Jesus and Mary. She made her solemn profession in 1894 and after serving as a novice mistress, archivist and general secretary, she became Superior General in 1911. Throughout her life Eugenia undertook many works of social charity, looking after the needy, the poor, and impoverished young families. As Superior General she led her Congregation more deeply into social concerns and this task became especially necessary during the First World War. Eugenia had a particular devotion to the Eucharist. She explained that 'as Jesus has chosen bread which is very common, so must my life be...common, approachable by all, and, at the same time humble and hidden like bread'. Eugenia had a degenerative bone condition which led to the amputation of her right leg in 1919. She died in 1921 and was beatified by Pope John Paul II in 2001.

Saint Arcangelo Tadini

1846–1912
Poor health, lame
Feast Day 20 May

Arcangelo was born on 12 October 1846 in the small village community of Verolanuova, Brescia in Italy into a noble Italian family. His health was always precarious and when he was two he became so ill that his parents and doctors thought that he would die. He managed to survive several further health crises and when he was eighteen he entered the seminary at Brescia in 1864. However, a serious fall resulted in severe injury to his right knee and Arcangelo walked with a limp for the rest of his life. Eventually, he could only walk with the aid of a stick. Arcangelo was ordained in 1870 but for health reasons he spent his first year as a priest living with his family and ministering to the local village. After a time as a curate at a local mountain village he was appointed priest at the shrine of Santa Maria della Noce near Brescia. His next appointment was as parish priest in Botticino Sera where he was well known for the care he had for his parishioners, especially in times of adversity. On one such occasion he organised a soup kitchen in the parish house for people made homeless by severe flooding. He was particularly enthusiastic to provide catechesis for every age and was concerned with liturgy and the choir as well as with rebuilding the church. He was also keen to organise confraternities, groups of lay people who were entrusted with special works of charity. Arcangelo was well aware of changes happening in society, and recognising the new phenomenon of growing industrialisation, he saw the need for social action and he set up an association to help workers suffering from illness, accident, disabilities or old age. He also provided work and accommodation to women by setting up a spinning factory and place of residence using his own inheritance as funding. He founded the Congregation of Worker Sisters of the Holy House of Nazareth where the sisters were to work alongside women in the factories to teach them by example. Despite his disability he would stand for hours in front of the Blessed Sacrament in contemplation. Arcangelo died in 1912, he was beatified by Pope John Paul II in 2001 and canonised by Pope Benedict XVI in 2009.

Saint Caterina Volpicelli

1839–1894
Poor health
Feast Day 22 January

Caterina was born on 21 January 1839 in Naples in Italy. Since her family was well off she had the opportunity to develop a love of languages, music, ballet and theatre and she spent much time trying to outshine her sister in society. In her late teenage years Caterina fell into a period of existential crisis that led her at one stage to prefer death to the feeling of great turmoil that she was undergoing. She began to feel torn between her life of entertainment and society, and a life that would bring her closer to God. In her memoirs, written at the suggestion of her spiritual director, Caterina pinpointed her chance meeting with Ludovico da Casoria, later declared a saint, as a decisive moment. Ludovico suggested that rather than join a cloistered order Caterina should enter the Third Order of St Francis to become a 'fisher of souls' and to devote herself to the Sacred Heart of Jesus. In 1859 Caterina entered the Congregation of Perpetual Adorers of the Blessed Sacrament. However serious ill health forced her to leave and she returned home to look after her father who was now seriously ill. She also took it upon herself to teach catechism to poor and deprived children and she was a frequent visitor to a hospital for incurable people. Caterina's confessor introduced her to the ideas of the Apostleship of Prayer and Caterina set about forming an apostleship in Naples, as she wrote, to 'revive love for Jesus Christ in hearts, in families and in society'. Naples itself was undergoing traumatic social change. It had been downgraded from a capital city and generally marginalised and this resulted not only in social unrest and riots but also in extreme poverty. Caterina realised that the way to reach people in dire need would be to work among them without barriers, and for her that meant without a religious uniform to single them out. She founded the Servants of the Sacred Heart in 1874 to help families, to care for the sick and to improve people's lives through education and the provision of libraries. When in 1884 cholera ravaged the city, Caterina organised nursing facilities for the victims and orphanages for children who otherwise would have been abandoned. She had built a shrine next to the mother house dedicated to the Sacred Heart of Jesus specifically for adoration for reparation to support the Church in times of difficulty. In 1893 during a resurgence of riots, the Servants of the Sacred Heart took care of the wounded. Caterina died in 1894 and she was beatified by Pope John Paul II in 2001 and canonised by Pope Benedict XVI in 2009.

Blessed Edward Poppe

1890–1924
Heart problems, confined to bed, stroke

Edward was born on 18 December 1890 in Moerzeke in Belgium into a simple and pious family. His father was a baker who worked hard to support his wife and eleven children. Edward seems to have been a mischievous child, fond of teasing his sisters, and also rather hyperactive. When Edward was fourteen his father suggested that Edward join the family business but he told them that he wished to become a priest. His parents accepted his decision and they allowed Edward to join the minor seminary in Waas. Then, some three years later in 1907, Edward's father died and, being a dutiful son, Edward thought he should return to take over the bakery. However, his mother instead insisted that he continue with his studies as this was what his father would have wanted. At the age of twenty Edward's studies were interrupted when he was called up for military service and his time in the army proved difficult since he was often ridiculed for his beliefs and for his desire to become a priest. Finally, at the end of his military service in 1912 Edward resumed his theological studies, though he also began to have doubts over the possibility of keeping to a life time's vocation to holiness as a priest. At the outbreak of the First World War Edward was called up to serve as a nurse, but in 1914, as the Belgian army withdrew, he fell sick and after suffering extreme exhaustion from his duties, he was discharged in 1915. He returned to the seminary in Ghent where he was ordained in 1916. He began his priestly ministry as a curate to a working class parish in Ghent where he involved himself with the special needs of children, the poor and the dying. Concerned with the increasing levels of secularisation, he promoted catechesis and associations for veneration of the Eucharist. His ill health meant that he was transferred back to Moerzeke where he became rector of a religious community. Although he spent four years there, for half of these he was confined to bed and he suffered the first of several serious heart attacks in 1919. He took the opportunity of this forced rest to write articles and letters and to concentrate on issues causing specific problems for Flanders, notably the issues of Marxism, secularism and materialism. Having visited the tomb of Thérèse of Lisieux in 1920 he adopted her 'little way' as a pattern for his life. He began a campaign for re-evangelisation based first on reform of the self, and the focus for this campaign was on the Eucharist, on catechesis and liturgical renewal and on developing the lay apostolate. Despite his increasing weakness, Edward was always happy to receive his many visitors, including a friend who had become a member of parliament and Edward took the opportunity to remind his influential friend of the importance of finding just solutions to the problems of workers. Edward suffered further cardiac problems at the end of 1923 before suffering from a final stroke. He died in 1924 and was beatified by Pope John Paul II in 1999.

Saint Filippo Smaldone

1848–1923
Diabetes, scoliosis, heart condition
Feast Day 4 June

Filippo was born on 27 July 1848 in Naples in Italy into a poor Christian family at a time of great political unrest and persecution of the Church. Initially Filippo was determined to become a missionary. However, he changed his mind and decided to study for the priest-hood after a chance meeting with a deaf-mute child in church. Filippo recognised that the deaf and mute community were particularly vulnerable since they were marginalised in society, deaf and mute children were often abandoned, and opportunities for their education and catechesis were virtually non-existent. While studying in the seminary, Filippo spent so much time helping people who were deaf and mute that he only just passed some of his exams. Fortunately, the archbishop allowed him to continue in the seminary and, even though he had not reached the mandatory age of twenty five, Filippo was ordained in 1871. Fillipo threw himself into his pastoral ministry. He formed evening catechesis classes and he worked with the sick, including those suffering from an epidemic of the plague. Although he still felt called to be a missionary, he was persuaded to carry on his work in Naples, especially his pioneering service to the deaf-mute community. In 1885 he founded an institute for deaf-mutes and trained sisters to work with them. This became the Congregation for the Salesian Sisters of the Sacred Heart. He founded other institutes for the blind, the abandoned and orphans. He served as confessor and as a spiritual director to priests, seminarians and religious. Filippo suffered from a serious and long lasting diabetic condition. This condition coupled with a heart problem and scoliosis led to his death in 1923. Filippo was beatified by Pope John Paul II in 1996 and canonised by Pope Benedict XVI in 2006.

Blessed Frederic Ozanam

1813–1853
Poor health, kidney disease
Feast Day 9 September

Frederic was born on 23 April 1813 in Milan and was brought up in Lyons in France where his father worked as an eminent mathematician, tutor and later physician. Frederic's parents had fourteen children in all. However, only three of their children survived beyond childhood and Frederic himself had poor health as a child and so was a worry to his parents. At seven he nearly died from a serious illness and a few years later his schooling was interrupted by an enforced stay in the country to recover his health. Despite setbacks due to his health, Frederic was a keen student. His studies in philosophy at sixteen made him briefly doubt his faith but this period of academic questioning eventually led him to develop a more robust approach to the intellectual aspect of his faith and he decided to commit himself to a defence of the truth. Although Frederic had an aptitude for literature and history, Frederic's father was determined that his son should become a lawyer and so apprenticed him to a local attorney. Whilst working Frederic still found time to write about philosophical, historical and social issues. He also wrote for the new Propagation of the Faith publication. In 1831 Frederic went to the University of Paris to study law and he met up with many people interested in the Catholic revival. In the rather anti-religious, materialistic, rationalistic and anti-clerical atmosphere of university life of the time Frederic gathered some like minded friends and they set up religious discussions including ones that focused on the social teachings of the gospel. Their Society of Good Studies became the Conference of History and eventually the Conference of St Vincent de Paul. After his bar exams Frederic began to practise law in Lyons even though he remained more interested in literature and publishing. Having completed a thesis on Dante, Frederic was offered an assistantship and then full professorship of Foreign Literature at the Sorbonne and as part of his research he lectured on the importance of Christianity in the growth of European civilisation. He married in 1844 and four years later his only daughter was born. By 1846 his increasing work with the Conference of St Vincent de Paul and his academic commitments took its toll on his health which had always been fragile. Frederic suffered a severe kidney infection that was mistaken for lung disease. He was obliged to take a year of rest in Italy to try and regain his health and during that time of convalescence he continued to devote himself to those in need. On his return he made it his particular concern to champion the rights of the poor and working class. The academic year of 1851 to 1852 brought another crisis in his health and although he stopped teaching in the Sorbonne he continued to work for the Conference. He retired to the Italian coast in 1853 for a rest but, realising he was dying he wished to return to France. He died in Marseille in September 1853 and he was beatified by Pope John Paul II in 1997.

Blessed Giuseppina Nicoli

1863–1924
Tuberculosis, bronchopneumonia
Feast Day 31 December

Giuseppina was born on 18 November 1863 at Casatisma, Pavia in Italy where she had a fairly privileged upbringing since her father was a magistrate and her mother a lawyer. Initially, Giuseppina gained a diploma in teaching because she wished to teach poor children. However, she was also drawn to religious life and the care of the poor so at the age of twenty she entered the Daughters of Charity of St Vincent de Paul in Turin. Two years later in 1885 she was sent to Sardinia to teach at the Conservatory of Providence of Cagliari and she took her simple vows in 1888. When she was thirty she contracted tuberculosis and its affects remained with her for the rest of her life. In 1899 she was sent to the community at Sassari in north-west Sardinia who had need of a superior and to begin with she ran the orphanage. She then set up a Daughters of Charity society to sew and mend clothes for distribution to the poor. She also organised a school for religious studies so that older students could be trained to teach the faith. In a further outreach to those in need, she ensured that the sisters visited women in prison. In 1910 she returned to the

province of Turin as bursar of the Daughters of Charity
and in 1912 became director of the novitiate in Turin.
She was not able to remain long in this position
because her lung condition worsened and her superiors sent her back to the more beneficial climate of
Sardinia. However anti-clericalism, general political
unwillingness and a drive towards civic education
meant she could not return to her previous adminis-
trative position at the orphanage in Sassari. Moreover,
it was said that she was incapable of administering the
orphanage, a charge that was later withdrawn. Instead,
she was sent back to Cagliari in 1914. During the First
World War Sister Giuseppina and the other sisters
nursed those wounded in the conflict as well as
continuing their care of the poor. Poverty and war and
disease were taking their toll on the most vulnerable,
and in 1917 at the request of the local bishop Sister
Giuseppina organised a group of consecrated lay
women and these became the Young Women of
Charity who ministered in the poorest suburbs of the
town, caring in particular for the many children who
were suffering from rickets and tuberculosis. In her
service to the poor, Giuseppina was acutely aware of
the need to engage with women and so she also
founded the St Teresa Circle, later to become the
Women's Catholic Action and the Josephite Association whose patron saint was St Joseph, for furthering
religious education. She was always mindful not only
of the physical needs of the poor but also of their
spiritual needs and so she organised retreats for
workers. Guiseppina had never managed to recover
from tuberculosis. By the age of sixty one her lung
condition had developed into bronchopneumonia, she

was confined to bed and she died in 1924. Giuseppina was beatified by Pope Benedict XVI in 2008.

Saint Laura Montoya Upegui

1874–1949

Prolonged illness, inflammation of the lymphatic system, wheelchair user

Feast Day 21 October

Laura was born on 26 May 1874 in the town of Jerico in the south west region of Antioquia in Columbia. When Laura was two, her father was killed in the Columbian civil war and as a result, the family property was confiscated and Laura, her mother and her two siblings were left poverty stricken. Laura was sent to live with her grandmother who did not show the little girl much care or affection and her upbringing was marked with neglect. Laura's isolation and loneliness led to her feeling a severe sense of abandonment but she found refuge in praying through scripture and in attending Mass. As Laura grew older, her mother played more of a role in her life and when Laura became sixteen her mother decided that Laura should apply to become a teacher so that she could help the family financially even though Laura had not had any formal education up to that point. Laura excelled in her studies and she began teaching in Antioquia. She found it natural to teach her young charges not only the set subjects but also values from the Gospel. Laura felt called to the religious life of a cloistered nun but was torn between that and her desire to be a missionary. In particular she noticed that the local native Indian population were generally marginalised, often treated with racial discrimination and frequently denied the dignity that belongs to all human beings. In 1914, amid local derision for attempting to bring the Gospel to what were regarded as animals, Laura and four companions went to live among the native Indians in Dabeiba and they became known as the Missionaries of Mary Immaculate and St Catherine of Sienna. Laura began to suffer from a long and painful illness, inflammation of the lymphatic system, and for the last nine years of her life she became a wheelchair user. She died in 1949, was beatified by Pope John Paul in 2004 and was canonised by Pope Francis in 2013.

Blessed Luigi Boccardo

1861–1936
Hunchback, poor health
Feast Day 9 June

Luigi was born on 9 August 1861 in Moncalieri in Italy. His parents were farmers but they recognised that Luigi wanted to study so they enrolled him with the Barnabite fathers where his older brother, Giovani, had also been educated. Luigi was always very close to his brother and when Luigi decided that he wanted to become a priest he appealed to his older brother for moral support. Giovani convinced their reluctant parents, moreover, he paid for his little brother's studies at the seminary in Turin. Luigi began his studies in 1875 but in 1877 he fell ill to severe typhus fever and he came close to death, saved, he believed by drinking Lourdes water. By this stage Giovani was now a priest and he became Luigi's spiritual director. In 1884, the same year that Luigi was ordained, a cholera epidemic struck Turin and the two brothers worked hard with victims of the disease. Giovani gave particular care to his flock at this time and founded the Poor Sisters of St Cajetan to minister to orphans and the elderly who survived the epidemic; Luigi later took over responsibility for this congregation. In 1886 Luigi became vice rector at a school that also provided formation for priests. By 1914 Luigi had been appointed Superior General of the Poor Sisters and so found himself responsible for several convents, hundreds of sisters and thousands of sick, elderly people, children and ageing priests. He also managed to turn around the failing fortunes of an institute for the blind in 1913. His work continued even though he was in poor health, prematurely aged and hunchbacked. As spiritual director at the institute for the blind, Luigi discovered that some blind people felt called to a life of service to God but were refused the possibility of pursuing their vocations due to their blindness. Recognising that every person has a particular call and in order to help some of these disabled people to consecrate themselves to God through a specific charism, Luigi instituted a contemplative branch of the Poor Sisters, the Sisters of Christ the King, whose work it was to pray for the pope, priests and people most in need. Luigi died in 1936 and he was beatified by Pope Benedict XVI in 2007.

Venerable Manuel Aparici Navarro

1902–1964

Heart problems, organ failure, wheelchair user

Manuel was born on 11 December 1902 in Madrid in Spain the son of an official of the General Treasury.

Although brought up as a Catholic, in his youth Manuel led a rather frivolous and secular life much to his mother's disappointment and he was particularly fond of smoking. In 1922 Manuel applied to join the customs offices and he was set on course for a good career in state administration. During the Lent of 1925, to keep his mother happy, he took up some spiritual exercises and began to recover some of his faith. Then at the age of twenty five in 1927 he underwent a conversion experience possibly from his contact with friends in the Catholic Youth Action and from that moment he practised his faith with fervour. However, he was always conscious that in his case the spirit was willing but the flesh weak. He was particularly irritated that he was wasting money on smoking, money that could have been spent on the poor, yet he was unable to give the habit up. Manuel was appointed vice president then president of the Catholic Youth Action and he went on the first Spanish youth pilgrimage to Rome in 1934. He began to think about a vocation to the priesthood but the bishop asked him to delay since his work at that stage with revitalising the Catholic Action movement was bearing fruit. Manuel himself did not consider that he was worthy of the office entrusted to him. Nevertheless, he obeyed and he concentrated on organising a great pilgrimage of young people to Santiago de Compostella as well as founding a Catholic youth paper. However, in 1936 with the outbreak of the Spanish Civil War and general persecution of the Church the project was postponed. Although not called up to fight, Manuel did what he could helping priests and caring for the wounded. Moreover, he endeavoured to keep Catholic Action going albeit as an underground movement. After the war in 1941 Manuel joined the seminary. He was ordained in 1947 and in 1950 he was appointed chaplain to the Catholic Youth. In 1955 Manuel began to suffer from circulatory problems, heart problems, organ failure, swollen legs and fatigue and was practically confined to bed throughout 1956 and 1957 so much so that he had to resign as chaplain. He kept in good spirits even when he was not able to say Mass and began to use a wheelchair to get around. Manuel described his feelings of being abandoned and needing oxygen to breathe as part of his climb to the summit of holiness, a climb that consisted of so many downs as well as ups. He wanted to dedicate his sufferings for the good of the Church but he himself recognised that theory is one thing, practice another. He continued with the spiritual exercises throughout his illness, wrote letters of encouragement especially to those working in Catholic Action, and commended himself to the will of God. Manuel died in 1964 and he was declared venerable by Pope Francis in 2013.

Blessed Manuel Lozano Garrido

1920–1971
Spondylitis, spinal deformity, wheelchair user, blind

Manuel was born on 9 August 1920 in Linares in Spain. He was one of seven children and his father died when he was young, his mother died when he was fourteen. From an early age Manuel was passionate about the Eucharist and had a strong devotion to Our Lady. Keen to put his faith in action and to play a part in his community, at the age of eleven Manuel joined the Catholic Action League. In the 1930s, during the Spanish Civil War when many priests had been arrested, Manuel took the Eucharist to local villagers and to prisoners even though on one of these visits the sixteen year old Manuel was caught and imprisoned. At the end of the Civil War, Manuel organised centres for Catholic action, gave catechism classes, and as a journalist he prepared radio broadcasts for evangelisation. Perhaps as a result of his own experience of imprisonment, Manuel developed a particular ministry to people in prison, notably those who were about to be executed. As was usual, Manuel was called up for military service and it was during this time in the army and at the age of twenty two that he was diagnosed with spondylitis, severe spinal arthritis, so he was discharged on health grounds in 1942. His condition resulted in increasing deformity and some paralysis and he became a wheelchair user in order to live life as fully as possible. Further paralysis and then blindness meant that he could no longer type so he dictated his work into a tape recorder. In 1956 Manuel formed an association of chronically ill people to pray for journalists. Manuel died in 1971 and he was beatified by Pope Benedict XVI in 2010.

Saint Paulina of the Agonizing Heart of Jesus (Amabile Lucia Wiesenteiner)

1865–1942
Diabetes, amputee, late onset blindness
Feast Day 9 July

Amabile was born on 16 December 1865 in the town of Vigolo Vatarro in Trentino in Italy then part of the Austro-Hungarian Empire. The family was poor and, in the company of other local people, they migrated to the state of Santa Catarina in Brazil. Here the new settlers founded the village of Vigolo, now known as Nova Trento. From the age of twelve Amabile began to take part in parish life by helping with catechesis, visiting the sick and cleaning the local chapel. In 1890 Amabile and her friend looked after a woman suffering from cancer and from this act of mercy the Congregation of the Little Sisters of the Immaculate Conception began its work. Amabile took her religious vows in the same year taking the name Sister Paulina of the Agonizing Heart of Jesus. In 1903 the Congregation moved to Sao Paolo with Sister Paulina as its superior general. Its mission was to look after orphans and in particular to care for the children of slaves and slaves that had been left destitute because they could no longer work. A series of disputes within the congregation meant that Sister Paulina was removed as superior general and she went to work with the sick and elderly in a hospice though later she was acknowledged as the founder of the congregation. In 1938 her health slowly deteriorated from her diabetes, her arm had to be amputated and she became blind. Paulina died in 1942. She was beatified by Pope John Paul II in 1991 and canonised in 2002.

Saint Richard Pampuri (Erminio Filippo Pampuri)

1897–1930
Poor health, pleurisy, bronchopneumonia
Feast Day 1 May

Erminio was born on 12 August 1897 in Trivolzio in northern Italy. When Erminio was three his mother died and he went to live with his grandparents and his aunt and uncle. Some seven years later his father died in a road traffic accident. Although he was interested in missionary work, Erminio's health was too fragile and so the option of joining a missionary order was out of the question. Instead Erminio joined the Franciscan Third Order and became involved in Catholic social action. Erminio continued to search for a vocation and he became increasingly impressed by the work of his uncle who was the village doctor. Through the inspiration of his uncle he decided to study medicine at Pavia University. His studies were interrupted by the outbreak of the First World War and his training in medicine led to a posting in the medical corps, first as a sergeant and then as an officer. It was during this time that he suffered from the pleurisy that would later return more virulently. After active service, Erminio resumed his medical studies. He graduated with high honours and became a rural health officer in Morimondo near Milan where he treated the poor for free, organised charity for them and founded a group to care for their medical needs. He set up music in the local parish, a Catholic action youth club, and organised retreats for young people and workers. In 1927 Erminio decided to join the Hospitaller Order of St John of God so that he could use his medical talents and also lead a holier life. He completed his novitiate year at Brescia and made his vows in 1928 taking the name Brother Richard and he began work in the St John of God Brothers' Hospital. Richard suffered another bout of pleurisy and this developed into bronchopneumonia. In 1930 he was taken back to Milan where he died at the age of thirty three. Richard

was beatified by Pope John Paul II in 1981 and canonised in 1989.

Saint Zygmunt Gorazdowski

1845–1920

Lung ailment, respiratory problems, poor health

Feast Day 1 January

Zygmunt was born on 1 November 1845 in Sanok in
the Ukraine. His family lived in very poor conditions
and this may have contributed to his serious lung
condition and ongoing respiratory problems. Initially,
Zygmunt intended to pursue a career in the law but
he soon abandoned his legal studies in favour of
studies for the priesthood at the seminary in Lvov.
After finishing his theological studies, Zygmunt
underwent two years of intensive medical therapy
before being ordained in 1871. Faced with a cholera
outbreak, the young priest worked tirelessly to care
for the sick, minister to the dying and bury the dead.
He took great interest in improving the educational
and social situations of the local people. He wrote a
catechism to help parents in their children's upbringing, and started an association to help in priestly
formation. Zygmunt was all too well aware of the
significant needs in his region and so he started a
refuge for homeless people and beggars, as well as a
kitchen that served food to the poor. He set up schools
for the poor, a teacher training college and an institute
for single mothers and their children, and he organised
a health centre for terminally ill patients. In order to
continue these missions, he founded the Congregation
of the Sisters of Mercy of St Joseph in 1884. Zygmunt

died in 1920. He was beatified in 2001 by Pope John Paul II and canonised in 2005 by Pope Benedict XVI.

Notes

1   Saint Augustine, *Sermon,* 103.
2   Pope Saint John Paul II, *Christifideles laici,* 53.
3   Pope Saint John Paul II, *Homily* (7 October 2001).

3

BEING A GOOD DISABLED SHEPHERD TO THE FLOCK

I am the good shepherd; I know my own and my own know me.

John 10:11

Introduction

N HIS APOSTOLIC Exhortation on the formation of priests, *Pastores Dabo Vobis* issued in 1992 Pope Saint John Paul II gave a meticulous account of the very many services offered by the priest. Among these he listed the duty to deepen the laity's sense of vocation and to bring comfort, healing and guidance to people through the administration of the sacraments, and to build up the body of Christ, the Church.[1] Certainly, all Christians are called to holiness and this vocation is rooted in their baptism. However, by virtue of Holy Orders, priests are specifically called to strive for holiness.[2] Not infrequently priests and their assistants have been faced with the tension between the requirement to deliver this pastoral need and the dangers that may ensue in times of persecution. A notable example was the situation of the second century bishop Saint Cyprian who prudently took refuge outside of Carthage during the Decian persecution in AD 250 but was later martyred in another wave of persecution in AD 258. There has never been an obligation on the priest to put himself at risk. However, many priests have shown themselves to be configured to Jesus as the 'head and shepherd' who lays down his life for his flock,[3] and in this act they show particular heroic virtue. This calling to heroic virtue is not restricted to priests. Catechists also have shown the considerable courage required to stay and teach the faith. Moreover, in times of persecution many lay people have themselves chosen to stay and serve their communities to the best of their abilities. Nevertheless, being a good shepherd does not require martyrdom. There are many situations where a person could reasonably retire to a more comfortable life on account of disability. However, some good shepherds decide to stay with their flock because they realise there is still work to be done, and some, like Saint Teresa of Avila, are keen to remind their flock of the need to be true to their calling, and in this they show heroic virtue.

Blessed Alojzije Stepinac

1898–1960

Polycythemia rubra vera, thrombosis of the leg, bronchial catarrah

Feast Day 10 February

Alojzije was born on 8 May 1898 in the village of Brezaric near Zagreb in Croatia, part of the Austro-Hungarian empire. Although Alojzije felt called to the priesthood, the First World War was looming and he was conscripted into the Austrian army where he trained as an officer before being sent to the Italian front. After some fighting he was imprisoned in Italy and then released and sent home in 1918. He began to study agriculture at Zagreb but soon realised that this was not the path for him and he returned home to work. After a brief marriage engagement, he began his studies for the priesthood in 1924 in Rome at the Pontifical Germanicum-Hungaricum College and then the Pontifical Gregorian University. He was ordained in 1930 and served in parishes in the Archdiocese of Zagreb. Alojzije worked in the city's poorer neighbourhoods and he proved himself to be skilled at calming disputes. He was always interested in finding ways to involve young people and lay people in parish and social life and as Archbishop of Zagreb he continued this interest by encouraging Eucharistic and Marian devotions with a special emphasis on participating in the sacramental life of the Church.

In the face of the rise of Nazism in 1936 Alojzije supported efforts to help those fleeing persecution and in 1938 he instituted the Action for Assistance to Jewish Refugees. Although a supporter of Croatian independence, Alojzije found himself at odds with the ruling fascist party, Ustasa. He spoke out publicly against the killing and deportation of Jews and allowed Jews to be hidden in monasteries. Where life was at stake, Alojzije did accept the baptism of Jews all the while believing that those who converted out of necessity would return to Judaism. Alojzije also condemned the revolutionary government's policy of forced conversion of Orthodox Christians to Catholicism. From May 1942 he used his sermons to speak out against injustice and in particular the failure to respect the right to life. He proclaimed the full dignity and rights of every human being, regardless of colour or religion. After the Nazi defeat the communists took over the government of the country. Alojzije spoke out against the persecution and execution of Catholic priests by communist militants. He was arrested and less than a month later was released. Tito, the new Yugoslavian leader, tried to persuade Alojzije to help him break the ties between the Catholic Church in Croatia and Rome but the Archbishop refused.

In 1946 Alojzije was put on trial for war crimes and collaboration with the Ustasa. He was sentenced to sixteen years hard labour but was released on the grounds of ill health in 1951 and offered either expulsion to Rome or house arrest. Alojzije chose house arrest because he felt his duty was to stay with his people. He was made a cardinal by Pope Pius XII in 1953 and in the same year he was diagnosed with the rare blood disorder polycythemia rubra vera, an excess of red blood cells. Apparently, he joked 'I am suffering from an excess of reds'. Although Alojzije was not physically tortured there were moves to expel him from Croatia. Alojzije refused all these moves because he was determined not to desert his flock, and he did not want to be replaced by a puppet Catholic hierarchy independent of the universal Church. This meant that he also refused to seek treatment abroad for his lethal blood condition because he feared that he would not be allowed to return. Alojzije eventually succumbed to his illness, though there has been further evidence that he was in fact poisoned. Alojzije died in 1960 and he was beatified by Pope John Paul II in 1998.

Venerable Aloysius Schwartz

1930–1992

Hepatitis, amyotropic lateral sclerosis (Lou Gehrig's disease, motor neuron disease)

Aloysius was born on 18 September 1930 in Washington DC where his father sold furniture door to door. Aloysius was one of eight children and when he was sixteen his mother died from cancer. Aloysius decided at an early age to become a priest and he was particularly interested in a mission to the poor and needy. He began his seminary studies in 1944 in Maryland and in 1947 he joined the Maryknoll missionaries. However, he felt called to minister to those in extreme poverty and so he became involved with the Belgian Société des Auxiliaires des Missions, a group set up to provide Western secular priests for mission under the jurisdiction of African and Asian bishops. Aloysius was ordained a priest in 1957 and, even though initially he thought that his poor health might count against him, he was allowed to go to Korea. Aloysius found that in the aftermath of the Korean War people were living in dire poverty with little chance of employment, and there were many widows, orphans, beggars and street children. He worked tirelessly to help his flock, but he soon collapsed and was diagnosed with hepatitis. His recovery was so slow that he was sent back to the United States where he spent much of his efforts raising money for the Korean mission. By 1961 he felt well enough to return to Korea and he resumed his work among the poor. Aloysius soon realised that a religious congregation would best be suited to the work he was trying to accomplish and so he founded the Sisters of Mary in 1964 and then the

Brothers of Christ in 1981. The congregations educated and took care of orphans, street children and children from impoverished homes. Aloysius became involved in the building of hospitals, hospices and homes for the elderly, the disabled and for unmarried mothers. In 1985 Aloysius brought the work of the Sisters of Mary into Manila. In 1989 Aloysius was diagnosed with Lou Gehrig's disease, amyotropic lateral sclerosis, a form of motor neuron disease. As his muscles began to waste away, Aloysius used a wheelchair so that he could carry on for as long as possible. Aloysius died in Manila in 1992 and was declared venerable by Pope Francis in 2015.

Saint Charles Borromeo

1538–1584

Speech impediment, skin infection

Feast Day 4 November

Charles was born on 2 October 1538 in the family castle in Arona in north Italy. His father, a count, married into the Medici family and in 1559 his mother's younger brother was elected Pope, taking the name Pius IV. At the early age of twelve, Charles was given permission to receive the tonsure, a ceremonial rite of preparation for clerical orders, and he began his studies in Latin first in Milan and then at the University of Pavia. To begin with, Charles was regarded as a slow learner because he had a speech impediment. However, he soon proved himself to be thorough and conscientious even though his impediment made preaching difficult for him. Charles was created titular abbot of the abbey at Arona and his studies were often interrupted by the need to deal with the family estate and business as well as affairs at the abbey. In 1560 his uncle, Pope Pius IV, called Charles to Rome and made him a cardinal-deacon, an administrator for the papal states, and secretary of state. In particular, Charles worked to re-assemble the Council of Trent which had been suspended since 1552. Using his considerable diplomatic skills, Charles ensured that the Council resumed in 1562 and he steered the Council through to the confirmation of the decrees in 1564 despite disagreements and difficulties. During these negotiations, his brother died and since Charles had not yet been ordained, pressure was put on him to marry for the sake of the family. However, Charles was ordained in secret in 1563 and later the same year he was consecrated bishop. Although Charles expressed the wish to retire to a monastery, he was persuaded to remain as bishop in his diocese and put the reforms of the Council of Trent into action. He was also given charge of visitations to Italy and Switzerland. He was especially concerned with reform and education of the clergy and in his work he demonstrated that change could take place from within the Church. Charles survived an attempt on his life by some who were against the reforms. Charles was also keen to encourage systematic teaching of children and he set up what became the forerunner of Sunday schools. In 1571 Charles suffered a bout of serious illness from which he only partially recovered. Despite the continuation of fever and catarrh, Charles prepared for his next diocesan synod and, on the death of Pope Pius V, he attended the conclave that elected Pope Gregory XIII in 1572. By 1576 plague had broken out in Milan. Charles took it upon himself to visit personally some of the worst affected areas so that he could offer comfort to sufferers who, from fear of contagion, had been abandoned. The plague gradually subsided and had disappeared by 1578. Charles resumed his visitations and his reforms. Moreover, he founded a congregation of secular priests, encouraging the setting up of seminaries and schools. At the end of 1584 an attack of erysipelas, an acute skin infection, in one leg left him confined to bed. Nevertheless, he continued to serve the needs of the diocese and he oversaw the beginnings of work on a hospital for invalids. After a prolonged bout of fever during which Charles pressed on with his work as far as he could, Charles died. Charles was beatified in 1602 and canonised in 1610 by Pope Paul V.

Blessed Elias del Socorro Nieves

1882–1928

Tuberculosis, bad eye sight, general poor health

Feast Day 10 March

Elias was born on 21 September 1882 in Yuriria, Guanajuato, in Mexico into a family of poor farmers. He was a very sick baby and his parents had him baptised quickly as a matter of urgency since they feared he would die. Although he survived this initial illness, at the age of twelve Elias contracted tuberculosis and suffered temporary blindness that left him with very bad eyesight. Elias was keen to join the Augustinian Order. However, various factors made this impractical. His father was murdered thus plunging the family into poverty. This and his poor health prevented him from pursuing the further studies that would have enabled him to join the Order. Instead, he supported his family as best as he could and committed himself to pastoral work in his parish. Eventually he managed to be admitted to the Augustinian Order and he gratefully accepted both the practical and economic help he needed in his studies to catch up on the education he had missed and to cope with his near blindness and frail health. Elias made his profession in 1911 and in 1916 he was ordained a priest. Elias carried on his pastoral work in and around Yuriria and then he was assigned to the larger town of La Canada de Caracheo. The community was impoverished, with no adequate sanitary services, electricity or schools. However, his own experience of hardship and poverty meant that Elias fully understood the difficulties of his flock and could offer practical as well as spiritual support. The political situation deteriorated and there were calls for revolution. The government ordered the Church to concentrate its activities in the larger urban areas but Elias refused to leave his small town since that would mean abandoning his flock. Instead, he took refuge in a local cave and in this way he ensured that his people always had access to the sacraments, though often under the cover of darkness. He was eventually captured by soldiers who realised that his peasant clothes were concealing his priestly vestments. He was executed in 1928 by firing squad after he had blessed his executioners. Elias was beatified by Pope John Paul II in 1997.

Blessed Isidore Ngei Ko Lat

c.1918–1950

Asthma

Little is known about the early life of Isidore. His family were peasant farmers who became Catholics through the work of the missions in Burma, now known as Myanmar, and Isidore was baptised in 1918. His parents died when Isidore was young, and he and his brother were sent to live with their aunt and uncle.

Isidore joined the minor seminary in Taungoo however he was forced to leave because he suffered from asthma. On his return home he decided to become a teacher and he opened a school offering free education and catechesis for the village children. In about 1948 the missionary Father Mario Vergara met Isidore and Isidore helped him as the catechist in Shadaw in the eastern part of Burma. The political situation in Burma was complex after Burma's independence in 1948, with rival groups fighting for power. Some of the rebel forces had begun to persecute Catholics and Father Vergara acted strenuously in the defence of those who were oppressed. On 24 May 1950 Father Vergara and Isidore approached a group of rebels in order to secure the release of a fellow catechist. Father Vergara and Isidore were both arrested and shot. Their bodies were put in bags and thrown in the river. Father Vergara and Isidore were beatified by Pope Francis in 2014.

Blessed James Alberione

1884–1971

Poor health, scoliosis, spinal arthritis

James was born on 4 April 1884 in San Lorenzo di Fassano, Cuneo, Italy. He was one of six children and his parents were farmers. As a young child, James felt that he was called to the priesthood and his family supported his decision to enter the seminary of Alba at the age of sixteen. At the turn of the century on the night of the 31 December 1900, James experienced a summons to put the new emerging innovations of human ingenuity, notably new methods of communication, at the service of the Church and the proper progress of human beings. This summons bore fruit later in his vocation. He finished his theological and philosophical studies and was ordained a priest in 1907. After some pastoral experience in a local parish, James became a spiritual director and teacher at the seminary in Alba. He also helped with preaching, catechesis and conferences in the diocese. In 1914 James founded the Society of St Paul, and a year later, with the help of Teresa (Thecla) Merlo, he set up a second Congregation, the Daughters of St Paul. Faithful to his earlier summons to develop modern communication methods for the service of the Church, James began a magazine for parish priests, *The Pastoral Life*, in 1912. Gradually he utilised the power of communication by producing various periodicals, including one for the family, *The Christian Home*, first published in 1931; *Mother of God*, dedicated to Mary in 1933; *Good Shepherd* a monthly magazine published in 1937; *Way, Truth, Life* a monthly publication on Christian teaching, first produced in 1952; *Life in Christ and in the Church* also produced in 1952 on the liturgy; and a weekly magazine for children, *The Little Newspaper*. James also organised the building of several churches and he encouraged his 'Pauline Family' in devotions to Jesus Master and Shepherd, Mary Queen of the Apostles and the Apostle Paul. By 1960 the 'Pauline Family' consisted of four congregations and several secular institutes for the consecrated life. The underpinning of the apostolate was to bring Jesus Christ Way, Truth and Life to the world through social communication. For some forty years, James suffered severe scoliosis that was accompanied by painful spinal arthritis. James died in 1971 and he was beatified by Pope John Paul II in 2003.

Saint John Dukla

About 1414–1484

Late onset blindness

Feast Day 29 September

John was born in about 1414 in Dukla, Galicia in Poland into a middle class family. At first as a young man John embraced the life of a hermit but then studied theology in Kracow. Apparently well versed in theology and the German language, he joined the Franciscans and was ordained. John rose to be superior in monasteries in Krosno and Lvov. From 1440 to 1463 he travelled as a missionary and preacher in the Ukraine. In later life he became blind. Nevertheless, he continued with his pastoral duties and found his way to the confessional using the pews as a guide. John died in Lvov in 1484. He was beatified by Pope Clement XII in 1733 and he was canonised by Pope John Paul II in 1997.

Saint José de Anchieta

1534–1597

Spinal problems

Feast Day 9 June

José de Anchieta Llarena was born on 19 March 1534 in the Canary Islands. His family was both prominent and wealthy moreover his mother was related to the family of Ignatius Loyola. At the age of fourteen José was sent to Portugal for his education and in 1551 at the age of seventeen he was admitted to the Jesuit College at Coimbra as a novice. During his studies he began to suffer problems with his spine that left him in constant pain. However, he was a diligent student, gifted at languages and poetry. The Jesuits sent him to Brazil hoping in vain that the mild climate would alleviate his pain. José and his companions arrived in Brazil on the feast of St Paul and they founded a mission that they named Sao Paulo. José set about learning the language of the local Tupi Indians and he worked on a dictionary for the incoming Portuguese missionaries. He spent much time trying to keep peace between the colonisers and the local tribes. In particular, he was keen to promote the spirituality and dignity of the local people. He wrote plays for the Indians and at one stage, while being held hostage by another Indian tribe, he composed a 4,000 line prayer to Our Lady that he was only able to write down on his release some five months later. Despite his poor health he travelled the local area to expand and consolidate the Jesuit mission. He died at Reritiba, renamed Anchieta in his honour in 1597. José was beatified by Pope John Paul II in 1980 and he was canonised by Pope Francis in 2014.

Saint Joseph Cafasso

1811–1860

Spinal deformity, stomach haemorrhage, pneumonia

Feast Day 23 June

Joseph was born on 15 January 1811 in the small town of Castelnuovo d'Asti, Piedmont in Italy into a peasant family. He was born with a marked spinal deformity and was frail and small in stature. His parents recognised early on that Joseph had a vocation to the priesthood and they allowed him to join the seminary in Turin. He excelled at his studies and obtained a dispensation to be ordained in 1833 despite being only twenty three years old and below the usual age. Joseph became a theology lecturer and then rector at the Institute of St Francis of Assisi. Joseph developed a

particular mission to prisoners, especially those waiting execution, and he ensured that many came to
repentance and to God before their deaths. Despite his
frailty he was known for his persistence with even the
most hardened criminals and he would refuse to give
up on those whom others judged to be hopeless causes.
Moreover, he inspired many local people to work for
social reform and he became a mentor to John Bosco.
He attended to the poor and was well known for his
patience in the confessional. Joseph died in 1860 from
pneumonia, stomach haemorrhage and complications
from his deformity. He was beatified by Pope Pius XI
in 1925 and canonised by Pope Pius XII in 1947.

Saint Junípero Serra (Miguel José Serra)

1713–1784

Leg and feet ulcers, possible asthma, severe chest pains

Feast Day 1 July

Miguel was born on 24 November 1713 at Petra,
Majorca in Spain where his family owned a small farm.
Miguel combined helping on the farm with attending
school at the Franciscan Friary at Petra and he was
particularly fond of singing in the choir. At the age of
fifteen, Manuel announced that he wanted to be a
priest and in 1729 he began his studies at the Friary of
St Francis in Palma. By 1730 Miguel had decided that
he wanted to become a Franciscan and he entered the
novitiate that same year. Apparently, Miguel was too
short, at five feet two inches, to turn the pages of the
Gradual, the huge plainchant book placed on the
lectern in the centre of the choir, so he was not able to
sing with the other novices and he had to serve the
private masses of the fathers instead. Miguel made his
religious profession in 1731, taking the name Junípero

after one of the companions of Saint Francis known for his humility and simplicity. Brother Junípero was ordained in 1738 or 1739 and he became a philosophy lecturer at the Friary, then professor of theology at the University of Palma. In response to appeals made to the Franciscans to help in missionary work, Brother Junípero volunteered to go to Mexico and he and another friar set off in 1749. When they arrived at Vera Cruz, the two friars decided to remain faithful to the rule of Saint Francis that forbade friars to ride on horseback except in cases of necessity, and they began the walk of some two hundred and seventy miles to Mexico City. During the journey, Brother Junípero suffered severe swellings on his feet and legs, possibly due to mosquito bites, and these swellings developed into a wound that lasted for the rest of his life.

Between 1750 and 1758 Brother Junípero worked with the Pame Indians, teaching, building mission churches and introducing European agricultural methods which, unbeknown to Brother Junípero, would eventually lead to the demise of the Indian traditional way of life. He then preached missions throughout Mexico before setting off for a new expedition to California in 1769. By this time Brother Junípero had developed aggravated varicose veins and an infected ulcer so he had to be carried on a stretcher for the last part of the journey. Although Brother Junípero took a rather paternalistic attitude towards his native Indian flock, seeing them as little children on their journey to the faith, he frequently criticised the notion that they were less rational than the ruling Spanish population. Moreover, he fought for the rights of the natives against the new settlers, Spanish soldiers and various governors of California. Brother Junípero died at the native mission of San Carlos in 1784 after suffering from increasing cardiac failure. He was beatified by Pope John Paul II in 1988 and canonised by Pope Francis in 2015.

Saint Lucy Yi Zhenmei

1815–1862

Poor health

Feast Day 19 February

Lucy was born on 9 December 1815 in Mianyang in Sichuan, China and as a child she loved to read and study. Lucy was known to be a pious child, but when she became seriously ill in her twenties she decided to commit herself more seriously to deepening her spiritual life. After her recovery she took up the same work as her mother, spinning, in order to help support her family all the while trying to live a religious way of life through prayer and devotions. The parish priest asked Lucy to teach at the school in Mianyang and Lucy also taught the faith to all the local children of the parish. On the death of her father, Lucy and her mother moved to Chongqing where her brother was a doctor. Once again Lucy was asked to teach, though this time the women in the parish, and although she was offered money she did it gladly and for free. After the death of her mother, Lucy continued to do missionary work and she moved to a convent that was seen as offering a level of protection to Christians under threat. However, she was forced to move back home as her health grew worse. In 1861 the bishop asked her to return and teach at the convent. Her relatives were concerned for her safety nevertheless Lucy wanted to remain with the community as their catechist. During an open mission in Jiashanlong, Lucy was arrested and sentenced to death because she refused to renounce her faith. Lucy was beheaded in 1862. Lucy was beatified by Pope Pius X in 1909 and canonised by Pope John Paul II in 2000.

Blessed Mario Vergara

1910–1950

Appendicitis followed by peritonitis and poor health, kidney problems

Mario was born on 16 November in the town of Frattamaggiore near Naples. His father, a factory owner and city councillor, was frequently absent from the family on business leaving his mother to bring up the rather boisterous Mario and his eight siblings. In 1921 Mario joined the junior seminary in Posillipo and then in 1929 he was admitted to the seminary for the Pontifical Institute for Foreign Mission in Monza. However, he was forced to leave his studies after suffering appendicitis and then a life-threatening bout of peritonitis. Although he was able to resume his studies, he remained in poor health. Mario was ordained a priest in 1934 and was sent to Burma, then a British colony. He had an aptitude for languages and he found and trained local people to be catechists, he set up a sanatorium and an orphanage.

During the Second World War in 1941 Mario was sent to a British concentration camp with other Italian missionaries. Although conditions were not bad, Mario's health suffered and he had to have one of his kidneys removed. When he was released he was concerned that he would be forced to retire on health grounds but instead he was sent to Taungoo where he learnt the tribal dialect, acquainted himself with the local customs and set about finding catechists. One such catechist was a local man, Isidore Ngei Ko Lat. In the aftermath of the war the area was stricken with poverty, lack of food and poor transport facilities. Mario lived in a bamboo hut and he cheerfully reported that if it rained he could have a bath at home like a king. In the general disorder following Burma's independence, there were many rival factions jostling for power and the Catholic missionaries were regarded as heirs of the old colonial order. The locals were oppressed by the rebels who frequently seized their food. Mario was known to champion the cause of the people against the rebels. In May 1950 one of the catechists was arrested and Mario set out with Isidore to secure his release. Instead, Mario and Isidore were taken prisoner themselves and were shot. Their bodies were dumped in the river. Mario and Isidore were beatified by Pope Francis in 2014.

Saint Maximilian Kolbe (Rajmund Kolbe)

1894–1941

Tuberculosis

Feast Day 14 August

Rajmund was born on 7 January 1894 in the town of Zduńska Wola in central Poland. His parents worked as weavers and they also belonged to the secular order of the Franciscan lay tertiaries. By all accounts Rajmund was a difficult child. However, when he was twelve he had a vision of Our Lady and this changed his life. It seems that when Rajmund asked Our Lady what would become of him, she offered him the choice of two crowns: a white crown of purity and a red crown of martyrdom. Rajmund chose both. In 1907, at the age of thirteen, Rajmund began his further education at the Franciscan junior seminary in Lvov and for a time toyed with the idea of having a career in the military. However, the call to the religious life was stronger and he joined the Franciscans as a novice in 1910. Rajmund took the name Maximilian and made his final vows in 1914. He studied at a seminary in Rome where he and his friends founded the Immaculata Movement, devoted to the conversion of sinners. In Rome Maximilian developed tuberculosis and this seems to have been a factor in his subsequent work as priest. On his return to Poland in 1919 Maximilian had hoped to be sent on missionary work, but instead he was given the job of teaching history in the seminary in Kracow. Maximilian's tuberculosis grew worse and so he was sent to the Tatra Mountains for treatment. Maximilian still worked with the Immaculata Movement and he started a publication, *Knight of the Immaculate*, as a response to religious apathy. In 1927 he helped found a monastery west of Warsaw called Niepokalanów, the City of the Immaculate Mother of God, and he then engaged in a mission to take the Immaculata Movement to Japan in 1930, founding a monastery in Nagasaki. In 1936 poor health forced him to end his missionary work and return to Poland to Niepokalanów where the monastery continued with its publications and, in addition, radio broadcasts.

Following the Nazi invasion of Poland in 1939, Maximilian and some of the brothers were arrested on the grounds that, not only were the publications viewed as anti-Nazi, the monastery also employed Jews. In 1941 Maximilian was transferred to the camp at Auschwitz. After a prisoner escaped from the camp, the guards planned to execute several prisoners in retribution and as a deterrent to the others. Maximilian offered to take the place of one of the selected prisoners who was married with children because, as a priest, Maximilian realised the importance of being with those who faced death. After three weeks of starvation during which Maximilian ministered to those who were dying with him, Maximilian was given a lethal injection and he died in 1941. Maximilian was beatified by Pope Paul VI in 1971 and canonised by Pope John Paul II in 1982

Blessed Miguel Pro

1891–1927

Stomach problems

Feast Day 23 November

Miguel was born on 13 January 1891 in Guadalupe in Mexico where his family was commercially successful in the mining industry. Miguel entered the Jesuit novitiate in 1909 in Mexico but the revolution in 1914 forced the Jesuits to leave and Miguel continued his training abroad in the United States and in Spain. He was ordained in Belgium in 1925 though his health had deteriorated. Miguel suffered from severe stomach problems and had numerous unsuccessful operations for ulcers. Despite the upheaval in Mexico, his superiors allowed him to return to Mexico in 1926 hoping that his health would improve at home. However, persecution had left churches closed and priests were in hiding. Miguel began secret missionary activity in Mexico City, ministering to the Catholics and assisting the poor. He used various disguises from that of a beggar to baptise infants, to that of a police officer to take viaticum to condemned prisoners. Falsely accused of being involved in an assassination attempt on the Mexican president, Miguel was executed in 1927 without trial by firing squad and he was shot at point blank range. He was beatified by Pope John Paul II in 1988.

Saint Nicholas Owen

c.1550–1606

Crippled, unusually small stature, hernia

Feast Day 22 March

Nicholas was born in Oxford in about 1550. His father was a carpenter, two of his brothers became priests and a third brother was involved in the underground Catholic printing trade. In about 1580 Nicholas joined the Jesuits as a lay brother, and he put his skills as a carpenter and stone mason to good use. Catholic households employed Nicholas to do general work around their houses. Then at night and alone, Nicholas built hides for priests, ingeniously concealed in the fabric of the house with sophisticated systems of entry, false facades, and ways in which liquids could be secretly delivered so that priests could be hidden for days. Nicholas was given the nickname Little John because of his very small stature though there is no evidence he was a dwarf. He was crippled in an accident when a packhorse fell on top of him and later in life he suffered from a hernia. Nicholas became a servant to Father Edmund Campion. Nicholas was first arrested in about 1582 after the priest's execution, when he publicly declared that the priest was innocent. He was tortured but revealed nothing and a wealthy Catholic paid for his release. He then became the servant of Father John Gerard and was arrested again in 1694, was imprisoned in the Tower of London and once more tortured but gave away nothing. Thought by his jailers to be too insignificant, he was able to buy his freedom with the help of another wealthy Catholic family. Some three years later, he helped to engineer the escape of Father John Gerard who was imprisoned in the Tower of London. Nicholas resumed his occupation of building priest holes and he was at Hindlip Hall in Worcester with Father Henry Garnet, Father Edward Oldcorne and Oldcorne's assistant, Ralph Ashley when the pursuivants, officials charged with hunting down Catholic priests, arrived after a tip off. Nicholas had already constructed eleven hiding places in Hindlip Hall so members of the group hid in different places. After three days, Nicholas and Ralph Ashley emerged hoping that if they gave themselves up the search would end and the priests would remain undiscovered. Unfortunately, the search continued for another week until the two priests also surrendered. Both priests were hung, drawn and quartered. Nicholas was taken to the Tower of London to be tortured since by this time his captors realised that, of all people, he would know where other priests were hidden. Under the law, torture was forbidden in cases of people who were maimed or crippled, however this did not stop the torturers. He was even given an iron waist girdle to prevent him dying from a ruptured hernia before they had managed to get out all the information. Nicholas was hung in iron manacles from a wall with heavy weights on his feet. He did not divulge any of his secrets and he died when his hernia and stomach finally burst. His jailers put forward the story that he had committed suicide but this was not believed. Nicholas was beatified by Pope Pius XI in 1929 and canonised by Pope Paul VI as one of the Forty Martyrs in 1970.

Blessed Ralph Ashley

Died 1606

Unspecified illness

Feast Day 9 April

Nothing is known about Ralph's birth and early life. Ralph was a cook at the English college of Douai in France and then in 1590 cook and baker in the college in Valladolid in Spain. He had tried to enter the Jesuit Order but ill health prevented him from completing his novitiate. Instead, he decided to return to England and in 1598 he became a Jesuit lay brother and assistant to the Jesuit priest Edward Oldcorne. The two worked together serving English Catholics for eight years. They were eventually captured and imprisoned in the Tower of London where they were tortured, tried and condemned to death. Father Edward was executed first and then Brother Ralph followed. They were martyred in 1606 and were beatified by Pius XI in 1929.

Saint Teresa of Avila

1515–1582

Angina, heart complaint, fainting fits, weakness, nausea, severe headaches, broken and badly set arm, paralytic stroke

Feast Day 15 October

Teresa was born on 28 March 1515 in Avila in Spain into a wealthy family. Her father and his second wife had nine children, Teresa being the third, and her father also had three children from an earlier marriage. As a child, Teresa loved the stories of the saints and at one stage she and one of her brothers set out intending to become martyrs. They had not gone far when they were found and were brought back home to their anxious parents. The two children then determined to become hermits in the garden. When Teresa was fourteen her mother died and Teresa became interested in the romantic chivalrous literature of the day. Her father decided that an education at the Augustinian convent in Avila with other young ladies of her position would be the suitable course of action. However, after a year and a half Teresa fell ill, possibly with a form of malaria, and her father brought her home. Teresa began to think about her future and, concerned that a marriage would be arranged for her, she told her father that she wished to become a nun. He refused his consent and even though Teresa was devoted to her father, she decided to apply for admission to the convent in secret. Teresa took her vows in 1536 but two years later she became very ill with heart pain, fainting fits and extreme weakness so her father removed her from the convent. At one point Teresa had a seizure and fell into a coma. Her family thought she had died and prepared a grave for her. During her convalescence, Teresa took comfort from a form of mental prayer that progressed to the quietness of the soul in contemplation of God. Her health slowly improved and Teresa returned to the convent and to a relaxed life where the young nuns would receive visitors and happily chat with friends in the convent parlour. She gave up her custom of mental prayer convincing herself that her health was too fragile. After a while she realised the unsatisfactory state of her life in the convent and returned to her mental prayer and a more austere way of living. She then began to have visions and to hear voices but these were dismissed as delusions or the action of evil spirits by her spiritual directors. In 1557 the Franciscan friar St Peter of

Alcantara came to Avila and found that Teresa's experiences were the work of the Holy Spirit. At about this time Teresa experienced her deepest ecstasy and her spiritual marriage to Christ. At the age of forty three Teresa began to feel that the Carmelite inspiration in her convent had drifted and she was determined to found a new convent that would return to the basic Carmelite understanding of a life of poverty and devotion to prayer. Although she faced considerable opposition, Teresa founded seventeen reformed convents for what later became the Discalced Carmelites, and she wrote spiritual books and her own autobiography. Throughout the years of reform Teresa still suffered from recurrent illness and severe headaches. In 1577 at the age of sixty two Teresa fell and broke her arm. It did not heal properly and caused her great pain leaving her unable even to dress herself. Teresa may have suffered a series of paralytic strokes in 1580. Teresa died in 1582 and she was beatified by Pope Paul V in 1614 and canonised by Pope Gregory XV in 1622. Teresa was proclaimed the first woman doctor of the Church by Pope Paul VI in 1970.

Notes

[1] Pope Saint John Paul II, *Pastores Dabo Vobis*, 3–4, 17.

[2] *Ibid*, 19–20.

[3] *Ibid*, 21–22.

4

HOLY VICTIMS: DISABLED PEOPLE LIVING OUT THE PASSION OF CHRIST

If it is possible, let this cup pass me by. Nevertheless, let it be as you, not I, would have it.

Matthew 26:39

Introduction

ANY PEOPLE WITH disabilities do not see themselves as suffering and, according to one of the models of disability, the social model, impairment or falling short of some apparent norm of health are not significant issues. Rather, what is at issue is the notion that there is a norm in the first place. For many people, attitudes to impairment are themselves impairing. Those who follow a strong version of the social model of disability are keen to point to the disabling attitudes of society that are the cause of suffering, marginalisation and discrimination. Some people who advocate for disability rights movements reject the way in which people with disabilities have been cast into a 'sick role' and above all they draw attention to the problem of seeing suffering as virtuous, as if suffering is of and by itself a good to pursue.

What then is to be made of people with disabilities who fully embrace an apostolate of suffering, especially those who, like Blessed Alexandrina Maria da Costa, see themselves as 'victim souls,' and those who ask to share more and more in Christ's suffering? Certainly not all people with long term disabilities, especially those whose illness confines them to bed and so potentially isolates them, see themselves as 'victim souls'. However, a significant number of the saints and blessed who find themselves in this situation, rather than give in to despair, decide to unite their sufferings with those of Christ where all suffering is redeemed.

In his encyclical *Evangelium vitae, the Gospel of Life,* Pope Saint John Paul II identified two opposing cultures: the culture of death and the culture of life.[1] He explained that in the culture of death, the spiritual aspect of human beings has been neglected or even replaced by an excessive materialism. This culture either elevates physical beauty, or reduces the human being to a complex set of organs, and it sees the person only in terms of what he or she can do, or how useful the person is. Anyone who does not have a role or a function is considered a burden, a drain on resources, something redundant or to be eliminated. And of course, in this culture of death the first to suffer are the weak, the sick, the very young or the very elderly and the disabled. According to the Pope, the problem with the culture of death was not only that it endorses abortion, euthanasia and assisted suicide. To be sure he regarded these actions as veritable crimes against humanity, especially where they have become legislative rights[2] or where they are motivated by a mistaken sense of compassion couched in terms of relieving suffering, when it fact the method for achieving this is to eliminate the sufferer him or herself. Rather, the Pope's main concern was that people are losing the sense of the fullness of life, that is, life in eternity. He was clear that this life is 'a sacred reality entrusted to us', nevertheless, he explained that earthly life is only the 'penultimate reality'.[3] However, for people who think that this earthly life is all there is, then suffering can have no place in it. As the Pope acknowledged, suffering is one of the greatest stumbling blocks in the effort to challenge this culture of death.[4]

Certainly, Pope Saint John Paul did not think that suffering can be easily explained. In his extensive writings on suffering, from his encyclical *Salvifici Dolores, On the Christian meaning of human suffering,* issued in 1984, to his speeches on the World Days of the Sick, the Pope talked essentially of witness and discipleship. Above all, he pointed out that although efforts should be made to relieve suffering, suffering itself is an inescapable reality of every human life.[5] In contrast to those who see no use or meaning in suffering, Pope Saint John Paul II saw people who suffer from disability as entrusted with a 'special mission': to see illness and disability in the light of Christ's death and resurrection and so be witnesses to 'the Gospel hope' in a world desperate for hope that human beings are destined for future glory brought about through the Passion of Jesus.[6] There is no doubt that Pope Saint John Paul II believed that suffering is an experience of evil.[7] However, he also thought that through the Passion of Christ all human suffering has found itself in 'a new situation'.[8] As the Pope explained just as Jesus shared in the reality of human suffering, so too do all human beings share in the reality of his redemp-

tion: suffering has been redeemed.[9] The Pope made it
clear that the apparent glorying in suffering of 'victim
souls' then is not found in suffering for its own sake.
Rather, it is found in sharing the sufferings of Christ
and so sharing in his resurrected glory.[10]

It has to be said that in today's world, exacerbated
perhaps by a cultural denial of death and a reluctance
to see meaning in difficult situations, the notion of
'victim souls' creates unease and for many it is disturbing. Nevertheless, in today's world where the chronically sick are seen as useless and potential subjects
either of euthanasia or of assisted dying, then the
witness of a life that involves prayer for others, consolation to visitors and contemplation of Christ can be
particularly instructive. Embracing the reality of suffering and seeing in it the possibility of redemption can be
seen as the opposite to a giving in to despair, despair
that the saints and blessed have often themselves
experienced and yet overcome. They lived the sorrow-
ful Passion of Christ in their bodies especially on behalf
of those who see no meaning in suffering or those who
are particularly in need of God's grace. Their willingness to take on suffering becomes a giving of the self,
an opening out to the possibility that God's grace can
transform a negative situation and release hope. In
particular, by looking outwards towards a world that
is suffering, they face and overcome the temptation to
self-absorption and a sense of isolation that often
accompanies chronic illness. They offer a new attitude
to disability that takes account of impairment and
brings it into the redemptive action of Christ. In his
homily on the beatification of six servants of God,
among them Alexandrina Maria da Costa, Augustus
Czartoryski and Eusebia Palomino Yenes, Pope John

Paul II declared that these sufferers were 'eloquent examples of how the Lord transforms the existence of believers when they trust in him'[11] and, in embracing this transformation that is at times painful these servants of God show in their own way heroic virtues.

Blessed Alexandrina Maria da Costa

1904–1955

Sickness from infection and later confined to bed by paralysis

Feast Day 13 October

Alexandrina was born on 30 March 1904 in Balasar, a small rural village north of Porto in Portugal. After her father died, Alexandrina worked for a farmer, though her employment with him did not last long since he made her work harder than was agreed. Moreover, it appears that the farmer had possibly tried to assault her. Alexandrina returned home and soon after she fell seriously ill with an infection, possibly intestinal typhoid fever, and the consequences of this illness remained with her for the rest of her life. Since she was no longer fit for arduous outside work she took up sewing and she also helped the local catechist with instructing younger children. One day, when Alexandrina was only fourteen, her former employer and two other men arrived at her house. They were drunk and abusive. Alexandrina fled by jumping from a window that was twelve feet to the ground and in doing so she injured her spine. Her condition deteriorated and by the age of nineteen she struggled to get to church. By twenty she was completely paralysed and was confined to bed, cared for by her sister and mother. She was often in severe pain, her condition worsened and serious worries about her health meant that she was given the last rites on several occasions. Alexandrina found it hard to come to terms with her condition, she felt she was a burden on her family and she prayed continuously for a cure.

Her priest organised a parish pilgrimage to Fatima, but since Alexandrina was too ill to go herself, her priest brought back a medal, rosary and some holy water. Alexandrina drank the holy water and instead of a cure she became more accepting of her suffering. She determined to use her situation in the best way that she could as a disciple of Jesus and so she called herself a 'victim soul' and dedicated herself to praying for the conversion and salvation of sinners. She began to dictate a diary of her experiences that included ecstasies, visions, premonitions and mystical experiences. However, she also frequently experienced the feeling that all her prayers were useless and she was tempted by suicidal thoughts. From the 3 October 1938 to the 24 March 1942 Alexandrina lived out the three hour passion of Jesus every Friday during which her paralysis seemed to be overcome. From Good Friday, 27 March in 1942 to her death thirteen years later Alexandrina fasted from all food and liquid and miraculously lived on the daily Eucharist alone, a fast that was independently tested and confirmed by doctors from the Faculty of Medicine in Oporto. Much to her consternation, her fame spread. However even her assailant repented and came to visit her. She began to offer prayers for the salvation of young people in particular. Thousands of people came to visit her and she exhorted them constantly with the message of Fatima to make reparation, to repent, to pray the rosary and to be consecrated to the Immaculate Heart of Mary. Alexandrina died in 1955 and she was beatified by Pope John Paul II in 2004.

Saint Aleydis

Died 1250

Leprosy, paralysis, blind, confined to bed

Feast Day 15 June

Aleydis was born in Schwaerbeek near Brussels in Belgium. When she was just seven she joined a Cistercian convent south east of Brussels but her life in the community did not last. While she was still young she contracted leprosy and had to be isolated from her beloved community. Although she accepted this isolation and used it as a path for greater opportunity for contemplation, she was devastated at being denied the chalice at communion. She was finally consoled by a vision where Jesus told her that to receive Him in part in the Bread was to receive Him in whole. In 1249 Aleydis became seriously ill and was anointed. As her sufferings increased she prayed more and more for the souls in purgatory. She also experienced more visions and ecstasies and focused all the energies left to her on the Cross of Christ. Eventually she was confined to bed, she became blind and was paralysed. Aleydis died in 1250. Her cult was confirmed by Pope Pius X in 1907.

Blessed Anna Katharina Emmerick

1774–1824

Incurable illness and confined to bed by paralysis

Feast Day 9 February

Anna Katharina was born on 8 September 1774 in Flamsche near Coesfeld in Westfalia Germany. She was one of nine children and she lived and worked in a farming community where opportunities for education were few. Although she was drawn to life in a convent, her family was too poor to provide the requisite dowry and Anna's applications to difference convents were all rejected, so Anna became a seamstress. As part of her normal routine she often walked the Way of the Cross in Coesfeld and had a strong devotion to Christ. Eventually, Anna was able to enter an Augustinian convent and she enthusiastically undertook all the tasks given to her even though they were often the most menial and unpleasant. From 1802 to 1811 Anna became very ill and was often in pain but she was still happy in the convent despite the fact that some of the sisters showed her little respect since she came from such a poor background. Then, with the rise of secularisation in Germany, Anna's convent was suppressed in 1811 and Anna became the housekeeper for a priest in Dulmen. But she soon became ill again and was confined to bed. The priest agreed that Anna's younger sister could take over the household duties under her direction. Having already suffered considerable pain, Anna then received the stigmata. She also had visions of the life of Christ and of Our Lady. Anna offered up her sufferings for the salvation of others and in particular the souls in purgatory. During her illness Anna was still concerned with the sufferings of the poor. She sewed clothes for poor children and received many visitors offering them religious assistance and consolation. She was known for her service and solidarity with others even though she was confined to bed. Anna died in 1824 and she was beatified by Pope John Paul II in 2004.

Saint Anna Schaffer

1882–1925

Paralysis, problem with speech and sight, spinal disorder, cancer

Feast Day 5 October

Anna was born on 18 February 1882 in the village of Mindelstetten, near Regensburg in Germany. Her father was a carpenter and she was brought up in a modest and religious household. When she was thirteen, Anna took work in Regensburg hoping to be able to earn enough money to enter a religious order since she wanted to become a missionary sister. However in 1901 she suffered a serious accident at work when her legs were severely scalded. The hospital was unable to cure her injuries and she left the hospital as an invalid in 1902. Her condition deteriorated and soon she was bed ridden. Anna and her now widowed mother lived in poverty on a disability pension in a rented room. To begin with, Anna found it difficult to be reconciled to her situation of suffering but despite her anxieties she remained close to her faith and she had a spiritual director who brought her daily communion. With support from her spiritual director and after much prayer she came to offer her life with its sufferings to God and she received the stigmata. In 1910 she started having dreams and visions and the idea of a different apostolate emerged. She promised God to pray for others and to offer consolation to those suffering. Many people wrote to her for her help from across the world. By 1923 she suffered complete paralysis of the legs, cramps from a spinal disorder and intestinal cancer. A fall out of bed resulted in a brain injury that affected her ability to speak and deterioration in her eyesight. She died in 1925, was beatified by Pope John Paul II in 1999 and canonised by Pope Benedict XVI in 2012.

Blessed Augustus Czartoryski

1858–1893

Tuberculosis

Feast Day 2 August

Prince Augustus was born on 2 August 1858 in Paris. His parents belonged to a Polish royal family and they had been exiled from Poland by the Russians. The family pinned their hopes for a restoration of the royalty and the continuation of the Czartoryski name on their only son. When Augustus was only six years old his mother died from tuberculosis and Augustus himself suffered from the disease. Anxious about the health of his son, his father took the boy from spa to spa and to various health resorts in order to cure him, but all efforts failed. From 1874–1877 Joseph Kalinowski, a soldier, patriot and fellow Polish exile, became tutor to the young prince and by all accounts Augustus was greatly impressed with Kalinowski, who later became a Carmelite and still later was declared a saint in 1991.

When Augustus was twenty five he met Don Bosco in Paris. Augustus found great inspiration from this meeting and, despite his frequent bouts of ill health and opposition from his father, he began to attend spiritual retreats organised by the Salesians in Turin. Initially, when Augustus applied to join the Salesians, Don Bosco was reluctant to accept him but Augustus managed to speak to Pope Leo XIII who invited Don Bosco to take the young man into the congregation. Against the wishes of his family who continued to try and dissuade him, Augustus renounced his earthly possessions and his royal title and in 1887 he entered the novitiate to become a Salesian. He sought in particular to forget his privileged upbringing and to be treated without exception in the same way as everyone else. Augustus was ordained in 1892 and his family chose not to attend, though a month later his father came to accept his decision. The tuberculosis that had affected Augustus for most of his life grew worse and Augustus offered his life and his sufferings for the good of the young and for the Congregation. He died in 1893, only a year after his ordination. Augustus was beatified by Pope John Paul II in 2004.

Blessed Elizabeth of the Trinity (Elizabeth Catez)

1880–1903

Addison's disease

Feast Day 9 November

Elizabeth was born on 18 July 1880 in the army camp of Avor, France since her father was a captain in the French army. Her father died when she was seven and Elizabeth grew to be a difficult child. Although she was strong willed and prone to sudden outbursts of rage, at the same time she was drawn to prayer and once she had made her first confession and communion, she resolved to control her temper. From an early age Elizabeth wished to join the Carmelites but her widowed mother was opposed to the idea and insisted that she wait until she was twenty one. Perhaps this obstacle to her hopes caused Elizabeth to undergo something of a dark night of the soul and to deal with this she decided to follow the little way of St Thérèse of Lisieux by herself. Although she was involved in normal social life, Elizabeth also helped out in her parish in the choir and in catechesis, and by this service she felt herself to be a 'Carmelite on the inside'. In 1901 Elizabeth entered Carmel in Dijon where she wrote many poems, prayers and retreat guides. For some time Elizabeth had suffered from the symptoms of Addison's disease which at that time was incurable, and she offered herself as a victim soul. She then developed chronic fatigue, abdominal pain, the inability to digest food, as well as tremendous thirst. Elizabeth died in 1903 and she was beatified by Pope John Paul II in 1984.

Saint Josep Manyanet y Vives

1833–1901

Chronic ill health, open sores

Feast Day 17 December

Josep was born on 7 January 1833 in the city of Tremp in north eastern Spain where his father worked as a farmer. His father died suddenly when Josep was only twenty months old, leaving his mother to bring up Josep and his eight siblings on her own. Josep's mother often felt overwhelmed and when Josep was five years old his mother offered him to Our Lady. This act seems to have deeply affected the young Josep. The family lived next door to the church and the priest took charge of Josep's education and encouraged him to be an altar server. When Josep was twelve years old he started school with the Piarist fathers in Barbastro, combining his studies with running errands and assisting the priests. In 1850 he joined the seminary at Lleida and worked as a private tutor to pay his way. He finished his studies in 1853 in Urgell and was ordained in 1859 after which he worked for the diocesan bishop of Urgell for twelve years.

Then in 1864, with the bishop's approval, Josep founded the Sons of the Holy Family Jesus, Mary and Joseph and in 1874 he founded the Missionary Daughters of the Holy Family of Nazareth. The mission of these two foundations was to spread the example of the Holy Family and to support the formation of Christian families especially through education of children and young people. The congregations opened houses in other countries and Josep followed all these centres with loving care. He wrote several books and pamphlets to promote the holiness of Christian families. He never refused a child in need of an education and would work into the night to complete his own tasks. For most of his life Josep had chronic ill health and for the last sixteen years of his life he had open sores on his side following three surgical operations. He referred to these painful sores as 'God's mercies'. Josep died in 1901, he was beatified by Pope John Paul II in 1984 and canonised in 2004.

Saint Lydwine

1330–1433

Paralysis, multiple disabilities, possibly multiple sclerosis
Feast Day 14 April

Lydwine was born on 18 April 1330 in Schiedam in Holland. Although her father was from a noble family, he married a poor girl and after his fortune declined the family lived in poverty. In 1395, when Lydwine was fifteen she was out skating with friends and she fell on the ice, causing her to break a rib. She then suffered walking difficulties, muscle spasms, eye sensitivity, headaches, sores, stomach bloating and violent pains in her teeth. Eventually, Lydwine's legs became paralysed and she was confined to her bed. She became progressively more disabled and eventually fully paralysed. It has been suggested that in fact Lydwine suffered from multiple sclerosis. To begin with Lydwine suffered depression and her illnesses were regarded by some as the result of demonic possession. However, she came to accept her situation and she soon experienced visions and ecstasies. Through her own quiet surrender she was able to offer comfort to others and was able to heal people. She died in 1433 and her grave soon became a place of pilgrimage. Her cult was confirmed by Pope Leo XIII in 1890.

Blessed Margaret Ebner

1291–1351

Confined to bed with a general illness, depression

Margaret was born in about 1291 in Donauworth, Bavaria into a noble and wealthy family. It seems that there was no opposition to her entering the Dominican convent of Maria Medingen at fifteen years of age, possibly because her aunt was already a nun. According to her own account of her spiritual experiences, Margaret said that in fact her true conversion only began in 1311 when she was twenty. Just one year later she then became seriously ill and suffered frequent bouts of illness for the rest of her life. Describing her condition in her reflections she said that at times she had no control over herself, and she would laugh or cry continuously for days at a time. On other occasions she was paralysed and in constant pain. At other times she was not able to speak and could not pray, she had pain around her heart, she could not bear disturbance and her mood darkened. For nearly seven years she was at the point of death, then for the next thirteen years she had to remain in bed for six months of the year. Margaret was forced to return home during political unrest when the convent was closed. On the death of her beloved old nurse she sank into a deep depression where she saw no one and she did not go out. However, in 1332 a secular priest became her spiritual advisor and she began to see God's mercy in everything. In particular she developed a Christ-centred mysticism where she fixed her gaze on Christ as her source of hope. Margaret died in 1351 and she was beatified by Pope John Paul II in 1979.

Blessed Sister Maria Giuseppina of Jesus Crucified (Giuseppina Catanea)

1894–1948

Multiple sclerosis, labyrinthitis

Feast Day 26 June

Giuseppina was born on 18 February 1894 in Naples in Italy into a noble family. At a young age she would accompany her mother and grandmother when they went out to help the poor, and she prayed the rosary. Although she felt called to a life with the Carmelites, she followed the wishes of her parents and took a course in business studies. Eventually she managed to persuade her family that she had a vocation and she entered the Carmelite convent in Ponti Rossi in 1918. Giuseppina suffered severe angina attacks, tuberculosis of the spine and paralysis. However, she was completely cured with the application of a relic of St Francis Xavier. As a result of this cure a life of solitude became more difficult since many people came to her to seek advice and consolation. In 1932 the convent house at Ponti Rossi was finally recognised as a

convent of the Discalced Carmelites. Giuseppina
received the Carmelite habit and took the name Sister
Mary Giuseppina of Jesus Crucified. She became the
sub-prioress in 1934. By 1943 she began to suffer from
failing eyesight and she had a physical impairment
that left her confined to a wheelchair. She had labyrinthitis, an ear problem that affects balance and creates
dizziness, nerve pain, and she developed multiple
sclerosis. In spite of her disabilities, in 1944 she was
elected prioress. At the request of her spiritual director,
Sister Mary Giuseppina wrote her autobiography and
a diary charting her desire to share her sufferings for
the benefit of others especially for the good of priests.
She died in 1948 and was beatified by Pope Benedict
XVI in 2008.

Venerable Marthe Robin

1902–1981

*Encephalitis, severe headaches, acute pain, despondency,
paralysis, partial sight*

Marthe was born on 13 March 1902 in the small village
of Châteauneuf-de-Galaure in south-east France. Her
parents were farmers, and although they were not
practising Christians, Marthe had a Christian education
at the local school. As a baby, Marthe contracted
typhoid and as a result her health was frail and her
schooling limited. Nevertheless, with the other local
children, she would walk to school and help out on the
farm. In 1918, at the age of sixteen, Marthe became ill
with severe headaches and possible encephalitis. Following this she also suffered from acute pains, fits and
paralysis. Gradually, her legs grew weaker so that she
had to use crutches, and her eye sight deteriorated.
Although she prayed for a cure, sought thermal reme-

dies and took up needlework to buy medicine, nothing seemed to work. By the age of twenty three, Marthe had numerous disabilities and she suffered from an acute sense of abandonment, desperation and loneliness.

In 1928 Marthe had a transforming spiritual experience of the infinite love of God. This personal encounter with Jesus enabled her to hand herself over completely to God and to make the decision to unite her sufferings with those of Jesus. By twenty eight Marthe's digestive tract was paralysed and she was unable to eat or drink. She could however swallow the Eucharist and she lived on this for her remaining years. She also received the stigmata. Even though her health grew worse, Marthe listened to, advised and consoled the many people who came to see her. People who visited her testified to her sense of serenity and joy. In 1934 Marthe set up a local school and in 1936, with the help of a priest from Lyons, she began the first Foyer de Charité, a place of welcome and prayer for consecrated lay people who live in community with a priest. By the age of thirty seven Marthe's ocular nerves were so affected that she could not bear the light and had to live in darkness. Over subsequent years, through prayer and conversation with others, Marthe supported many new spiritual and charitable initiatives in France. She continued to receive visitors and offer them spiritual comfort. Marthe died in 1981 and she was declared venerable by Pope Francis in 2014.

Blessed Mary Bartholomea Bagnesi (Marietta Bagnesi)

1514–1577

Confined to bed, asthma, pleurisy, kidney ailment

Feast Day 27 May

Marietta was born on 15 August 1514 in Florence in Italy into a wealthy family. However, she was neglected by her mother, she was under sized, possibly malnourished, and was left in the casual care of others. Marietta was not left purely on her own since her sister was a Dominican nun and the sisters of the convent allowed the little girl to play in the cloisters. Marietta had hoped to follow her sister into the convent but when her mother died she had to take over the running of the family household instead. When Marietta's father arranged a marriage for her, Marietta reacted badly and fell into a faint remaining like that for days. Marietta appears to have suffered from a spastic nerve problem that confined her to bed and although her father engaged a series of doctors to relieve her malady through various quack remedies, her ailment continued for thirty four years. During this illness it appears that one of the servants mistreated her, yet Marietta endured her sufferings with no complaint. Marietta still hoped to enter the convent where four of her sisters were already nuns. However, it soon became clear that convent life was impossible for her due to her disabilities and so her father arranged for her to be accepted into the Dominican Third Order. She was excused the obligation of saying the Office because of the desperate nature of her condition. She had now succumbed to asthma, pleurisy and a kidney ailment. Marietta's room became a sort of oratory where Mass was said and

Marietta herself had mystic experiences. People would come to her for advice, reconciliation with their neighbours and for comfort. Marietta died in 1577. Her cult was confirmed by Pope Pius VII in 1804.

Blessed Nunzio Sulprizio

1817–1836
Lame, amputee, bone cancer
Feast Day 5 May

Nunzio was born on 13 April 1817 in Pescosansonesco a small town in the Abruzzo region of Italy. By 1823, at six years old, Nunzio was left an orphan and was brought up by his maternal grandmother who took him to Mass and sent him to a school for poor children. His grandmother died in 1826 and his uncle took the nine year old, who could barely read, out of education and set him to work in his own blacksmith shop. Nunzio worked as best he could with no complaint and still found time to pray and attend Mass. It seems that the young Nunzio may have already been ill with a bone deficiency and hard working conditions, lack of food and other privations made his condition worse. Nunzio damaged his ankle in an accident and, possibly through bathing it in dirty water, the wound became infected with gangrene. In 1832 he was moved to Naples for medical treatment at the hospital for incurable diseases but there was no remedies for his condition, and after suffering excruciating pain his leg had to be amputated. Nevertheless, much to his delight Nunzio was able to make his First Communion and he was able to move around using just a stick. He spent his time praying, helping prepare other hospitalised children for their Communion, and comforting them in their pain. Those that met the young Nunzio recognised a vocation in the making and he was promised that he could enter the Congregation of the Sacred Heart despite his infirmities. However, Nunzio's condition began to deteriorate and he was diagnosed with bone cancer. Nunzio offered his sufferings for the conversion of sinners. In 1836 he developed fever and his heart began to fail. He received the last sacraments and he died at the age of nineteen. Nunzio was beatified by Pope Paul VI in 1963.

Padre Pio da Pietrelcina (Francesco Forgione)

1887–1968

Poor health, fevers, chest pains, respiratory and digestive problems, headaches, severe rheumatism, asthma

Feast Day 23 September

Francesco was born on 25 May 1887 in the small farming town of Pietrelcina in southern Italy. He was named after his brother who had died in infancy and after St Francis of Assisi. When Francesco was only five years old, he decided to dedicate his life to God and it seems that he had already experienced visions. From an early age Francesco suffered from poor health. At the age of six he came down with severe gastroenteritis that confined him for some time to bed and when he was ten he contracted typhoid fever. However, these illnesses did not prevent him from working as a shepherd looking after the family's small flock of sheep though this work did delay his schooling. At the age of sixteen in 1903 Francesco entered the novitiate of the Capuchin Friars and he took the name Brother Pio. He made his solemn profession in 1907 and, although he was forced to spend a period at home to recover from severe headaches and chest pains in 1909, Brother Pio became Padre Pio when he was finally ordained in 1910. From

1911 to 1916 Padre Pio had recurring health problems, he was diagnosed with chronic bronchitis and he was sent back to the family home in Pietrelcina to recover. He managed to return to the small friary of San Giovanni Rotondo but then in 1917 he was called up to serve in the First World War even though he had also been diagnosed with tuberculosis.

After spending much of his time in a military hospital near Naples and then a short spell in a military barracks, Padre Pio was discharged from the army and in 1918 he returned to San Giovanni Rotondo where he continued to suffer physically from various debilitating illnesses. It was in 1918 that Padre Pio also received the stigmata. However, this was viewed with some suspicion in many quarters and the faithful were discouraged from visiting him. In 1956 Padre Pio helped to establish a hospital complex where he insisted that care be truly human, and patients be treated with utmost respect and attention. Padre Pio was especially noted for his prayer life, his devotion to the Eucharist and his spirituality in the confessional. People began to flock to hear him say Mass and there were long queues for the Sacrament of Reconciliation. Seeing his own life and sufferings as a way of the Cross, Padre Pio offered himself as a victim soul for the souls in purgatory. In his last years he suffered from asthma and gradually withdrew more and more from the world. He died in 1968. Padre Pio was beatified by Pope John Paul II in 1999 and canonised in 2002.

Saint Thérèse of Lisieux

1873–1897

Haemoptysis, tuberculosis

Feast Day 3 October

Thérèse was born on 2 January 1873 in Alençon, in France. Her parents, Louis, a watch maker, and Zelie, a lace maker, both came from military families. Thérèse was their ninth child and she was considered to be a highly strung child who liked to get her own way. When Thérèse was four years old her mother Zelie died from breast cancer, and the family moved to Lisieux to be nearer Zelie's family. Thérèse's oldest sister, Marie took over the running of the household and her second sister, Pauline, organised religious instruction for the younger children. Thérèse herself was very affected by the death of her mother and became rather withdrawn and shy. When Thérèse was nine years old, Pauline entered the Carmelite convent at Lisieux, and Marie followed her four years later so it came as no surprise when Thérèse expressed the hope to join them.

At fourteen, Thérèse experienced what she called her conversion and the following year she told her father about her wish to enter the convent. Both the bishop and the Carmelites decided that Thérèse was too young and so her request was refused. However, in 1887 during a visit to Rome with pilgrims from Lisieux, Thérèse managed to have an audience with Pope Leo XIII and he gave permission for her to enter Carmel at the age of fifteen in 1888. Thérèse received the habit the following year and made her profession in 1890. She took the name Thérèse of the Child Jesus and of the Holy Face. She believed that by contemplating the sufferings in the face of Jesus we can become closer to him and so be able to unite our sufferings with him. Her spiritual life blossomed and, by placing love at the centre of everything, Thérèse discovered, lived and taught the little way of spiritual childhood. She prayed in particular for souls and for priests, and she was dedicated to Eucharistic devotions. In 1895 Thérèse offered herself as a sacrificial victim to the merciful love of God and she also began to write her autobiography, *The Story of a Soul,* to help draw everyone on her little path to holiness. In 1896 Thérèse began to cough up blood, haemoptysis, and she found in her illness a new vocation to God. As her health declined she was transferred to the infirmary all the while her spirituality deepened with her sufferings. She proclaimed a spirituality of simplicity without pretence and with absolute trust in God. At the age of twenty four Thérèse received the Eucharist and died of tuberculosis. Thérèse was beatified by Pope Pius XI in 1923, was canonised by Pope Pius XI in 1925 and was declared a Doctor of the Church by Pope John Paul II in 1997.

Notes

1   Pope Saint John Paul II, *Evangelium vitae,* 28.
2   *Ibid.,* 11.
3   *Ibid.,* 2.
4   *Ibid.,* 31.
5   Pope Saint John Paul II, *World Day of the Sick,* V, 4.
6   Pope Saint John Paul II, *World Day of the Sick* II, 5.
7   Pope Saint John Paul II, *Salvifici Dolores,* 7.
8   *Ibid.* 19.
9   *Ibid.* 19.
10   *Ibid.* 21.
11   Pope Saint John Paul II, *Homily* (25 April 2004).

5

SLOW LEARNERS, FOOLS FOR GOD, THE SIMPLE AND THE PURE IN HEART

I bless you, Father, Lord of heaven and of earth,
for hiding these things from the learned and the
clever and revealing them to little children.

Matthew 11:25

Introduction

DISABILITY RIGHTS MOVEMENTS quite correctly point to the discrimination that exists in society, where people with disabilities are not given equal access to opportunities, to work, to participation in society, and where, more often than not, they live in poverty and isolation. According to some of these disability movements, the answer is to give people with disabilities a voice, to ensure respect for their choices, to enable them to gain independence. But what about people with intellectual disabilities who will never have a voice, who may find it difficult or perhaps impossible to make meaningful choices, who will never be independent? For many people, a life of physical disability may be challenging, but a life of intellectual disability is on a different plane altogether.

It seems that people with disabilities are as likely as the abled to hold attitudes of discrimination, attitudes that point to a hierarchy of disability where more often than not people with cognitive disability are at the lower end of the hierarchy. Of course, what that tells us is that people with disabilities, just like all other human beings, are equally prone to spiritual sins like pride and so are equally in need of God's grace to lead them to holiness.

When it comes to holiness and intellectually disabled people, it is common to call a profoundly disabled person an angel, particularly if the disability means that the person remains childlike in his or her abilities. Sometimes such a person is described as already a saint since he or she does not have the cognitive capacity to do wrong. However, human beings are not angels. Every human being is in need of salvation, of grace, of redemption. Moreover, every human being is asked to do what he or she can, as far as he or she is able, to co-operate with God because that in itself is recognition of the dignity of the human person. There are only a few saints and blessed who appear to have had some sort of intellectual disability. It is difficult to find the evidence for this because, perhaps unsurprisingly, people do not want to accept that there may have been cognitive impairment as if by admitting this it means that the person cannot also voluntarily pursue a life of holiness. There are cases where it is argued that the person is only pretending to be a 'holy fool', or is keeping silent as a discipline rather than as the result of finding communication difficult. However, there are also clear cases where a person has found learning difficult and as a consequence when they have tried to follow Christ they have found themselves with the most basic of jobs as the porter, the kitchen staff, the gardener. Yet they have also found themselves at the heart of a community as a listener, a friend, as someone who accepts others without question or judgement. On his pilgrimage to Canada in 1984, Pope John Paul II spoke about at that time Blessed, but now Saint, André Bessette as 'one of the most humble' among us, one who lived in the light of Christ without pretension.[1] In his homily on the canonisation of six new saints, including Blessed André, Pope Benedict XVI talked about the hidden and 'intense inner life' of those, like Blessed André, who lived 'the beatitude of pure of heart'.[2]

In declaring people with intellectual disabilities and slow learners saints and blessed the Church reminds us that everything is possible to God, that God works through all kinds of capacities and that the path to holiness begins with Him. After all, as the first letter of St John says, we love because God first loved us.[3] Moreover, as Pope Pius XI explained using the examples of Saint John Vianney and Saint Joseph Cupertino, without holiness 'other gifts will not go far' and, 'even supposing other gifts to be meagre,' with God's help a person can work marvels.[4] It is perhaps easy to notice heroic virtue in people who strive to overcome physical disabilities or who fight against illness. However, people can also display heroic virtue in what to others are simple everyday activities.

Saint André Bessette (Alfred Bessette)

1845–1937

Poor health, stomach problems, difficulty learning

Feast Day 6 January

Alfred was born on 9 August 1895 in the village of St Gregoire d'Iberville near Montreal in Canada. He was a sickly baby and the midwife was so concerned that he was baptised the day after he was born. He had severe stomach problems and his illnesses impeded his schooling so at the age of twelve he still could not read or write. By 1857 both his parents had died and Alfred was sent to live with relatives. He was not physically strong enough to work on his uncle's farm so he was apprenticed to a cobbler, then a baker, then a tinsmith and then a blacksmith, but each time the work was too strenuous. Finally, he was taken in by the parish priest and lived in the rectory earning his keep by doing odd jobs. After time spent in the United States looking for work, Alfred returned to Canada in 1867. In 1870 he joined the Holy Cross congregation as a lay brother where he received the name Brother André. At the age of twenty five, André still could not master reading and writing. Moreover, he nearly had to leave the congregation because his health was so poor, but at the intervention of a visiting bishop he was allowed to stay.

After taking his vows, André was given the job of door keeper, laundry worker and messenger at Notre Dame College at Cote-des-Neiges in Montreal at the foot of Mount Royale. André was particularly helpful with sick people, and he used holy oils from the college chapel to great effect, so much so that many people were cured of their ailments. In 1904 he came up with the idea of building a chapel to St Joseph on the mountain near the college. Anxious not to let the diocese get into debt, the local bishop refused André any money but he gave permission for André to use what money he had to build what he could. Starting with the few coins he had collected as donations for St Joseph from the haircuts he did for local people André built first a small wooden shelter, a shrine and finally, as news spread of the work he was doing and the healings that were taking place, a basilica. André did not see the completion of the basilica. He died at the age of ninety two in 1937. André was beatified by Pope John Paul II in 1982 and canonised by Pope Benedict XVI in 2010.

Saint Anna Pak Agi

1782 or 1783–1839

Naturally slow, simple

Feast Day of the Korean Martyrs 20 September

Anna was born in either 1782 or 1783 in Korea. By all reports Anna was known to be naturally slow and it seems that she may have had learning difficulties in general as well as finding it difficult to learn about the truths of the faith. She used to say that if she could not learn about God as she wished to do at least she could try and love him with all her heart. She married a Christian and became especially drawn to pictures of the Passion of Jesus. Anna was arrested for her faith with her husband and eldest son. Her husband and son eventually renounced their faith but Anna did not. She was tortured and then martyred at the age of fifty-seven in 1839. With other Korean martyrs she was beatified by Pope Pius XI in 1925 and canonised by Pope John Paul II in 1984.

Saint Bertilla Boscardin (Ann Frances Boscardin)

1888–1922

Slow learner, painful tumour

Feast Day 20 October

Ann Frances Boscardin was born on 6 October 1888 in Brendola near Vicenza in Italy. She grew up in a simple peasant family but her father was an alcoholic and often violent. She attended school infrequently because she was needed in the fields and she also worked as a domestic servant in a house nearby. Ann Frances was thought to be of low intelligence and was slow at learning. This made her the butt of many jokes and insults and even a local clergyman called her 'the goose'. However, her parish priest allowed her to receive her First Communion early and when she was twelve he accepted her into the Children of Mary Association. He gave her a catechism as a gift and it was found in the pocket of her habit when she died some twenty two years later.

Ann Frances hoped to be a nun but the first order to which she applied rejected her on account of her slowness. Eventually, in 1904 she was accepted by the Teachers of Saint Dorothy, Daughters of the Sacred Heart at Vicenza and she took the name Maria Bertilla. She worked in the convent as a kitchen maid and laundress for three years. She was then sent to the municipal hospital at Treviso to learn nursing. Initially she was placed in the kitchen but later she worked in the children's ward with victims of diphtheria. During the First World War the hospital was taken over by Italian troops and the nurses were moved to a military hospital. Treviso soon became on the front line and during air raids on the hospital Maria Bertilla was noted for her calmness and the care of her patients, particularly those who were too ill to be moved. However, her superior felt she was more suited to the laundry so she worked there until a higher superior who had recognised her talents put her in charge of the children's isolation ward. Meanwhile, Maria Bertilla's health which had been poor grew worse. For some years she had had a painful tumour and it now required an operation. Maria Bertilla did not survive the operation and she died in 1922. She was beatified by Pope Pius XII in 1952 and canonised by Pope John XXIII in 1961.

Blessed Eusebia Palomino Yenes

1899–1935

Simplicity, unknown illness resulting in twisted limbs, asthma

Feast Day 10 February

Eusebia was born on 15 December 1899 in Cantalpino in Spain. The family was very poor and her father had to beg for food when he had no work, while her mother collected firewood. Eusebia worked to help support the family and she was especially good at looking after young children. She came to know some sisters from the Congregation of the Daughters of Mary Help of Christians and they asked if she would like to volunteer some time helping them. Eusebia helped in the kitchen, in collecting firewood, in cleaning and in running errands. Although she wished to join the sisters she was conscious of her lack of education and poverty. A visiting superior recognised something deeper in her simple way of going about things, and Eusebia was accepted into the novitiate in 1922. Two years later she made her profession and was assigned to a convent in Valverde del Camino, south western Spain. She cheerfully took up her duties in the kitchen, laundry, garden, and among her tasks Eusebia answered the door and looked after the smallest of the children. At first the older children mocked her for her simplicity but she soon proved that she had a gift for telling the stories of the saints and she showed obvious care for all her charges. During the 1930s the Church in Spain suffered persecution and Eusebia offered herself for the salvation of her country. In 1932 she was struck by an illness that was never diagnosed and that twisted her limbs, and this was made worse by aggravated asthma. Eusebia died in 1935 and was beatified by Pope John Paul II in 2004.

Saint Isadora the Simple of Egypt

Died c. 365

Holy fool

Isadora lived at the convent of Tabennisi and is one of the earliest people known as a fool for Christ. Isadora did not dress in the same way as the other nuns in the convent, but instead she went bare foot and wore a rag cloth on her head. Nor did Isadora eat with the others, though it is unclear whether this was the decision of the convent or Isadora's own choice. It appears that Isadora lived in isolation, shunned and mocked by the nuns. She did all the chores in the kitchen and seemed to live by eating crumbs and food that was left over and by drinking the water that had been used for the washing up. The nuns regarded her as stupid and treated her with contempt, giving her the most menial tasks to do, though she never complained. However, Isadora was recognised as particularly blessed by St

Pitirim a hermit who was told in a vision to find a true example of holiness at the convent. Afraid of the number of people coming to visit her, Isadora left the convent and escaped into the wilderness, possibly to live the life of a hermit. Her whereabouts were never discovered and she is thought to have died in about the year 365.

Saint John Vianney

1786–1859

Slow learner

Feast Day 4 August

John was born on 8 May 1786 in the town of Dardilly in the south of France. His parents owned a small piece of farm land and as a boy John looked after the cattle. With the closure of churches and exile of priests during the French Revolution, the family had to travel around to local farms and secret meeting places in order to hear Mass and to pray with others. John's religious education, his first communion and confirmation took place in the context of this secrecy and the heroism of Catholic priests. In 1802 the Catholic Church was re-established in France and at the age of twenty John began to think of his future vocation. Realising that John lacked education, his parish priest got him a place at a local school at Ecully. However, John found himself struggling in his lessons, particularly in Latin.

In 1809 his studies were interrupted when he was drafted into Napoleon's army, though he soon became ill and was hospitalised. When he left the hospital he was ordered to report for duty but on the morning of departure he went into a church to pray and when he emerged he found he had missed his comrades. A man who offered to take him to join his fellow soldiers instead took him to meet a group of deserters in the mountains and John stayed with them for fourteen months. An amnesty was given to deserters and John resumed his studies at Ecully, though by now he was much older than the other students and they frequently ridiculed him. In 1812 he was sent to the seminary at Verrieres, but he did not pass the examinations for entry to the seminary proper. Considered too slow a learner, he was sent back to his parish priest who managed to convince the vicar general that what John lacked in education he surpassed in piety. John was ordained in 1815 and was appointed assistant to his parish priest in Ecully. In 1818 John became parish priest at Ars, a village near Lyons, though on his first visit to the town he got lost. At Ars he discovered that in the aftermath of the French Revolution the people had forgotten their faith and so he set himself the task of rekindling their sense of religion and spirituality. He founded an orphanage in Ars and instructed children in the catechism. He became well known for his patience and wisdom in the confessional and pilgrims came from far and wide to listen to him. John died in 1859 and was beatified by Pope Pius X in 1905. He was canonised by Pope Pius XI in 1925.

Saint Joseph of Cupertino

1603–1663

Intellectual disability

Feast Day 18 September

Joseph was born in 1603 in the town of Cupertino in south eastern Italy into an impoverished family. He was born in a shed because his family home was being auctioned. His widowed mother had become destitute and she regarded her son as a burden since he was profoundly absent-minded, clumsy, unable to hold a conversation or take proper care of himself and incapable of many daily tasks, He would wander with his mouth open all the time, going nowhere, so he was given the nickname 'the Gaper'. His mother apprenticed him to a shoe maker but he was a failure. He tried to enter two monasteries but was refused.

Finally, at the age of twenty he was taken on as a servant in a Franciscan convent. He managed to do the most menial duties with cheerfulness and humility though he was also known as 'Brother Ass' by his fellow monks. His superiors saw sufficient piety to suggest he tried for the priesthood, however he could not learn. The only thing he grasped was a passable discussion on the biblical passage 'Blessed is the womb that bore thee'. When it came to the exam before being ordained deacon, the bishop asked him to explain precisely this piece of scripture. When it came to the exam before ordination the first few of his colleagues had so impressed the examining bishop that all subsequent students, including Joseph, were excused the exam. Joseph became well known as a healer and confessor but also as someone who could levitate during prayers. Arrested during the Inquisition in the belief that his gifts were the result of demonic forces, Joseph was vouched for in person by Pope Urban VIII who had witnessed his levitations and Joseph was released with the proviso that he live in monastic exile. People flocked to see him and eventually he had to be moved from monastery to monastery because of the number of people seeking him out. Joseph died of fever in 1663. He was beatified by Pope Benedict XIV in 1753 and canonised by Pope Clement XIII in 1767.

Blessed Joseph Marie Cassant

1878–1903

Learning difficulties; tuberculosis

Feast Day 17 June

Joseph-Marie Cassant was born on 6 March 1878 at Casseneuil in south west France where his family were orchard keepers. He was sent to board with the La Salle Brothers in Casseneuil, however he found study difficult since he had such a poor memory. Although he wanted to become a priest, Joseph-Marie found that his learning difficulties meant that he could not enter the junior seminary. Nevertheless, his priest recognised the boy's obvious vocation and love of contemplation and suggested that Joseph-Marie join the Trappists. So at the age of sixteen, Joseph-Marie began a trial period, entering the Cistercian Abbey of Sainte-Marie du Desert in the diocese of Toulouse in 1894. The novice master happened to be particularly understanding of Joseph-Marie's difficulties and he helped Joseph-Marie to develop an affective rather than intellectual approach to his formation, concentrating on the 'way of the heart of Jesus'. The novice master taught Joseph-Marie to live in the present moment with hope, patience and love, so that Joseph-Marie came to realise that through his own weakness and lack he could come to depend more and more on Christ. Joseph-Marie's simplicity, kindness as well as his ordinariness endeared him to the monks. He made his final vows in 1900. With great difficulty and despite having a less than understanding teacher, but with the support of the novice master, he managed to pass his exams and he was ordained a priest in 1902. It then became clear that he was suffering from advanced tuberculosis. Over the year his health gradually deteriorated and he suffered more and more from physical pain. After receiving communion he died in 1903. Joseph-Marie was beatified by Pope John Paul II in 2004.

Saint Peter of St Joseph Betancur

1619 or 1626–1667

Slow learner

Feast Day 18 April

Peter was born in possibly 1619 or 1626 in Tenerife into a poor family and until the age of twenty four he worked as a shepherd. In 1649 he decided to set out for Guatemala with the intention of helping the poor in the New World but he ran out of money even before he arrived and had to work to find enough money to complete the journey. When he finally arrived he was so destitute and ill that he joined the bread line set up by the Franciscans. Peter had a strong desire to become a priest and, with the help of one of the friars, he entered the local Jesuit seminary. However, he was unable to learn what was required and he failed his studies. He then joined the Third Order of St Francis in the convent of Costa Rica in Antigua Guatemala, taking the name Peter of St Joseph. Peter visited hospitals, prisons and ministered to the young and unemployed. He opened a hospital for the poor, a shelter for the homeless, free schools for the poor and for street children, an oratory and a place for priests to stay. At a time of considerable marginalisation and racial discrimination, he showed special care for African slaves and native Americans. He was so passionate about his faith and his charitable foundations that he became well-known in the city streets as the Franciscan brother who would ring a bell calling for donations and he led weekly rosary processions. Peter died in 1667 from bronchial pneumonia. He was beatified by Pope John Paul II in 1980 and was canonised in 2002.

Venerable Solanus Casey (Barney Casey)

1870–1957

Slow learner, diphtheria, weakened health, eczema, erysipelas

Bernard Casey, known as Barney, was born on 25 November 1870 in Wisconsin in the United States. His parents were Irish immigrants and they lived on a farm with their sixteen children. At the age of eight Barney contracted diphtheria and this permanently affected his general health and damaged his vocal cords leaving his voice weakened, high-pitched and thin. As with many rural children, schooling fitted around the needs of the farm and Barney spent much of his time working in the fields or hunting. In 1885 and 1886 the harvests were particularly disappointing so Barney had to find extra work to help support the family, and so his education fell further behind. By the age of sixteen Barney was working in a lumber mill and he went on to work as a handyman, a relief guard at the local prison and then in a brick yard. It was when he had a job as a street car operator and witnessed a brutal murder that he began to re-evaluate his life. At the age of twenty one, Barney decided to apply for the priest-hood and in 1892 he was admitted to the St Francis de Sales seminary in Milwaukee. However, given the large number of German immigrants, all the classes were taught in German and Latin. Barney, who did not know either German or Latin, unsurprisingly did poorly and he was asked to leave.

The diocesan officials thought that Barney had limited academic abilities, but they also recognised that he had a vocation to religious life, and so they suggested that Barney became a religious brother. In 1896 Barney joined the Capuchin seminary in Detroit and in 1897 he took the name Solanus after St Francis Solano, a seventeenth century Franciscan missionary to South America. Brother Solanus struggled through his classes in seminary and at the age of thirty three in 1904 he was ordained as a simplex priest, a priest who could not hear confessions or preach homilies. Father Solanus acted as porter and sacristan in several parishes. He also conducted services for the sick and people began to flock to him for blessings. In his position as door keeper, he was the first port of call for many people who needed someone who would listen to them and he never turned anyone away. By 1946 his health had begun to fail, he suffered from severe eczema over his whole body, and he was moved to the Capuchin novitiate in Huntingdon, Indiana. He developed erysipelas, an acute skin infection, and died in 1957. Father Solanus was declared venerable by Pope John Paul II in 1995.

Blessed Ulrika Nisch (Francesca Nisch)

1882–1913

Simple, skin infection, tuberculosis

Francesca was born on 18 September 1882 in Oberdorf-Mittelbiberach in Germany. Her parents were very poor and she was brought up by her grandmother and aunt. Francesca was a sickly child and missed out on her schooling. When she did attend school her educational results were not good and she was seen as rather simple, she was always breaking things, she was awkward but also very kind. At the age of twelve, she took work as a maid first in Germany and then later in

Rorschach in Switzerland. In 1901 she contracted a severe form of erysipelas, an acute infection of the skin, and she was sent to the hospital in Rorschach where she received assiduous care from the Sisters of the Holy Cross. Through the example of these nuns Francesca decided to enter their convent in the German village of Hegne on the shore of Lake Constance. In Hegne she worked in the kitchen and then she was sent to a sister convent in Zell-Weierbach where once again she worked in the kitchen and cared for the few elderly and sick nuns. She returned to Hegne and took the religious habit in 1905 taking the name Ulrika after her father Ulrich. She then found herself back at work in the kitchen where she did everything for the glory of God though not at times without some mishap. Sister Ulrika made her religious profession in 1907. She was moved to Bühl in Germany to work in the hospital kitchens and then to Baden-Baden and she got on with all the staff however demanding they were. She put up with humiliations and taunts with great fortitude. Sister Ulrika developed severe headaches and sinusitis that required surgery but took up her work again as soon as she had recovered sufficiently. In 1912 her health suddenly deteriorated. She was diagnosed with an advanced case of tuberculosis and she was sent back to a hospital in Hegne. Without proper spiritual direction and without any form of consolation she felt abandoned by God, however she still spent her time in prayer. On the evening of 8 May 1913 a nurse came to see if Sister Ulrika needed anything. Sister Ulrika sent the nurse to another sister who was having a coughing fit. When the nurse returned Sister Ulrika had already died. Sister Ulrika was beatified by Pope John Paul II in 1987.

Notes

1   Pope Saint John Paul II, *Speech* (11 September 1984).
2   Pope Benedict XVI, *Homily* (17 October 2010).
3   1 Jn 4:19.
4   Pope Pius XI, *Ad Catholici Sacerdotii*, 85.

6

BEARING THE WEIGHT OF THE WORLD

In his anguish he prayed even more earnestly, and his sweat fell to the ground like great drops of blood.

Luke 22:44

Introduction

HE FOCUS OF this chapter is on those saints and blessed who have such an intense interior life that they feel the weight of the world, often to the neglect of themselves. At a time when people with mental health issues are often stigmatised or marginalised, it is important to remember that people who live with such a concentrated inner life that life becomes a struggle, can also live a holy life. Of course, the spiritual life is the life of the whole person, mind and body, soul and spirit. As the early second century writer Tertullian said, the body is the 'minister and servant of the soul,' and the two are so united that the flesh is 'the hinge of salvation'.[1] The Church does not despise the body, after all the Church recognises the goodness of creation and she professes belief in the resurrection of the body. In fact, for the desert fathers the body was seen as a God-given field to cultivate[2] and the Church has always encouraged the faithful to be good stewards of human bodily life.

In early Christianity extreme forms of asceticism such as some of the early encratic movements were regarded as more pagan than Christian. *Enkrateia* means self-control and in its extreme version it forbade marriage and saw women as the work of Satan, it showed hatred of the body and a desire to escape what was seen as bondage to a circle of birth and death. Extreme encratism was more about self-absorption and pride in self-control. In contrast, the traditional spiritual learning process recognises that although we think we are in control, our wills are twisted, we choose lower goods over higher ones, we are never satisfied with what we have whether that is material things or significantly the spirituality that God has given us. For the ascetic monks who lived when encratism was at its height, the spiritual life was not about hating the body but about training a body that is ruled by this twisted will that always wants more, that puts goods like food above higher goods. Practical activities like fasting both unite the activities of body and soul, pointing to the fact that we are embodied and not minds or souls occupying a body, and they show up our shortcomings.

For the early monks, gluttony was the primary sin and as the fourteenth-century monk Saint Gregory of Sinai explained 'to abstain, means to remain a little hungry after eating; to eat adequately, means neither to be hungry, nor weighted down; to be satiated, means to be slightly weighed down. But eating beyond satiety is the door to belly-madness'.[3] Fasting demonstrates that absolute autonomy is an illusion, because we really do depend on things other than ourselves, food for example, and during fasting even the simplest of things tastes wonderful. Fasting draws attention to how clever we can become at developing strategies to avoid change, at how we can become slaves to self-absorption. In the tradition, while moderation is recommended as the norm, fasting always takes place in set periods and it is not undertaken where it may damage health. Thus, in the earliest monastic rules and in today's directions the very young, the elderly and above all the sick and disabled do not fast: the body is after all the temple of the Holy Spirit. Moreover fasting is not performed for its own sake: denying the self also leads to thinking about others and giving to the poor out of our excess.

The interior life is perhaps most tempted towards self-absorption if the focus remains only on the self and the self's successes or indeed failures. In her description of the garden of Jesus, Saint Thérèse of Lisieux reminds us that everyone, however small or apparently insignificant, has been given a vocation from God. For Saint Thérèse 'perfection consists in doing His will, in being what He wills us to be,' and this involves doing the smallest things with love.[4] In the task of paying attention not only to what you are doing but also to how you are doing it, nothing is too trivial. This is why Pope Saint John Paul II said that the way of holiness is also found in everyday things and daily activities. If I do a simple action like washing dishes in a thoughtless way all the while focusing on what I want, on my sense of control or irritated at my lack of it, then this is a good indication of how I may be approaching life.

This chapter makes no judgment about disability, and in particular it does not suggest that any of the saints or blessed suffered from mental disability or mental health issues other than the issues they themselves had already identified. In some cases, illness may have an effect but it never causes the saints and blessed to abandon God or be abandoned by God: a person can be ill and holy, for illness neither causes holiness nor destroys holiness nor indeed proves holiness. However, the chapter does recognise that some people live with such intensity that life is a struggle. In his homily on the beatification of Marcel Callo in 1987, Pope John Paul II acknowledged this and gave the answer:

> although he [Marcel] was talented and full of good will, he had to engage in a long struggle with the spirit of the world, with himself, and with the weight of people and things. But he was fully open to the workings of grace and allowed God to lead him by degrees—to the very point of martyrdom.

There may be ups as well as downs but being open to grace, sharing with God an intense inner life rather than focusing in on the self, uncovering the many layers of self-absorption that inevitably are replaced by other layers, allowing resistance to God's will to be broken down, being committed to spiritual change and above all learning to trust in God, are signs of heroic virtue.

Saint Benedict Joseph Labre

1748–1783
Difficulty coping with the world, poor health
Feast Day 17 April
Benedict was born on 26 March 1748 in the village of Amettes near Boulogne in France. His parents were prosperous shopkeepers and they were keen to ensure

that their fifteen children were well educated. Benedict, the eldest, was a serious and religious child who
did not quite fit in with the local children. He seemed
to prefer to be on the side lines, he was often misun-
derstood and he did not find it easy to express himself.
Benedict's parents thought that his education would
be better served elsewhere, and they possibly had the
priesthood in mind for their eldest son, so at the age
of twelve he went to live with his paternal uncle who
was a priest in Erin. Benedict took to his studies of
scripture, though he found Latin tedious, but he also
liked to wander away and mix with the poor and with
the more marginalised people of the neighbourhood.

When he was sixteen Benedict decided that he
wanted to pursue the religious life as a Trappist since
their apparently unconventional way of life appealed
to him. His uncle had already come to the conclusion
that the young man who liked to wander would not be
suited to the priesthood and he sent Benedict back to
his parents to ask their permission. Benedict's parents
refused saying that he was too young and Benedict
returned to live and study with his uncle. In 1766 a
cholera epidemic broke out in Erin. Benedict's uncle
took care of the sick at considerable to risk to himself
while the eighteen year old Benedict became a farm
labourer and looked after the local cattle, as he seemed
to prefer this to his studies. As the epidemic began to
subside, Benedict's uncle contracted cholera and died.
Benedict was now left without a home but he appeared
largely untroubled by this and he returned to Amettes
intent on becoming a monk with the consent of his
parents. Eventually his parents reluctantly agreed and
Benedict approached the Trappists. The Trappists

refused him admission both because he was young and because he had a delicate constitution.

At the suggestion of another uncle, Benedict applied to the Carthusians of Montreuil however he was again refused since he did not know enough philosophy or plainchant. He was accepted at another Carthusian monastery at Longuenesse for a trial period but this did not last long since the solitude filled him with darkness and despair and his superiors feared for the mental health of this rather odd young man. Undeterred, Benedict took a course in further studies and reapplied to the Carthusians in Montreuil who finally accepted him. Once again the superiors asked Benedict to leave on the grounds that he was not suited to monastic community life. This time Benedict decided that he had already caused his parents enough trouble so he did not return home.

After approaching the Trappists and being refused once more, he was given a place at the Abbey of Sept Fons. However, after an unsuccessful and unhappy few months he fell ill and was unable to do very much for two months, after which the monks sent him home. Instead of going home Benedict, who could not live in the cloister and who found life in the world hard, decided to set off as a pilgrim. The attire he chose made him look rather eccentric: he dressed in a long cloak with a rope round his waist, he had large rosary beads round his neck, he wore makeshift shoes, and he carried a sack with his prayer book and bible. Washing was of little interest to him and he did not keep food since he relied solely on what people gave him or on what he could forage from the countryside. He visited all the religious shrines he could throughout Europe and ended up a few times in hospitals suffering from fever, exhaustion, sores and ulcers or malnutrition. Stories abounded of this peculiar young man especially since he always refused to sleep in a bed. If he was given money he tended to pass it on to other beggars instead of spending it. He did not accept friendship and when a convent of nuns showed concern at his situation he left never to return. Benedict took to living in the ruins of the Coliseum in Rome, attending confession, Mass and going to holy sites. In 1783 in Holy Week Benedict collapsed on the steps of one of the churches he frequented. He was taken to the house of the local butcher, the priest was called, and after he had received Viaticum, Benedict died. He was thirty five. Acclaimed a saint almost immediately by the people, Benedict was beatified by Pope Pius IX in 1860 and canonised by Pope Leo XIII in 1881.

Saint Catherine of Siena

1347–1380

Severe pain, eating and swallowing problems, paralysis, stroke

Feast Day 29 April

Catherine was born on 17 March 1347 in Siena in Italy, the daughter of a prosperous cloth dyer. Catherine was a happy child and her family gave her the nick name, Euphrosyne, the Greek for joy. Catherine is believed to have had her first vision of Christ in glory at the age of five, and from the age of seven she secretly decided to consecrate her life to God. Catherine was deeply attached to her older sister Bonaventura who was married to a difficult man and Bonaventura often resorted to refusing to eat in order to change his ways. When her sister died in childbirth, Catherine's parents proposed that she should marry her brother-in-law and Catherine adopted her dead sister's strategy of refusing to eat to avoid the marriage. Moreover, she cut her hair in an attempt to make her less attractive to possible suitors. Eventually Catherine's parents realised that their daughter would not marry and they allowed her to live as she wished. Catherine kept to her small room where she spent her days in prayer, fasting, and practising self-mortification. She was prone to rashes and fever but these conditions seemed to fade when she applied to join the Third Order of St Dominic and was accepted. Nevertheless she still suffered from bouts of severe physical pain. Catherine continued to live outside the convent at home, in prayer, in virtual silence, and in solitude following the rule of St Dominic. She ate little and slept even less.

In 1368 Catherine experienced what she described as a mystical marriage with Jesus who told her to leave her life of solitude and enter the world. To begin with, Catherine took to helping the poor and the sick in the same way as other Dominican tertiaries and she soon found herself caring for plague victims and visiting prisoners. She also acquired a reputation for being able to persuade people in dispute to reach amicable solutions. In spite of being regarded by some as a fanatic, Catherine drew many more people to her and she travelled in north and central Italy with some of her followers preaching reform of the clergy, repentance and conversion to God.

In 1375 Catherine was invited to Pisa and it was here that she became involved in Church politics. At a time of insurrection in the papal states, confusion and frequent changes in government, she dictated letters asking for peace and calling for the papacy to leave Avignon and return to Rome. She also dictated papers to encourage a spiritual revival in the Church. Catherine returned to Siena in 1377 to found a monastery, and she spent considerable time in preaching and peace-making as well as in learning how to write.

In 1378 she was called to Rome to assist Pope Urban VI through support of his papacy and at the same time Catherine worked tirelessly for the reformation of the Church. However her strength was beginning to fail and, she wrote, it seemed that the Bark of Peter (the papacy at the helm of the Church) was laid on her shoulders and that it was crushing her to death with its weight. Over the years Catherine had eaten less and less and soon she survived principally only on the Holy Eucharist. Her spiritual director and her monastic sisters saw this extreme fasting as unhealthy and urged her to eat. However, Catherine said that she could not and she described her inability to eat as *infermita,* an illness. By 1380 Catherine could no longer eat or swallow water. Her legs became paralysed and she suffered a stroke. Catherine died at the age of thirty three in 1380. Catherine was canonised by Pope Pius II in 1461 and she was given the title of Doctor of the Church by Pope Paul VI in 1970.

Blessed Eustochium of Padua (Lucrezia Bellini)

1444–1469

Battling demons

Feast Day 13 February

Eustochium, baptised Lucrezia, was born at San Prosdocimo convent in Padua, in 1444 and she was possibly the illegitimate daughter of one of the nuns. She was educated at the convent, but even as a child she was believed to be possessed. Eustochium applied to join the congregation however the nuns were reluctant to accept her. Nevertheless, with the bishop's support her application succeeded and she began her novitiate. For most of the time Eustochiuim was a model nun and she was well known for her gentleness and obedience. However, at other times she became violent, convulsed and behaved with madness, hysteria and fits of screaming. At such times she was restrained in much the same way as the insane were treated, by being tied to a pillar. When the Abbess fell ill it was suggested that Eustochium had poisoned her, so the townspeople threatened to burn her as a witch. In order to protect her, the bishop tried to keep her locked up in her cell where she continued to suffer from violent spells and self-harm. She once escaped and the sisters found her on a high beam in the roof where the slightest false move would have resulted in her death.

The Abbess recovered and declared that Eustochium was innocent. Nonetheless, Eustochium was shunned by her religious community who tried to persuade her to leave since she had not yet made her final vows. Eustochium believed that she was called to the religious life and refused. In her obedient and quiet moments she was always ready to do acts of charity for anyone even those who had avoided her. Eventually she was allowed to take her final vows and slowly won round her congregation. Further illness meant that she was confined to bed and she died at the age of twenty six in 1469. The name Jesus was found as if cauterized on her chest. The cult of Eustochium was confirmed by Pope Clement XIII, a former bishop of Padua, in 1760.

Saint Flora

About 1309–1347

Depression, pain, haemorrhage

Feast Day 5 October

Flora was born in France in about 1309 into a noble family. Although her parents wished her to marry, she felt called to the religious life and in 1324 she entered the Priory of Beaulieu of the Hospitaller nuns of St John of Jerusalem. The Priory also served as a hostel for the care of pilgrims. Flora found herself assailed by doubts and calls to return to a worldly life. Moreover, she suffered from periods of deep depression, intense pain and haemorrhages and became convinced that she was carrying the Cross of Christ inside her own body. Her problems of depression were exacerbated by the taunts of her fellow nuns who called her insane, who ridiculed her for her devotion, and who encouraged local people to stare at her and mimic her. However, Flora was granted particular spiritual experiences, she had ecstasies, could levitate, possibly had the stigmata and had prophetic knowledge. She remained humble and gave good advice to all who came to her. She died in 1347. The Holy See recognised her feast day in 1852.

Venerable Giunio Tinarelli

1912–1956

Arthritis, paralysis, depression

Giunio was born on 27 May 1912 in Terni in Italy. His father vehemently opposed the Church so Giunio was baptised in secret. Although his father worked in the local steelworks, the family's economic situation was difficult and from the age of twelve Giunio worked in various factories, beginning in a print works with his father and then becoming a locomotive mechanic. However, at the age of twenty five he was diagnosed with debilitating rheumatoid arthritis and spondylitis deformans. By the age of twenty eight he had become paralysed and, with no prospect of an improvement in his condition, he felt obliged to call off his engagement to be married. Giunio suffered depression and a crisis of faith. However, his local priest and his friends rallied to his aid and Giunio began to see how he could offer a ministry through his illness as 'an apostle of the sick'. He organised a pilgrimage to Loreto for sixty other patients and there he became involved in the new association of the Silent Workers of the Cross established in 1950. Through the Association he helped to organise spiritual retreats for the severely ill and for disabled people and he entered into written correspondence with many of the sick patients he had met. Giunio died in 1956. He was declared venerable in 2009 by Pope Benedict XVI.

Saint Heimrad

c.970–1019

Holy fool, eccentric

Feast Day 28 June

Heimrad was possibly born near Baden, the son of poor serfs working on a large estate in Swabia, south west Germany. Presumably seeing some potential in the young man, the lady of the estate had him trained as a priest so that he could be her chaplain. However, Heimrad proved to be unfit for the post and he asked to be released. He took to wandering and embarked on pilgrimages to Rome and Jerusalem, begging for food on the way and sharing whatever he had with other poor people. He had a nomadic existence in west Germany gaining the reputation of, if not a lunatic, certainly an eccentric, with his rather gaunt, sickly and ragged appearance. Despite his often strange behaviour, Heimrad was noted for his life of prayer and preaching such that the abbot of Hersfeld invited him to join the Benedictine monastery. Heimrad refused to wear the habit or to take monastic vows, though he did live for a very short while with the community. Soon after his admission, Heimrad asked permission to leave. He finally settled as a hermit in Kessel and led a life of austerity, penance and prayer. Heimrad died alone in 1019 and his tomb became a popular medieval site of pilgrimage.

Saint John of God

1495–1550

Mental health issues

Feast Day 8 March

John was born in 1495 in Montemor O Novo in Portugal and his family appear to have been fairly well-off. When he was eight John disappeared from home and ended up living in Spain on the estates of the Count of Oropesa. It has been suggested that John's parents had Jewish origins and, in the religious climate of his day, even if Jews were converts, it was not unknown that children would be removed from the family and be given to Christian households to ensure their religious upbringing. John worked as a shepherd on the estate and then had two spells in the army. The first spell ended in a dishonourable discharge for dereliction of sentry duty, for which he nearly faced execution. After the second spell, he decided to return to Portugal but when he arrived at his home village he discovered that both his parents had died. Perhaps seeking adventure, John set off for Gibraltar intending to sail to the Portuguese colony of Ceuta on the North African coast. At the port and possibly to help with his passage, John entered the service of a noble family who were on the way to exile in Africa, possibly after being involved in political intrigue. To begin with, in Ceuta the family lived a modest life but illnesses and lack of opportunity meant they fell on hard times and John found himself working as a labourer on the city defences in order to help the family out.

Eventually, John returned to Granada and became an itinerant book peddler. John's life appears to have been completely shattered at the arrival of the theologian and spiritual master, Father John of Avila and John, now in his forties, reacted explosively when he heard Father John of Avila preach in the city. John destroyed many of his possessions including his books, he went about half clothed and, calling himself a great sinner, he covered himself in mud and filth. His behaviour was seen as evidence of a severe mental breakdown and John was taken to the city mental asylum for treatment. This involved flogging and drenching with cold water, the recognised treatment for mental illness, designed to bring people back to their senses.

By 1539 John was sufficiently restored that he began to work in the hospital as a cleaner and he volunteered as an unpaid auxiliary nurse so that he could go some way to alleviate the dreadful conditions of some of the patients. Father John of Avila seems to have recognised John's hospital experience and growing spirituality. He organised for John to study for a while in Baeza and then to learn healthcare at a hospital in Guadalupe before encouraging him to return to Granada. In

Granada people still remembered John as the mad man. Despite this stigma, John gathered together the many poor, needy and sick and he set up a hospital that would refuse no one. John himself worked tirelessly in the hospital and sought out charitable donations for its support. John and his followers organised themselves into the Order of Hospitallers with a special ministry to those suffering mental illness. John died in 1550. He was beatified by Pope Urban VIII in 1630 and canonised by Pope Alexander VIII in 1690.

Venerable Ludovico Necchi

1876–1930

Mental health issues, anxiety, cancer

Ludovico was born on 19 November 1876 in Milan in Italy. When Ludovico was five his father, who possibly had already separated from his mother, died and his mother married an atheist so there was little interest in Christianity at home. Moreover, Ludovico's education took place in a culture of anti-clericalism and hostility to religion. Through the influence of his maternal aunts, Ludovico's faith remained strong and seemed to grow with the challenges he faced at school and at university. However, Ludovico was also prone to attacks of anxiety and scruples and this gave him a lasting empathy with people who suffered from mental illness. At secondary school Ludovico met Edward Gemelli and theirs became a life-long friendship. Ludovico was known to be a committed Catholic interested in promoting the Christian Democratic Movement, a movement concerned with the interaction of religion and solutions to social problems. In 1902 Ludovico gained his degree of Doctor of Medicine from the University of Pavia and then completed his military service at a military hospital. Possibly at this time Ludovico joined the Franciscan Third Order. While his friend Edward was drawn to the Franciscans, after some considerable discernment, Ludovico decided that his vocation lay in the world as a consecrated person.

In 1904 Ludovico began a postgraduate course in neuropathology in Berlin University where he also helped the university chaplain. He married Vittoria in Milan in 1905 and they went on to have three children. During the First World War Ludovico served as a doctor with the Italian army. After the war, Ludovico and Edward founded the first Catholic university in Italy, the University of the Sacred Heart in Milan where Ludovico took the post of professor of biology. Ludovico continued to minister to the sick as a doctor and he had special sympathy for people with mental illness and for children with disabilities. In 1929 Ludovico began to suspect he had cancer and tests proved that he was right. Ludovico died in 1930 and he was declared venerable by Pope Paul VI in 1971.

Blessed Marcel Callo

1921–1945

Depression, illnesses related to imprisonment in a concentration camp

Feast Day 19 March

Marcel was born on 6 December 1921 in Rennes, France and his father, once a farmer in Brittany, worked in the chemical factory in Rennes. To help the family financially, at the age of twelve Marcel became an assistant in a printing house. However, he found it difficult to settle in with his work colleagues who did not share his religious sensibilities and his sense of perfectionism. At his parish he joined the Eucharistic Crusade, a children's and youth movement, and when he became fourteen he joined the Christian Young Workers' Movement though he reluctantly had to give up his role as a scout leader. Realising that he had a vocation to bring Christianity into the workplace, and that for this he needed a solid Catholic foundation, he began to study Catholic social teaching in the evenings and he took more of a leadership role in the Christian Youth Workers' Movement. At the onset of the Second World War and at the age of twenty Marcel became engaged to a fellow youth member, Marguerite Derniaux.

In 1943, after a bomb attack on Rennes that killed his sister, Marcel was deported against his will to Germany to work in a factory producing bombs to be used against his own country. He missed his family and fiancé and Mass was not available so he fell into deep depression. He managed to find a room where he could hear Mass and this helped in his recovery. As he reportedly said, 'finally Christ reacted. He made me understand that the depression was not good. I had to keep busy with my friends then joy and relief would come back to me'. While suffering from boils, headaches and infected teeth he took it upon himself to care for other deportees, he began a Christian group that did activities together, he organised theatre and he found a way of having Mass said in French. Marcel wrote about his love for Christ to his newly ordained brother explaining, 'fortunately, He is a Friend, who never deserts me for an instant. He supports and consoles me. With Him, you can bear everything, even those terrible hours so filled with torment. How grateful I am to Christ'. The Nazis arrested him in 1944 for activities against the Third Reich and he was eventually sent to a camp at Mauthausen. Here he suffered other ailments including bronchitis, malnutrition, dysentery, fever, swelling, stomach problems and generalised weakness. He also had further bouts of depression. Marcel died from dysentery in 1945. He was beatified by Pope John Paul II in 1987.

Saint Marie de Saint Just (Anne-Françoise Moreau)

1866–1900

Depression

Feast Day 8 July or 28 September

Anne-Françoise Moreau was born on 9 April 1866 in La Fate in France, the daughter of a sharecropper who was known for his charitable works. She was regarded as a sensitive child who preferred her own company and she was perhaps happiest when looking after the animals in the fields. Her father died when she was young and Anne-Françoise helped to support the family by selling farm produce in the town. Although her mother had already arranged a marriage for her, Anne-Françoise felt called to the religious life and in particular to serve in the mission to China. In 1890 she entered the novitiate of the Franciscan Missionaries of Mary taking the name Marie de Saint Just. However, Marie suffered from severe depression, doubts about her vocation, her faith and her sanity. She was helped through this period of darkness by one of the sisters. In the mission to China during the Boxer Rebellion Marie was arrested and beheaded with her companions in 1900. Marie was beatified by Pope Pius XII in 1946 and canonised by Pope John Paul II in 2000.

Blessed Otto Neururer

1882–1940

Depression, illnesses related to torture

Feast Day 13 August

Otto was born on 25 March 1882 in Piller in Austria into a family of peasant farmers. His father died when he was young and throughout his life Otto, like his mother, suffered from long periods of deep depression. In 1895 he attended the minor seminary and after graduation joined the main seminary at Brixen. He was ordained in 1907 and taught religion at Innsbruck where he was especially interested in Catholic social teaching. He was then appointed as parish priest in the village of Gotzens in 1932. The Nazis occupied the Tirol in 1938 and there was general persecution of the Austrian Church. Otto came to the attention of the Nazis when, in his capacity as parish priest, he advised a local girl not to marry a divorced man who was leading a dissolute life. The man was a personal friend of a high ranking Nazi in the area. Otto was arrested for slandering German marriage and was sent to the camps of Dachau and Buchenwald. He was routinely tortured but continued to minister to his flock. In Buchenwald, where religious activity by priests was severely curtailed, Otto was approached in secret by a man for baptism and even though he suspected the man might be a spy, Otto baptised him. Two days later in 1940 he was executed by being hung upside down until he died. Otto was beatified by Pope John Paul II in 1996.

Saint Pompilio Maria Pirrotti (Dominic Pirrotti)

1710–1766

Depression, nerves, stomach complaints, convulsions, fever

Feast Day 15 July

Dominic was born on 29 September 1710 in Montecalvo Irpino in Italy into a noble family. His father was a prominent lawyer who had depressive tendencies, and Dominic also became prone to depression. In 1726 the sixteen year old Dominic heard a Piarist father preach during Lent and, fearing his parents would object, he decided to run away from home to join the Piarists. He received the habit of the Piarists in 1727 in Naples and took the name Pompilio Maria in recognition of his older brother who had died while studying in a seminary. Pompilio's poor health meant that he could not follow the usual curriculum and he was dispensed of the second year of the novitiate. He received minor orders in 1729 but his superiors sent him home so that he could recover his health. He continued his studies nearer his home all the while seeing his illnesses of headaches, stomach trouble, poor appetite, heart and blood pressure irregularities, vertigo, his nervous disposition and depression, as ascetic means of perfection.

In 1732 he began teaching, though by 1737 he suffered from what he termed an indescribable feeling of human misery. At times he found himself sunk in depressions that lasted for months but he continued, he said, to 'fight for souls', determined to unite his sufferings to the Cross. In 1739 he became professor at the diocesan seminary near Ortona a Mare on the east coast of Italy though he found the seminarians rather unruly and he himself had pain and heart discomfort. Pompilio also preached to the people advising them to take daily communion and to avoid the errors of Jansenism. He established a confraternity for the formation of lay people and an apostolate among some nuns.

In 1742 Pompilio was transferred to the town of Lanciano however for political reasons the new bishop prevented Pompilio from preaching so he moved to continue his work in Naples. He was expelled from some towns either because of the Jansenist tendencies of the town leaders or out of jealousy, and such persecutions only increased his nervous attacks and depression. In 1748 he was sent to Rome and then managed to return to Naples though once again there was conflict involving the tensions in Caravaggio over the leadership of the Arch-Confraternity of the Charity of God, an organisation Pompilio had established to promote the frequency of the sacraments, charity for all and social reform. Pompilio was censured for his over zealousness and his habit of going around the city at night and he was confined to his house. On receiving this order, Pampilio fell into a crisis of depression that forced him to remain in bed. He was then exiled from Naples, suspended from preaching, and could celebrate Mass only on his own.

He arrived in Lugo in 1759 and began work with the poor, giving spiritual retreats to the clergy and nuns and he was allowed to do some preaching. In 1762 jealousy and Jansenism once again came into play and by order of the Inquisition Pompilio was forced to leave Lugo for Ancona, although he felt especially ill. He was confined to bed at the end of 1763 with fever and stomach complaints. Pompilio was not allowed to hear confessions, to preach or to be a spiritual director. It appears that illnesses followed Pompilio whenever he was exiled and he suffered further from convulsions and sickness. This time his sickness lasted for six months and eventually in 1765 he was sent to the Piarists in Campi who were enduring rivalries of their own in the community. Pompilio took it upon himself to look after the novices and he began to see a change in attitude although he did feel that the whole weight of the house was upon his shoulders. In the wake of the famine of 1765 in 1766 Pompilio erected the Way of the Cross for the people and helped to distribute alms and what food there was to ensure the poor had something as well. Just before his death Pompilio celebrated Mass, preached and heard confessions. He fainted and was taken to his room where he remained in a chair. A few days later he received the Sacrament of the Sick. Pompilio died in 1766. He was beatified by Pope Leo XIII in 1890 and canonised by Pope Pius XI in 1934.

Notes

1   Tertullian, *On the Resurrection of the Flesh,* Chapters 7 and 8.
2   P. Brown, *The Body and Society* (New York: Columbia University Press, 1988), pp. 235–236.
3   Saint Gregory of Sinai, 'Instructions to Hesychasts,' in D. Fleming (ed.), *The Fire and the Cloud, An Anthropology of Catholic Spirituality* (London: Geoffrey Chapman, 1978), pp. 97–106 at p. 102.
4   Saint Thérèse of Lisieux, *Story of a Soul, the Autobiography of St. Thérèse of Lisieux,* translated by J. Clarke (Washington: ICS Publications, 1996), p. 14.

7

Belonging to Jesus to the End
Cancer, Tuberculosis and
Terminal Diseases

*Come to me, all you who labour and are over-
burdened and I will give you rest.*

Matthew 11:28

Introduction

THE HISTORY OF hospice care is complex, and it
is only in the late twentieth century that the
term hospice is used specifically to refer to care
of people who are dying. Before then, in the early
centuries there were some hospitals, for instance in
Roman times there were hospitals for military person-
nel, but these were few, they were not available to the
public and they were only for a very specific group of
people. Moreover they were set up for military or
economic reasons rather than being charitable foundations. One of the first documented hospices open to all
was set up in the fourth century by the theologian Saint
Basil the Great of Caesarea. Saint Basil was an active
diocesan bishop, and he founded a monastic community not only to pray and worship together, but also to
look after poor and sick people. He engaged in an

extensive building project that included a church
centre, a hostelry for travellers and a hospital for the
sick. He also built a centre, like a hospice, for long term
care of people with lasting conditions. In a letter Saint
Basil himself explained the bureaucratic difficulties of
funding his project,[1] and he is now known as the
patron saint of hospital administrators. Another
bishop, Saint John Chrysostom also set up some houses
for sick people, *nosokomeia*, and these catered for the
needs of the people in his diocese and for strangers
who fell ill.

The word hospice and hospital come from the Latin
root *hospes*, guest or host, and it is linked to hospitality.
Early hospices were associated with facilities to care
for pilgrims and one such hospice was founded by
Crusaders in 1099 in Jerusalem during the First Crusade, though it was built on an already existing
institution. The Jerusalem hospice looked after all sick
and weary pilgrims travelling to the Holy Land, both
Christian and Muslim. The brothers of the hospice
were recognised as an order of knighthood and they
became the order of the Knights Hospitaller of St John
of Jerusalem. Hospitals in medieval Europe were
associated with monastic orders, and in the fourteenth
century the Knights Hospitaller built a hospital in
Rhodes that was renowned for its advanced medicine.
Another notable hospital, the Hôtel Dieu, was built in
Beaume in Burgundy by a wealthy layman, Nicholas
Rodin, in 1443. Again, the hospital was not strictly a
hospice in our modern understanding of the word
since it looked after not only the dying but also
disabled people, the elderly, the destitute, sick people,
orphans and pregnant women. Rodin gathered

together a religious order of nuns to care for these otherwise marginalised people.

After the Protestant Reformation, some institutions continued, though under the control of the civil author-ities. Other institutions were set up later by religious foundations, indeed many saints and the blessed were involved in care for the destitute and dying. By the late eighteenth and early nineteenth centuries, more inter-est was shown in science and medicine, and the nineteenth century saw an expansion in hospital building. However, the object of these early modern hospitals was to cure. This meant that futile conditions in the last year or months of life were seen as medical failure, and the dying were less welcome in hospitals. If they could find a place, people went to institutions and asylums to die or they died at home. A new approach was needed by the middle of the nineteenth century when illnesses such as consumption and tuberculosis became rife in overcrowded cities like Dublin and London. A number of charitable associa-tions, often organised by women, began to found institutions to cater for people who were dying from these specific diseases.

St Christopher's Hospice was the first modern hospice specifically dedicated to the care of the termi-nally ill and it was set up in 1967 in London by the nurse, and later doctor, Dame Cicely Saunders. Dame Cicely began working with people with terminal illness in 1948 and she was the first person to use the term hospice for places that specialised in the care of the dying. Another milestone in the hospice movement was the seminal work done by the Swiss-American psychiatrist Dr Elisabeth Kübler-Ross. Dr Kübler-Ross wanted to privilege the voice of the dying and so she entered into a documented dialogue with people with terminal conditions in order to let their stories be told and to have some basis for understanding the dying process. Through this research better help can be available for those who are dying, for their loved ones and carers, and for healthcare professionals. The work of Dr Kübler-Ross was not intended to provide a detail by detail account of how to manage terminally ill people, nor was it a complete psychological study and she noted that everyone goes through their own personal journey. Nevertheless, her identification of the five stages in the dying process offers a good reflection on what may be going on with a patient.

The five stages that Dr Kübler-Ross picked out, stages of denial, anger, bargaining, depression and acceptance, demonstrate the complexity of the dying process, even if these stages do not represent a rigid system, after all, these stages may overlap, that may not surface, or may indeed come in a different order. This complexity plays out in many different ways: some people with terminal illness decide to fight to the end, and some people rage against death. There are some people who simply give up and wait to die. There are others who have unrealistic expectations, who cling to all and any treatment option no matter how unreasonable or experimental. There are people who fear losing control and being dependent, and people who would rather be dead than disabled and so demand euthanasia or assisted suicide. There are also people who face their last years and months with patient endurance.

In a speech to scientists and specifically gastro-enterologists Pope John Paul II reiterated the Church's commitment to support speedy diagnosis and effective treatment for terminal conditions such as cancer. Nevertheless, he reminded his audience that human beings are limited and mortal. He pointed out that

> it is necessary to approach the sick with a healthy realism that avoids giving to those who are suffering the illusion that medicine is omnipotent. There are limits that are not humanly possible to overcome; in these cases, the patient must know how to accept his human condition serenely, which the faithful know how to interpret in the light of the divine will. The divine will is manifested even in death, the natural end of human life on earth.[2]

Certainly Pope John Paul II was right when he told physicians and healthcare workers that 'teaching people to accept death serenely belongs to your mission'. However, he added that the nature of the human being as spirit as well as body must be taken into account, and a focus merely on technology or on overzealous treatment may not fully respect the dignity of the human person who is in a terminal condition.

The mission to teach people to die well does not only belong to healthcare professionals. This is clear from the insight from Dr Kübler-Ross that the terminally ill also have a voice for us to hear. That voice is especially powerful when it belongs to the saints and blessed who are making the journey. That voice speaks not only about the fragility and limits of human life. In their lived experience the saints and blessed speak of common human feelings of hopes and despair, of spiritual questioning, of the sense that a person is more than just a condition or an illness or a transitory being. Some experience spiritual distress or feelings of abandonment as they struggle to come to terms with the reality of their situation. All demonstrate the need for a good preparation for death, spiritual reconciliation and reception of the sacraments. The final acceptance that this is the will of God, and entrusting oneself to God's mercy and goodness, are the signs of patient endurance and of heroic virtue.

Saint Alberto Hurtado Cruchaga

1901–1952

Pancreatic cancer

Feast Day 18 August

Alberto was born on 22 January 1901 in Viña del Mar in Chile into an impoverished family. When Alberto was four his father died and his mother fell into debt. As a result, Alberto and his younger brother and mother found themselves moved from one set of relatives to another. Alberto managed to gain a scholarship to the Jesuit College in Santiago and, when not studying, he spent time helping in the poorest neighbourhoods. Although he wanted to join the Jesuits, Alberto was concerned first and foremost with his family and so he found a job and worked afternoons and evenings to support his mother and brother, spending the mornings at the Catholic University studying law. After a brief spell in military service, Alberto completed his degree in 1923 and he immediately entered the novitiate of the Society of Jesus. He did further studies in humanities in Argentina and then philosophy and theology in Spain. However, the political turmoil in Spain brought an anti-clerical government to power and in 1931 the Jesuits were banned so Alberto was sent to Belgium to study theology at the Louvain. He was ordained there in 1933 and in 1935 he obtained his doctorate.

Alberto returned to Chile in 1936 and took up the post of professor of religion at the Catholic university in Santiago. Alberto was especially interested in encouraging lay people to work with those in need and he involved his students in teaching catechism to poor people. He also organised retreats both for those discerning a call to the priesthood and for lay vocations. Through his work with the Catholic Youth Movement he saw the need to provide not simply accommodation but a home life for the homeless and he opened *El Hogar de Cristo,* the home of Christ, first for homeless children then for women and men. Alberto was also concerned with social humanism and social action as well as how Catholic social action works with unions for the good of the whole of society. When he was just fifty one, Alberto was diagnosed with pancreatic cancer and he died in 1952. He was beatified by Pope John Paul II in 1994 and canonised by Pope Benedict XVI in 2005.

Blessed Antonio Rosmini

1797–1855

Liver disease

Feast Day 1 July

Antonio was born on 24 March 1797 in Rovereto, northern Italy into a wealthy and distinguished aristocratic family. Antonio was a keen student first at home, where he took full advantage of the extensive family library, and then with a tutor where with his friends he studied and discussed philosophy. By 1814 Antonio had decided to become a priest. At first his parents were reluctant to give their consent since they had hoped he would pursue a career and continue the family name. Finally, his father suggested that Antonio go to Rome for his theological studies so that at least he could make suitable connections for a successful Church career. Nevertheless, Antonio enrolled at the University of Padua in 1816 where he received doctorates in theology and canon law. Antonio was ordained in 1821 and he returned to Rovereto for further personal study and prayer since he felt God was calling him to found a religious order. He also began to publish some of his books. His spiritual experiences at this time helped him to formulate his principle of passivity that a person is to be concerned with his or her own personal sanctification until God's will manifests itself to undertake some external work of charity.

From 1822 he began to suffer symptoms of the disease that had already affected many of his family, inflammation of the liver, and over the years these symptoms grew in severity. In 1823 he had the opportunity to go to Rome where he met Pope Pius VII who encouraged Antonio to look into a reform of philosophy. Antonio settled for a few years in Milan where he wrote and published on many theological, philosophical and political themes. By 1827 Antonio was suffering an acute form of liver disease and his doctor predicted an early death if he did not give up some of his more austere practices. Antonio agreed to look after his health, to take the prescribed medication and to take regular periods of time in areas with purer air and water.

In 1828 Antonio headed for the retreat Sacro Monte Calvaria, Domodossola, where he began work on the constitutions for his foundation the Institute of Charity. Antonio returned to Rome late in 1828 to ensure he was indeed following the will of God, and in Rome he received the support first of Pope Leo XII then of Pope Pius VIII. Under orders from his doctors, Antonio was obliged to remain in Rome and his stay was extended by a serious bout of small pox. His Institute grew and spread to north Italy; by 1835 it became established in England. The Constitutions were approved in 1838 by Pope Gregory XVI and Antonio was appointed provost general for life. However, Antonio's published work proved controversial and generated much opposition. His works were examined by the Congregation of the Index and the case against them was only dismissed in 1854. By 1849 Antonio had moved to Stresa in northern Italy. His health grew worse and in 1854 he suffered intense intestinal pain that confined him to bed. At the news of the severity of his illness many friends came to see him and he welcomed them all reminding them to 'adore, be silent, rejoice'. Antonio died in 1855 and he was beatified by Pope Benedict XVI in 2007.

Blessed Chiara Badano

1971–1990

Bone cancer

Feast Day 29 October

Chiara was born on 29 October 1971 in the village of Sassello in Italy to parents who had been praying for eleven years for a child. Even as a young girl, Chiara was always concerned with those who were poor and she was especially interested in the work of the African missions. In 1981 Chiara, who was only nine years old, and her parents became involved in the Focolare movement, an ecumenical group that looks to building a united world of people of all faiths and none. Chiara herself was a typical teenager who loved outdoor activities, singing and dancing, and having coffee with her friends. These distractions perhaps contributed to

Chiara failing her first year of high school but she carried on with her studies undeterred. She joined a group of students on a trip to Rome arranged by Focolare and during this time she had a life changing experience where she felt she had encountered Jesus forsaken and crucified. The experience so affected her that she decided to think more deeply about her future. One day in 1988 while playing tennis Chiara had a severe pain in her shoulder. Later tests diagnosed cancer. During her time in hospital Chiara helped other young patients, accompanying them when she was needed despite her own pain. Chiara underwent painful operations and chemotherapy. Eventually she became unable to walk. Still, she wanted to offer up her pain for Christ. Chiara died in 1990 and she was beatified by Pope Benedict XVI in 2010.

Saint Gabriel of Our Lady of Sorrows (Francesco Possenti)

1838–1862

Tuberculosis

Feast Day 28 February

Francesco was born on 1 March 1838 in Assisi, Italy. His father was a government official and the family moved to Spoleto in 1841 when his father was appointed a magistrate there. In the same year two of Francesco's sisters and his mother died. Then in 1846 one of his brothers was killed in the Italian war against Austria and some years later another brother committed suicide. Francesco was known to be a difficult child who was prone to temper and, as a young man, he was fond of socialising, dancing and very keen on his own appearance. In 1851 Francesco became seriously ill, so much so that he promised he would join the religious life if he recovered. He did recover and soon forgot his promise. The same thing happened again when he narrowly escaped a bullet during a hunting expedition. In 1853 Francesco fell ill once more, this time with a throat abscess and he attributed his recovery to the intercession of the recently beatified Jesuit, Andrew Bobola.

Although Francesco did apply to join the Society of Jesus, he did not proceed with his application. Then his sister, who had cared for him after the death of their mother, died of cholera. Greatly affected by a procession of Our Lady organised after the cholera epidemic had ended, Francisco decided to enter the Passionist Congregation. At first his father refused permission and tried to persuade Francisco to change his mind but realising that his son was serious he allowed Francisco to enter the novitiate in Morrovalle in Italy in 1856. Francisco took the name Gabriel of Our Lady of Sorrows and made his vows in 1857. The community moved to the monastery of Isola Gran Sasso in 1859 where Gabriel excelled at his studies and deepened his spiritual life. Towards the end of 1861 he showed symptoms of tuberculosis. Efforts to treat the illness were unsuccessful but Gabriel remained cheerful throughout and supported his fellow students with his own particular devotion to Our Lady. Before he could be ordained a priest Gabriel died surrounded by his community in 1862. Gabriel was beatified by Pope Pius X in 1908 and he was canonised by Pope Benedict XV in 1920.

Blessed Isidore of St Joseph de Loor

1881–1916

Eye cancer, metastasis, pleurisy

Feast Day 6 October

Isidore was born on 18 April 1881 in Vrasene, a small town in Eastern Flanders, where his parents had a farm. Isidore went to school until he was twelve and then he joined his father working on the family farm. However, his health did not suit him to farm work, so he helped teach catechism. When the town received a mission from the Redemptorist Fathers, Isidore had the opportunity to discuss with one of the missionaries the possibility that he had a vocation to the religious life. The Redemptorist missionary advised him to join the Passionists, dedicated to the Passion of Jesus, with its goals of both missionary work and a contemplative life.

In 1907 the Dutch speaking Isidore joined the Passionist monastery as a lay brother at Ere in Belgium where French was spoken, so at first the move was difficult. However, a year later he professed his vows as a Passionist. He was sent to another Passionist monastery where, ready to do God's will in the smallest things of everyday living, he worked as a gardener and cook. A painful cancerous tumour was discovered in his right eye and he had the eye removed in 1911. The cancer had however spread and Isidore was given only a few years to live. He continued to serve at the monastery as porter and then, during the First World War, as an assistant to the many people who came to the monastery for help. By 1916 cancer had affected his inner organs and he prepared for death. He died in 1916 from cancer and pleurisy. Isidore was beatified by Pope John Paul II in 1984.

Blessed Louise Thérèse de Montaignac de Chauvance

1820–1885
Bone tuberculosis, confined to bed
Feast Day 27 June

Louise was born on 14 May 1820 in Le Havre, France into a noble French family and her father was a wealthy financier. She was known to be a fervent child and when she went to boarding school at the age of seven, Louise developed a deep devotion to the Sacred Heart that remained with her throughout her life. Louise was particularly influenced by her aunt and the two women gathered together a group of women to pray for the renewal of faith and moral life in France. Louise was at one stage drawn to life with the Carmelites, however, on the sudden death of her aunt in 1845 Louise continued their project and founded a society to help maintain rural churches and to encourage devotion to the Sacred Heart. Louise also noticed that there were a number of abandoned and destitute children, so in 1850 she lodged orphans in the family home opening an orphanage in Moulins in 1852.

Still concerned with the general lapse in faith and morals in France, Louise set up the Society for the Adoration of Reparation in 1854, whose members made the commitment to pray before the Blessed Sacrament specifically to make up for the ingratitude of human beings. At the age of twenty two Louise first began to suffer from tuberculosis of the bones and she endured increasing disability. However, Louise felt that there was more to be done and in 1874 she obtained permission to set up the Pious Union of the

Oblates of the Sacred Heart, a congregation for women who wished to serve either alone or in their families, and who sought to renew the faith of society by their examples of holiness. Louise became the superior and then the Mother General of this new congregation and the congregation enlarged its activities from running orphanages to organising religious education, retreats, Eucharistic adoration and raising funds for poor parishes. Louise's condition caused her considerable suffering and she was confined to her bed for some years before she died in 1885. Louise was beatified by Pope John Paul II in 1990.

Blessed Maria Teresa of Cascia
(Maria Teresa Fasce)

1881–1947

Breast cancer, heart problems, diabetes, asthma and circulatory problems, difficulty walking

Feast Day 12 October

Maria Teresa, known as Marietta was born on 27 December 1881 in the small town of Torriglia near Genoa in Italy. She came from a well to do family and had a good education. Marietta taught catechesis and singing in her parish and it was here that she also came to love the spirituality of Saint Augustine. In 1900 Pope Leo XIII canonised Saint Rita of Cascia and as the Augustinians set about making this new saint known, Marietta took this to be her particular task as well. In 1906 she entered the monastery of Saint Rita in Cascia though not without having to overcome considerable opposition. Marietta's family thought that the monastery was too remote, and the abbess of the monastery was concerned that a young lady used to the city would find the life too hard. Nevertheless, after six months Marietta, now once more known as Maria Teresa, received the Augustinian habit, and the next year in 1907 she made her vows of chastity, poverty and obedience.

Maria Teresa did not find monastery life in Cascia hard but instead she found that the community was in crisis with little meditation, silence and diligence, so, disappointed and with doubts about her vocation, she left in 1910. She returned in 1911 with the idea of renewing the monastery and in 1912 she made her solemn profession. Appointed mistress of novices in 1914 she was then elected abbess in 1920. With her experience of people, her practical sense, her authority and above all her motherly instinct she helped the monastery become a model community. She set up an orphanage for girls, a seminary and a hospital. She arranged for a publication to promote Saint Rita. For almost thirty years she suffered from a painful malignant tumour in her right breast which she saw as a gift from God, her 'treasure'. She also had heart problems, diabetes, asthma and circulatory problems. She had difficulty walking so had to be carried on a chair. Maria Teresa died from her illnesses in 1947 and she was beatified by Pope John Paul II in 1997.

Blessed Mary Anna Sala

1829–1891

Throat cancer

Feast Day 24 November

Mary Anna was born on 21 April 1829 in Brivio near Lecco in Italy, the fifth of eight children, and her father worked in the timber trade. Her parents recognised that she was a clever child and so in 1842 they enrolled Mary Anna in a new boarding school run by the Sisters of Saint Marcellina. Mary Anna gained a diploma in teaching and, at the same time, she made it clear that she wished to join the order. However, her father had just been defrauded of all his money, and her mother had become ill, so Mary Anna returned home to help support the family. Finally, she was able to join the order in 1848 and she made her profession of vows in 1852. She taught in several of the congregation's schools and was totally devoted to the welfare of her students. In 1883 Mary Anna was diagnosed with throat cancer. She continued to teach and to take part in community life for as long as she could and she bore her suffering and the debilitating medical treatments without complaint. After collapsing, Mary Anna was taken to the infirmary where she died in 1891. She was beatified by Pope John Paul II in 1980.

Venerable Nicola D'Onofrio

1943–1964

Lung cancer

Feast Day 12 June

Nicola was born on 24 March 1943 in Villamagna a town near Chieti in the east of Italy and a few kilometres away from the birthplace of Saint Camilles de Lellis. His family were farmers. The local priest was of the religious order of Saint Camilles and, recognising that Nicola was devoted at Mass and diligent at school, he suggested that Nicola join the Camillian seminary in Rome. Although Nicola was enthusiastic, his parents objected. His father was reluctant to lose his son from the farm; his mother wanted him to go to the local seminary in Chieti, and two of his aunts offered to make him their sole heir if he stayed at home. Family opposition continued for a year but eventually he was given permission, and at the age of twelve Nicola entered the Camillian seminary in 1955. He entrusted himself completely to the spiritual direction of his superiors and when he discovered two years later that his father wanted to withdraw him from the seminary he wrote strongly to his superiors convincing them of the resoluteness of his vocation. In 1960 Nicola began his novitiate year and in 1961 at the age of eighteen he started the period of formation as a professed Camillian religious, taking the usual vows of poverty, chastity and obedience with the additional Camillian vow to care for the sick even in cases of contagious diseases. He developed a strong devotion to Saint Thérèse of Lisieux, making her little way the path of his own spirituality.

In 1962 at the age of twenty he began to suffer symptoms of illness and after an operation the doctors diagnosed cancer. Known to be patient and always smiling, Nicola underwent radiotherapy and surgical operations while also beginning his studies at the Pontifical Gregorian University. In 1964 further investigations showed up lung cancer and although his superiors had tried to hide the severity of his condition from him, Nicola realised that he was dying. However, Nicola was more concerned at the effect this diagnosis would have on his mother. Nicola continued with the community life of the seminary though, it is reported, he lived aware of the reality of the life to come and he made the Crucified Christ his daily reference point. In obedience to his superiors who were praying for a miraculous cure, Nicola visited Lourdes and Lisieux. At times during his suffering Nicola prayed for healing, at times he said he would not pray any further for healing, however he also accepted God's will for him.

On his return from pilgrimage he was given a dispensation and allowed to take his perpetual vows. By this stage Nicola was so weak that he had to use a wheelchair but he consecrated himself to God and received the Anointing of the Sick. The lung cancer caused him considerable pain including moments when he felt he was suffocating. Nicola refused pain relief that would compromise his ability to remain lucidly listening to the prayers of the community of brothers round his bedside. He himself offered up his life and his sufferings to Christ and he died in 1964 at the age of twenty one. After a decree of heroic virtues he was declared venerable by Pope Francis in 2013.

Saint Rafqa (Butrusia Ar-Rayes)

1832–1914

Blind, paralysed, bone tuberculosis

Feast Day 23 March

Butrusia was born on 29 June 1832 in the town of Himalaya in the Lebanon to a poor family of Maronite Christians. Her mother died when Butrusia was seven and to support the family Butrusia worked as a domestic servant for a Christian family in Damascus. Her father remarried, and when Butrusia was fourteen years old the family called her home in order to arrange a marriage for her. However Butrusia wanted to pursue the religious life, so she managed to put off all attempts at marriage and at the age of twenty one she finally left home and entered the local convent of Mariamette Sisters, Our Lady of Deliverance, a new order of teaching sisters founded by the Jesuits. Her parents came to claim her back but the superior refused them. In 1855 Butrusia took the habit and was professed a year later taking the name Sister Anissa. While she studied at the convent she also worked as the cook. She then taught in various local schools, though at one of her postings she was deeply affected by the violence and deaths that so often took place in the area.

In 1871 the Jesuits decided to merge the Mariamette Sisters with the Daughters of the Sacred Heart but since no agreement was made between the two institutes both were suppressed. Although many of the nuns returned to a secular life, Sister Anissa felt called to a life of contemplation and she joined the monastic Order of St Antony the Great and she took the name of her mother, Rebecca, Rafqa. In this more contemplative setting Rafqa was known for her cheerfulness and her willingness to help anyone in need. However, she felt a lack in her spiritual life that she thought could be filled by suffering. In 1885 possibly as a result of a form of tuberculosis that affected the bones, Rafqa began to feel enormous pain and to lose the sight in her right eye. In an attempt at a cure she was sent to a doctor who removed the eye but with the result that the pain concentrated in her left eye. She was sent to a monastery where the climate might be more beneficial but her sight worsened, she eventually became blind and she suffered frequent bleeding from her eyes and nose. Meanwhile the pain increased. She became paralysed except for her hands and she spent her time in prayer, saying the rosary and knitting for the community. She did not complain, saying only that her sufferings were nothing compared to the sufferings of Christ. By 1907 she was completely blind and paralysed. Rafqa died in 1914, she was beatified by Pope John Paul II in 1985 and canonised in 2001.

Blessed Zepherin Namuncura

1886–1905

Tuberculosis

Feast Day 26 August

Zepherin was born on 26 August 1886 in Chimpay, a small town in Valle Medio in Argentina. His father, the chief of the Araucano Indians, handed his very young son over to the Salesian missionaries since he wanted the future leader of his people to be brought up in 'the white man's religion'. Zepherin was cared for by the local priest until 1887 when his father enrolled the eleven year old into military school at El Tigre, once again hoping that this would give the boy good leadership skills. However, Zepherin was the only native Indian in the military school, he was mistreated by the other students and soon became ill. His priest came to his rescue, and Zepherin was sent to the Salesian mission school in Buenos Aires where he proved to be popular and well liked even though some of his classmates were insensitive over his Indian heritage. Zepherin developed a deep love for the church and at the age of seventeen he joined the minor seminary. In 1903, with the permission of his superiors, he organised a procession in honour of Our Lady but fell ill with tuberculosis that same night. In 1904 he was sent to Rome in the hopes that a change of climate would help him but his health took a turn for the worse. His illness progressed and, praying continuously for his people, he died at the age of eighteen in 1905. Zepherin was beatified by Pope Benedict XVI in 2007.

Notes

1   Saint Basil, *Letter* 74.
2   Pope Saint John Paul, *Address to the World Organisation of Gastro-enterology* (23 March 2002).

8

DISCIPLES OF JESUS THE DEFORMED, THE STUNTED, THE CRIPPLED, AMPUTEES, THE PARALYSED, THE BLIND, THE DEAF AND STAMMERERS

When you have a party, invite the poor, the crippled, the lame and the blind.

Luke 14:13

Introduction

THE VERY WAY in which certain people with disabilities are described—the deformed, the stunted, the crippled, the blind, the deaf— suggests a certain attitude on the part of the person or society doing the describing. The person who is disabled appears to be missing and the focus is on the disability. This depersonalising language gives the impression that the disability is what matters or that there is a lack in the person, he or she is not whole, not 'normal'. Of course in the Christian mindset talk of the lame, the crippled, the deaf, the blind and the dumb immediately recalls the Gospels and the healing mission of Jesus. To find out if Jesus was the promised one, John the Baptist sent two of his disciples to ask Jesus and Jesus replied, 'Go back and tell John what you have seen and heard: the blind see again, the lame walk, those suffering from virulent diseases are cleansed, and the deaf hear, the dead are raised to life'.[1] For some people, scriptural emphasis on the fact that Jesus heals people is simply a way of saying that people with disabilities do not belong in the Kingdom, there is no wholeness or holiness in disability. Even more troublesome, they think, is the link made in Scripture between sin and suffering or disability. This emphasis, they say, is a tool of oppression and they call for a reinterpretation of Scripture. And if Scripture singles out certain disabled people then the question raised is 'why me'?

Of course, any reading of the healing miracles demonstrates beyond doubt that Jesus never depersonalised anyone. On the contrary, Jesus brings the human being before Him into a deeper way of being the person that God wants her or him to be. The 'why me' question is not so much why am I disabled or why has God created me this way. Rather it is 'why me', what vocation has God chosen for me? The healing miracles are primarily about Jesus and the reality of who He is, God and man. Miracles prove that time has been fulfilled, the Kingdom is near and that Jesus has the authority to do mighty deeds. Miracles are also stories about discipleship because they are about having faith in Jesus and in what He can do. They are also about vocation even if it is not what the person expected. For instance, Saint Mark tells the story of the Gerasene demoniac. After his cure the man begged to be allowed to stay with Jesus but Jesus told him to go home. Jesus asked him to be a disciple with a particular vocation: not to stay with Jesus but to follow Him by going home to his own people, not the Jews, and to 'tell them all that the Lord in his mercy has done for you'.[2] However the healing ministry of Jesus does bring with it some other important issues.

To begin with there is the issue of disability itself. Jesus did not heal anyone who did not want to be healed. Moreover, as the account of the cure of the paralysed man in the gospels of Matthew, Mark and Luke shows, Jesus is concerned first and foremost with the person's spiritual life. Jesus forgives the man's sins and it is only later, after the scribes have discussed this amongst themselves, that Jesus cures him.[3] Of course anyone whether disabled or not can sin. For those who maintain that their disability is not a defect or limitation, rather it is part of who they are, and for those who challenge the idea that there is indeed a norm of which people with disabilities fall short, Saint Augustine may help. In his book the *City of God* Saint Augustine discussed the diversity that exists among human beings.[4] Augustine mentioned people born with extra fingers or toes as well as people born so deformed that they appeared to be monstrous births. Saint Augustine was clear that these human beings, coming from human parents, were truly human. Moreover, he explained that they were not aberrations or accidents: God, he said, does not make mistakes, He knows what He is doing. According to Saint Augustine, people will have at the resurrection bodies that belong to them naturally. So who is to gainsay that if a person who is deaf believes that deafness is a part of who they are as a person, then they may be deaf in heaven?

A good example of someone healed by Jesus whose situation raises some significant questions is the man born blind and his story is told by Saint John. When the disciples came across the man blind from birth they asked a question particularly pressing among the Jewish scholars of the time: 'Rabbi, who sinned, this man or his parents, that he should have been born blind?'[5] There was much discussion about the priority of collective guilt over personal guilt: both the prophets Jeremiah and Ezekiel spoke about a common Jewish proverb, 'the fathers have eaten unripe grapes; the children's teeth are set on edge'. Both prophets questioned this proverb and both called for individual and personal conversion.[6] Putting aside for a moment the issue that for some people their disability is neither a suffering nor a particular evil, it is just an aspect of who they are, the reality of evil and suffering has always been a particularly intractable problem.

In the ancient pagan world, evil and its result, suffering, were accounted for by the imperfections in the material world: matter was to blame because matter was furthest from ideal of the Good. In some cults, notably Manichaeism, the material world was created by an evil demi-god, the vengeful god of the Old Testament, and not by the true God. In contrast, according to the tradition of the Jews and Christians as told in the Genesis creation story, the whole of creation including matter was created by the all good God and so was and is good. God gifted human beings, Adam and Eve, created in his image and likeness, with the ability to live and act in a godlike manner, they were free to live a life of virtue and love. However, Adam and Eve misused this freedom by seeking to be gods themselves and deciding for themselves what was true and good. This misuse of freedom, sin, brought the evil of suffering: human beings broke their relationship with God, they separated themselves from the God of life and they made themselves his enemies. This first sin devastated not only the relationship of Adam and Eve but also all human relationships and the whole of creation. In considering blindness, everything created is a good. Evil, as founded on sin, is a privation of good, it is a reality but attached to a good as a corruption of that good. So, in the tradition, for human beings sight is good since the possession of eyes means that human beings are intended to see. The reality of blindness is the absence of the good of sight. Nevertheless, if we return to the idea of creation as good and that God does not make mistakes, the person who is blind is not defective or falls short of a normal human being.

Although Jeremiah and Ezekiel wished to remind the Israelites of the personal nature of responsibility, suffering and disability are complex. There are situations where suffering is caused by the sin of others: foetal alcohol syndrome is perhaps a case in point. There are times when pain is actually a help: pain lets the person know that the body is in need of help, that something might be amiss. Moreover suffering, whether or not through illness and disability, may be the wake-up call, the *kairos* moment that calls a person to re-evaluate his or her life and relationships, a conversion moment. It is often through suffering that people come to grow in the virtues of patience and endurance and so is the means of heroic sanctity.

This leads us onto the response of Jesus to the question raised by his disciples. Jesus answered, 'he was born blind so that the works of God might be revealed in him'. Immediately we have a problem: if blindness is not due to sin, does God afflict people for His own glory? This problem points to the perplexity and mystery of suffering to which only God has the answer. Nevertheless, it can be said that disability and suffering is an inevitable part of earthly life and since it has happened, God may still bring some good out of it. Jesus healed the man born blind in Saint John's Gospel. This healing, with all the other healings, are examples of the mighty deeds, *dynameis,* of Jesus that affirmed the presence of the power of God and the in-breaking of the Kingdom. Clearly there are present day healings, after all the miracles that demonstrate that a person is now with God are the marks of the saints and blessed: God is still active and He works healing miracles through the intercession of His servants.

However, not all of God's servants are healed. Many saints and the blessed were disabled, crippled, blind, deformed and remained so for their earthly life. There are no cures here but also these holy men and women are not declared saints or blessed in spite of their disabilities. Scripture contains many examples of people with varying disabilities who God specifically chose to do his work. Isaac, grown old and blind, gave Jacob rather than Esau his blessing,[7] Jacob had a limp after he wrestled with God and received a special blessing from God on Israel,[8] God chose Moses the stammerer to bring His people out of Egypt,[9] Saint Paul had a 'thorn in his flesh' that reminded him that it is God who works through every weakness.[10] As Saint Paul told the community at Corinth, each person has a share in God's work.[11] In some cases the way in which the person centres his or her life on Christ is obscured in their life time by people who cannot see past the person's situation. Nevertheless, these people with disabilities not only draw closer to Christ, they also bring others with them through their heroic witness that God works through all people no matter what their state or condition.

Saint Albert Chmielowski (Adam Chmielowski)

1845–1916

Amputee

Feast Day 17 June

Adam Chmielowski was born on 20 August 1845 in Igołomia on the outskirts of Kracow into a wealthy and aristocratic family. When Adam was just eight years old his father died, and three years later his mother also died, leaving Adam and his three siblings in the care of relatives who ensured that the orphans were brought up well and received a good education. As the eldest son, Adam was sent to study agriculture so that he could manage the family estate. In 1863 at the age of eighteen he became involved in politics and lost a leg in the Polish nationalist uprising against Czar Alexander III. The uprising was followed by political repression and Adam was forced to leave Poland. He went to Belgium where he studied engineering and it was here that he discovered his talent for painting. He became an artist and studied in Warsaw, Munich and Paris. In 1874 he was able to return to Kracow as an accomplished artist however he was soon made very aware of the plight of the poor, destitute and homeless in the city. Adam now felt that he was called to serve the poor by living in poverty among them, so in 1887 he joined a secular order of Saint Francis and took the name Brother Albert. He founded the Brothers of the Third Order of Saint Francis, the Albertines and a community of Albertine sisters whose mission it was to organise food and shelter for the poor and homeless of any age or religion. He arranged homes for people with disabilities and for those with incurable illnesses. Brother Albert called on all to see the face of Jesus in every human being and to affirm the intrinsic human dignity of all no matter their situation. Brother Albert died in 1916 he was beatified by Pope John Paul II in 1983 and canonised 1989.

Saint Albert of Montecorvino

Died 1127

Blind

Feast Day 5 April

Albert was born into a Norman family and came to Montecorvino in Italy as a child. It seems that he became blind when young. Albert may have been a monk before reluctantly becoming bishop of Montecorvino apparently by acclamation, and he was known for his visions and healing powers. He died in 1127. A cult began soon after Albert's death, his cathedral became a pilgrimage site and today a procession still takes place in Montecorvino in honour of the bishop.

Venerable Brother Anthony Kowalczyk

1866–1947

Amputee, rheumatism, failing memory, paralysis, loss of speech

Anthony was born on 4 June 1866 in Dzierzanow near Poznan in south west Poland. His parents had a small farm and after a basic education in the village school he left school to help them. When he was fourteen years old Anthony was apprenticed to a blacksmith and when he was seventeen he left home in order to find work first in northern Germany and then in Cologne. He lodged with a Catholic family and the lady of the house recognised in Anthony a firmness of belief, a dedication to social action and missionary zeal. Anthony considered his lack of education and his advanced age of twenty five a bar to missionary work, nevertheless his land lady persuaded him to make contact with the Missionary Oblates of Mary Immaculate. Anthony joined them as a religious brother and as part of the mission he arrived in Canada in 1896 where as an immigrant he found the language and cultural differences and subsequent alienation difficult. The missionaries had opened a school for boys run by the nuns of the order and a work shop with a saw mill to provide timber for the missions further north.

While working in the saw mill, Brother Anthony had a serious accident and had to travel 120 miles to receive treatment by which time gangrene had set in and his arm was amputated. There was no anaesthetic available but Brother Anthony endured this without complaint and he was later fitted with an artificial arm with a hook in place of his hand. Although no longer considered fit for more arduous missionary activity, Brother Anthony spent the rest of his life dedicated to everyday service taking care of the heating at the religious house and school, doing any jobs needed by the nuns including work in the kitchen and garden, with the poultry, in the farm, cleaning the toilets, sharpening the skates for the school boys and repairing their hockey sticks. He showed a special devotion to Our Lady and constantly reminded the boys to pray to her. He was well known for being ready to listen to the boys, pray and give good advice. By 1945 Brother

Anthony's health had begun to fail, he had rheumatism, was beginning to lose his sight and his memory was deteriorating. A few days before he died, Brother Anthony suffered paralysis and lost his speech. He died in 1947 and was declared venerable by Pope Francis in 2013.

Venerable Mother Carmen Martinez Rendiles

1903–1977

Born without a limb

Carmen was born on 11 August 1903 in Caracas in Venezuela into a comfortably off family. She was born without a left arm and wore a prosthesis from an early age, however, she did not regard this as an impediment to normal life. At the age of fifteen Carmen felt called to the religious life and, having been refused by some convents possibly on account of her physical disability, she spent much time in prayer to find the right congregation. Finally, in 1927 she entered the French order of the Sister Servants of Jesus in the Blessed Sacrament and she made her perpetual vows in 1932. She became novice mistress and then superior for the Venezuelan congregation in 1945. In 1965 after a long and difficult process, the French order separated from the congregation and a new congregation with the same name was formed in Venezuela with Mother Carmen as Mother General. The sisters founded several houses and educational institutes. Devoted particularly to the Eucharist, Mother Carmen prayed constantly for the welfare of priests. She died after a bout of virulent flu in 1977, and was declared venerable by Pope Francis in 2013.

Saint Drogo

1105–1186

Physical deformity

Feast Day 16 April

Drogo was born on 14 March 1105 in Epinoy in Flanders into a noble family. When he learnt that his mother had died giving birth to him, he suffered terrible guilt. At the age of eighteen after his father had died he disposed of all his property and became a penitential pilgrim finally becoming a shepherd at Sebourg near Valenciennes. Reportedly he had the ability to bilocate so that he could both work in the fields and be at Mass. When he was in his twenties on one particular pilgrimage he was afflicted by an illness that caused gross bodily deformation. The villagers were so alarmed at his appearance that they demanded that he live apart from them. A cell was built for him with a small window so that he could receive Communion and food and the cell was attached to the church since he was known for his holiness. Although Drogo lived in isolation as a hermit in his cell for about forty years, he was known for his compassion for people who suffered mental illness. Drogo died in 1186.

Saint Genoveva Torres Morales

1870–1956

Amputee, illness, apoplexy, coma

Feast Day 5 January

Genoveva was born on 3 January 1870 in Almenara, Castille in Spain. By the time she was eight she had lost both her parents and four of her brothers and sisters. Genoveva was left to bring up her remaining and rather demanding brother on her own. Genoveva grew used to solitude and she took particular delight in reading spiritual books. At the age of thirteen she developed a malignant tumour and gangrene in her left leg. Doctors performed an amputation at her home and since there was no anaesthetic Genoveva had to endure tremendous pain. She had to use crutches and the effect of her amputation caused her pain and illness throughout her life. In 1885 she became ill again with sores, and so she went to live in a home run by the Carmelites for the next nine years where she learnt to sew. Life in the Carmelite home also allowed her to deepen her spiritual life where she developed a special devotion to the Eucharist, the Sacred Heart and Our Lady.

Genoveva gained much from her time in the convent and she hoped to join the Carmelites properly so she applied but they did not accept her because of her physical disability. A priest suggested that she set up her own religious community since there were many women who could not afford to live on their own and who therefore were suffering hardship. Genoveva began the first community in Valencia and there were soon many more communities throughout Spain. Despite longing for her former solitude, Genoveva continued to supervise the new communities and she was well known for her openness to others, her kindness and consideration. From 1950 Genoveva's health began to grow weaker and she suffered an attack of apoplexy. Genoveva died after falling into a coma in 1956, she was beatified by Pope John Paul II in 1995 and was canonised in 2003.

Saint Germaine Cousin

1579–1601

Deformed hand, poor health, neglect, scrofula

Feast Day 15 June

Germaine was born in the small village of Pibrac near Toulouse into a farming family. She was born with a deformed and paralysed right hand. Her mother died soon after she was born and her new step-mother took decidedly against this sickly child. Germaine suffered considerable abuse from her step-mother. Her step-mother made her find food from the meals put down to the dog, she poured boiling water on her and generally abandoned or neglected her for days on end. Germaine's health became worse and in this weakened state she contracted scrofula and swellings that deformed her face, as well as other illnesses. She was further tormented by her half brothers and sisters. She was made to live in the stable where she slept on straw or on vine-twigs. Germaine was given the job of tending the sheep. In the fields she prayed the rosary on string tied with knots and in this dire home situation she developed her relationship with God. She attended Mass daily, she shared what little food she had with beggars and she spoke about her faith with the village children. Germaine showed patience and forgiveness to her family but when they finally invited her back to the family home she decided to remain living in her poverty. One morning in 1601 her father found her dead on her pallet of vine twigs. She was twenty two. In recognition of the many miracles and healings that took place at her intercession, Germaine was canonised by Pope Pius IX in 1867.

Saint Gilbert of Sempringham

About 1083- 1189
Physical deformity, late onset blindness
Feast Day 11 February

Gilbert was born in about 1083 in Sempringham, near the Lincolnshire fens in England. His father was a wealthy Norman knight and landowner, his mother was Saxon. Gilbert was born with physical disabilities and was possibly a cripple. Much to his father's disappointment Gilbert's disabilities made him unfit for military service so instead he was sent to France to study. On his return to England his father gave him the livings, a benefice and source of income, of Semprington and Tirington where Gilbert established schools for both boys and girls. Gilbert himself became a clerk to the court of the Bishop of Lincoln in 1122 and he funded himself from the living from Sempringham. He used the living from Tirington for the poor. Gilbert was ordained a priest and he refused the position of archdeacon of Lincoln preferring to return to Sempringham in 1131. A group of devout women came to him for spiritual direction and, with the advice of the abbot at the Cistercian abbey of Rievaulx, Gilbert devised a rule for them based on the Rule of Saint Benedict. Gradually the order spread, and lay brothers were admitted so forming the Gilbertines with Gilbert as their first Master. Gilbert endured difficulties with King Henry II and problems within his order due to the austerities imposed by the Rule. Eventually at an advanced age Gilbert retired as Master. As he grew more and more infirm and almost completely blind, Gilbert finally decided to make his religious profession. Gilbert died in 1189 and he was canonised by Pope Innocent III in 1202.

Blessed Herman the Cripple (Herman Contractus)

1013–1054

Cleft palate, cerebral palsy, spinal deformities, blindness
Feast Day 25 September

Herman was born in Swabia in Germany, the son of Count Wolverad II von Altshausen. He was born with a cleft palate, cerebral palsy and deformities that suggest either spina bifida or spinal muscular atrophy. He had difficulty moving and could hardly speak. When he was seven his parents placed him in the Benedictine abbey of Reichenau and he was professed as a monk there at the age of twenty. Herman was confined to bed and his speech was nearly incomprehensible. However, he was intellectually gifted and he wrote on astronomy, theology, maths and history as well as composing poetry. He is perhaps best known for two hymns to Our Lady, *Alma Redemptoris Mater* and the *Salve Regina*. He knew Greek and Latin and possibly Arabic as well as German and he wrote one of the earliest chronicles of history and designed and made musical and scientific instruments. Eventually, he became blind and he died at the age of forty in 1054. His cult was approved by Pope Pius IX in 1863.

Saint Jeanne de Valois

1464–1505

Spinal deformity, physical disabilities

Feast Day 4 February

Jeanne was born on 23 April 1464 in a castle in Nogent-le-Roi, in northern France, the daughter of King Louis XI of France and Charlotte of Savoy. Louis XI was greatly disappointed that his second child was not a boy and moreover, the child was deformed and sickly. Shortly after her birth, Jeanne was betrothed in marriage to her father's infant second cousin, Louis Duke of Orleans. King Louis sent Jeanne away to live in an isolated chateaux where she was much loved by her guardians but neglected by her family. Jeanne learnt the skills appropriate to her station and she also developed a strong spirituality through prayer and devotion. She was admitted to the Third Order of St Francis. Louis Duke of Orleans was compelled to marry the twelve year old Jeanne in 1476 but the Duke made it clear that he was repulsed by Jeanne's looks and deformities. After the death of King Louis, the Duke was imprisoned for campaigning against the King's heir and Jeanne's brother, Charles. Jeanne herself sought to have her husband freed. On the accidental and untimely death of Charles, Louis was crowned King as Louis XII. He immediately petitioned for an annulment from Jeanne and among the grounds he cited her disabilities that prevented, he argued, consummation of the marriage. The marriage was annulled but on the grounds of lack of true consent. Jeanne, now Duchess of Berry, decided to follow the call to monastic life. She established the Order of the Virgin Mary, an independent branch of the Poor

Clares, and her rule for the new Order was approved by Pope Alexander in 1502. Jeanne died in 1505, she was beatified by Pope Benedict XIV in 1742 and canonised by Pope Pius XII in 1950.

Saint John the Dwarf

339–c.405

Short stature

Feast Day 17 October

John was born in 339 in Basta in Egypt. He was well known for being very short, very short tempered and full of pride. However, he decided to pursue a life of contemplation and so he travelled to the desert wilderness of Scetes in northern Egypt to become a disciple of Saint Pamboa. According to one account, John took off his clothes and walked off into the desert telling his spiritual father that he wanted to be free of care like the angels, and that he intended to do no work, but only praise God. On his return his spiritual father refused to recognise him saying that John had become one of the angels and was no longer among men. John was left outside the cell to think about his situation. His spiritual father then came out, warned him against the dangers of pride, and reminded him that human beings must work to eat. John gradually learned obedience, endurance and persistence shaped by following his spiritual father's commands. One such command was to water a dry stick every day until it flowered. The water source was twelve miles away and the stick took some three years to flower but John persevered in his task of obedience. John became an abbot and teacher of many of the desert monks. When Scetes was overrun by the Berbers in 395 John fled to the Nitrian Desert. He died on Mount Colzim in about 405.

Saint Leopold Mandic (Bogdan Mandic)

1866–1942

Physical disabilities, deformity, stunted growth, stutter, poor eye sight, stomach problems, arthritis, esophagus cancer

Feast Day 30 July

Bogdan was born on 12 May 1866 in Herceg Novi in Boka Kotorska, now Montenegro. He was physically malformed, weak, had stunted growth, stuttered, had poor sight, suffered abdominal pains and was gradually further deformed by chronic arthritis. At the age of sixteen he entered the Capuchin Seraphic Seminary at Udine close to the Italian border and took the name Leopold. He was ordained in 1890 and, although he had hoped to become a missionary to Eastern Europe, he spent seven years in the Capuchin monastery in Venice where he became well known for hearing confessions. He was sent to Dalmatia to take charge of a monastery, and then in 1909 he went to Padua where once again he spent most of his time in the confessional. Some of his fellow monks despised him for his disabilities and considered him to be too lenient in the confessional. Leopold's hope that he could be a missionary working for some kind of reunion with the Eastern Orthodox Church was treated with disdain by his superiors and he was never given the opportunity. However, his sympathetic and understanding approach in the con-fessional also meant that the bishop was keen he remained in Padua. Leopold was outspoken on many issues to do with dignity and respect for children and expectant mothers. He helped set up orphanages and visited the sick in their homes in hospitals and hospices. Leopold suffered from esophagus cancer and he died in 1942. He was beatified by Pope Paul VI in 1976 and canonised by Pope John Paul II in 1983.

Blessed Margaret of Castello

1287–1320

Deformed, crippled, dwarfism, spinal curvature

Feast Day 13 April

Margaret was born in Metola in Italy into a noble family. When their daughter was born Margaret's parents were so horrified that at first they spread the rumour that the baby had died. Margaret was born deformed, blind, crippled with one leg considerably shorter than the other, she had spinal curvature and dwarfism. They gave the baby to a maidservant in the castle who had permission to name the baby whatever she liked as long as it was not the name of Margaret's mother. Margaret had freedom of the castle until she was six when she accidentally came across a visitor who asked her who her parents were. Being an honest child she told the visitor, much to the embarrassment of her father.

Determined to keep her out of the public eye, Margaret's father had her removed from the castle and walled up into a room built onto the side of the parish church. Food and other necessities were passed to her through a window and through another window she heard Mass and received communion. The parish priest took it upon himself to educate her and he found her a willing student. Margaret lived like this for some years until her parents decided to ask God for a cure since they had heard that miracles had begun to happen at the nearby tomb of Fra Giacomo in Citta di Castello. They travelled to the shrine and when no miracle occurred they abandoned her. Margaret had to resort to begging to survive. Margaret was eventually taken in by some local nuns but their practice was lax and they regarded Margaret's fervour as an affront to their own behaviour so they forced her to leave. Finding herself alone once more she managed to stay at the homes of some of the townspeople who recognised that she had qualities of virtue and kindness, and at the age of fifteen she was able to enter a lay order of Dominicans. She spent the next eighteen years cheerfully caring for the sick and visiting prisoners as far as she was able, as well as living a prayerful life. She died at the age of thirty three in 1320 and was beatified by Paul V in 1609.

Blessed Maria Euthymia Uffing (Emma Uffing)

1914–1955

Rickets, stunted growth, poor health, cancer

Feast Day 9 September

Emma was born on 8 April 1914 in the small town of Halverde in northwest Germany. At eighteen months old she developed rickets that left her with stunted growth and permanently weak health, however as she grew up she was still able to help out on the family farm. Even though from the age of fourteen Emma had expressed the desire to become a religious sister, when she turned nineteen she took an apprenticeship in a nearby hospital in household management. Emma's training lasted from 1931 until 1933 though she spent some time in 1932 at home caring for her dying father. While at the hospital, Emma came to know some of the Sisters of Charity of Munster who were impressed by her hard work, diligence and dedication. Emma asked to be admitted to the congregation and the superiors eventually agreed though they initially hesitated on account of her poor health. Emma entered the congregation in 1934 taking the name Maria Euthymia and she made her simple vows in 1936. In 1939 she gained a nursing diploma and she made her final vows in 1940. During the Second World War Maria Euthymia nursed many sick soldiers and prisoners of war of all nationalities, particularly those suffering from infectious diseases, and she recognised that the ravages of war required more than just physical healing but also a sense of security and peace. After the war Maria Euthymia was put in charge of laundry duties even though her skills lay with dealing with people. Nevertheless, she bore this change with patience and did not neglect to spend time before the Blessed Sacrament. Maria Euthymia died in 1955 from virulent cancer. She was beatified by Pope John Paul II in 2001.

Blessed Michael Giedroyc

Died 1485

Dwarf, deformed, crippled

Feast Day 4 May

Michael was born in Giedroyc castle in Vilnius in Lithuania. Since this was a time of great political unrest, it was expected that the sons of noble families would be trained as soldiers. However, Michael was born deformed, a dwarf and crippled. Moreover, when he was a young boy he lost a foot in an accident. Instead of a military career, he took to study though his progress was hampered by his ill health. Michael found he had a particular talent for metal work and he made beautiful religious vessels and chalices. He also made pyxes for carrying viaticum to the dying. Michael entered the monastery of the Augustinian

Canons in Kracow in Poland and he was given permission to live the life of a hermit in a cell near the church. He spent most of his time in the church and he died kneeling in prayer in 1485.

Saint Notker the Stammerer (Notcerus Balbulus)

c.840–912

Delicate health, speech impediment

Feast Day 6 April

Notker was born in about 840 possibly in Jonschwil in the area of St Gall in Switzerland into what seems to have been a distinguished and landed family. According to the biographer of the monks of St Gall, Notker had delicate health and he stammered. Notker became an orphan when he was very young and to begin with, he was brought up in a foster family. His foster father, Adalbert, who had served in the army under Charlemagne, sent the young Notker to the Benedictine monastery of St Gall where Notker received a good education. He excelled at his studies and after he became a monk he became a teacher, librarian and guest master in the monastery. Notker was a prolific writer. He produced some historical works including *The Deeds of Emperor Charles the Great*, a guide to Christian writers, and a catalogue of saints. He also composed hymns and wrote poetry. His work on liturgical music had significant influence on later medieval chant. After his death Notker was much mourned by the monks and revered by the local people. His cult was confirmed in 1512.

Saint Pacificus of San Severino (Charles Anthony Divini)

1653–1721

Blind, deaf, crippled

Feast Day 24 September

Charles was born on 1 March in 1653 at San Severino near Ancona in Italy. At the age of about three he was left an orphan and was sent to live with his uncle who treated him as a servant. When he was twelve years old Charles asked to join the Franciscans at their monastery in San Severino. He was accepted and after a period of formation he was ordained, taking the name Pacificus. He was appointed professor of philosophy and then became a missionary preacher in the rural areas of Italy where he became known for hearing confessions. At the age of thirty five, Pacificus succumbed to an illness that eventually led to chronic disability leaving him blind, deaf and crippled for the next twenty nine years. As he could no longer act as a missionary, he decided to dedicate the rest of his life to contemplation and prayer and many penitents and sick people came to visit him for words of comfort. Pacificus was appointed superior of the monastery until his death in 1721. Pacificus was beatified by Pope Pius VI in 1786 and canonised by Pope Gregory XVI in 1839.

Saint Seraphina

1238–1253

Paralysis, deformed

Seraphina was born in 1238 in San Gimignano in Italy into a family that had been wealthy but had fallen on hard times. Although she was poor, she would give whatever she had spare to others in more need. When

Seraphina was very young her father died and soon after, in 1248 the once pretty girl succumbed to a series of diseases, possibly the bone infection osteomyelitis, that left her in constant pain, paralysed, unable to turn over, and deformed. Her mother died suddenly and Seraphina was left totally dependent on her devoted friend Beldia. Seraphina spent most of her time confined to her house and during a chance conversation she came to learn about the sufferings of Saint Gregory the Great. She began to pray to him and fixing her eyes on the Cross she united her sufferings with Christ. Her devotion and words of encouragement to the local people became an example to all. Seraphina died at the age of fifteen in 1253.

Saint Servulus

c.590

Paralysis, cerebral palsy

Feast Day 23 December

Servulus had been paralysed from infancy. He was unable to stand upright or lift his hand to his mouth or turn over. His family brought him to the Church of San Clemente in Rome where he stayed in the porch living off the alms given to him by passers-by. Whatever he had he shared with other poor people. He could not read but he obtained books on scripture and asked people to read them to him learning many of the passages off by heart. Much of his time was spent in singing the praises of God even though he was in constant pain. The poor and the pilgrims who were with him sang the psalms with him as he was dying. When he died he was buried in San Clemente.

Notes

1   Lk 7:22.
2   Mk 5.
3   Mk 2:1–12; Mt 9:1–8; Lk 5:17–26.
4   Saint Augustine, *City of God,* XVI, 8.
5   Jn 9.
6   Jer 31:29–30; Ez 18:1–3.
7   Gn 27.
8   Gn 32:32.
9   Ex 6:28–30.
10   2 Co 12:7.
11   1 Co 3:9.

9

THE CHURCH STILL NEEDS YOU
THE ELDERLY AND THEIR
AILMENTS

*In all truth I tell you, when you were young you
put on your own belt and walked where you
liked; but when you grow old you will stretch
out your hands, and somebody else will put a
belt round you and take you where you would
rather not go.*

John 21:18

Introduction

WITH BETTER NUTRITION, better health, better
hygiene and preventative medicine like
immunisations, more and more people are
reaching old age and in old age people are living
longer. Indeed, more and more people are aging
healthily and there are a growing number of the very
old, people over ninety. Chronological age is becoming
less significant as people feel and think themselves
young, or at least young at heart. Some even idolise
youthfulness. However, in today's society people are
also more and more fixated on function, efficiency,
speed and economic resources. This means that people

who are not productive, who are slow, who require a
level of care and acceptance become seen as redundant,
as burdens, as using up or even wasting limited
resources and this applies to people of all ages. Elderly
people, especially those who are disabled, sick or who
have chronic illnesses are seen as a problem. The desire
to remain young and active has a downside. It rein-
forces the negative image of ageing as a burdensome
inevitable decline and a traumatic experience. Younger
people have contempt for old age; older people won-
der whether their lives are still worthwhile. People fear
old age. They fear the natural accompaniments of age,
the ailments, the slowing down, and above all they
fear mental decline. With this fear and the added fear
of being seen or treated as a burden comes self-mar-
ginalisation and despair.

In his letter to the elderly Pope John Paul II wrote
that there is an 'urgent need to recover a correct perspective on life as a whole'.[1] For the Pope this correct
perspective is the perspective of eternity: earthly life is
both beautiful and precious and it is fragile and limited.
We are to be good stewards of life but our lasting hope
is in the life to come. According to Pope John Paul II,
elderly people have a particularly important role in
promoting this proper perspective and they have especially useful gifts for this role. The Pope noted that the
lived experience of elderly people helps them to see
things with greater wisdom; they are, he said, 'guardians of our collective memory' because they have witnessed the ideals and common values which support
and guide society; they give with no thought of return;
they offer a more complete vision of life that includes
the qualities of affection, simplicity and contemplation
in contrast to the busy-ness and distraction of a more

active life. He called those 'signs of human frailty' connected with advanced age 'a summons to the mutual dependence and indispensable solidarity which link the different generations'.

Certainly the Pope believed that the commandment to honour father and mother has a three-fold duty: to welcome the elderly, to help them and to make good use of their qualities, as well as the injunction to make sure that the elderly are and feel 'a vital part of society'. In accepting this commandment and faithfully observing it, elderly people are not regarded as useless, troublesome or as burdens. Rather, they are treated with respect since the commandment points to what the Pope called the 'bond between generations'. However the Pope added 'the Church still needs you': we have a vocation to fulfil right up to the end of our earthly lives. On a practical level many older people are actively engaged in evangelisation, in teaching their grandchildren, in parish catechesis, in volunteering and in activities of social action especially where they are no longer constrained by the demands of a career or paid work. But what about elderly people who are disabled and nearing the end of life?

Pope John Paul II realised that it is natural to look towards the 'threshold of eternity' when friends and family gradually become thin on the ground. Nevertheless, he also acknowledged that people find it difficult when approaching that threshold: we have the 'deep instinct' that we are 'made for life'. With chronic illness, constant aches and pains, becoming less and less able to do things, above all with increasing loneliness, there is a temptation to live out old age 'passively as the expectation of a calamity' or in constant fear of the next bad turn. Instead, the Pope reminded the elderly that faith illuminates the mystery of death and so can bring serenity into old age. Although growing old is a natural progression, how people face old age can be an indication of heroic virtue. By developing a trusting abandonment into the hands of God, by a commitment to others through offering prayers, understanding and comfort, by a deepening of the person's own spiritual life through the sacraments and the routine of prayer, the elderly person can live out the Christian hope that loves life and that at the hour of death asks Jesus to 'call me and bid me come to you'.

Saint Aidric

Died 856
Paralysed the last two years of his life
Feast Day 7 January
Aidric was possibly born in about 800 and he may have come from a noble Saxon Bavarian family associated with Aix-La-Chapelle in Germany. When Aidric was twelve years old he was sent to serve at the court of Charlemagne. At the age of twenty one he decided to leave the court and study for the priesthood at Metz in France. After his ordination he was called back to court by the emperor, Louis and he became the emperor's chaplain and confessor. He was later appointed bishop of Le Mans in 832 and he showed special concern for the situation of the poor, he provided public services and established churches and monasteries. Aidric was a legate to King Pepin of Aquitaine and took part in the Church councils at Paris and Tours. He was paralysed for the last two years of his life and he died in 856.

Saint Albert the Great

1206–1280

Memory loss and mental frailty

Feast Day 15 November

Albert was born in about 1206 at Lauingen in Swabia, Germany. His family were Swabian knights and he was the eldest son of a count. His family had great hopes for him since he was intellectually very gifted and he was sent to study at the University of Padua. However, against the wishes of his parents, Albert decided to join the Dominican Order in 1223. Albert's family may have regarded his choice of religious life as inappropriate since the Dominican Order was relatively new and, as a mendicant (begging) order, some viewed it with suspicion. Nevertheless, the Dominicans were particularly concerned with preaching and education and soon they had chairs in some of the most prestigious universities. Albert himself excelled in his theological studies and as soon as he had qualified he taught theology at Hildesheim, Freiburg, Ratisbon, Strasbourg and Cologne.

In 1245 Albert was sent to Paris where he received his doctor's degree and met the young Thomas Aquinas. Albert was elected Provincial of his Order in Germany in 1254 and he worked as a theologian and canonist in Rome. However, in 1257 Albert resigned the office of Provincial so that he could devote more time to his teaching. Although Albert was keen to teach, he reluctantly accepted an appointment as bishop of Ratisbon in 1260 and he guided his diocese until 1262, after which he returned to his teaching in Cologne. Albert had great knowledge and love of biology, chemistry, natural sciences, astronomy and geography. He wrote extensively on logic, metaphysics, mathematics and theology. He was particularly interested in how methods developed from Aristotle's philosophy could be used to serve Christian truths. He played an active role in defending the mendicant orders and he took part in the Council of Lyons in 1274. The early death of his pupil and friend, Thomas Aquinas affected him deeply and in 1277 he vigorously defended Aquinas from those who believed that Thomas had favoured unbelieving philosophers. Sometime in 1278 it appears that Albert's memory failed him suddenly during the delivery of a lecture and he may have had a stroke. Over the next two years he suffered from increasing mental and physical frailty. Albert died in 1280, he was beatified by Pope Gregory XV in 1522 and canonised and declared a Doctor of the Church by Pope Pius XI in 1931.

Blessed Andrea Giacinto Longhin (Giacinto Bonaventura Longhin)

1863–1936

Arteriosclerosis, late onset blindness, age related mental frailty

Feast Day 26 June

Giacinto Bonaventura was born on 22 November 1863 in Fiumicello in the diocese of Padua, Italy, the only son of poor tenant farmers. He was a deeply spiritual child and developed a vocation to the priesthood early in life. In spite of his father's objections, at the age of sixteen Giacinto became a novice of the Capuchin Order and he took the name Andrea. He completed his studies in Padua and in Venice and then he was ordained a priest in 1886 aged twenty three. Andrea was a spiritual director for young religious, a director of Capuchin teachers at Padua, and a director of theology students in Venice. In 1902 he was elected the Provincial Minister of the Capuchins of Venice and in 1904 Pope Pius X appointed him bishop of Treviso. Immediately Andrea set about implementing a reform programme following the initiative of the Pope. Andrea first embarked on a five year pastoral visit to get to know his diocese and to become personally acquainted with his clergy. He was also keen to foster lay associations and the rights of workers at a time when it was uncertain how lay Catholics should relate to the state and how they could undertake social action. His central concern, however, was to encourage a life of holiness for lay and clergy alike. In particular, and following the Pope's call to improve seminary education, Andrea set about reforming the diocesan seminary by improving both studies and spiritual formation. He encouraged clergy retreats and organised an annual programme of ongoing formation for his priests.

During the First World War Treviso found itself at the front line and much of the town was destroyed by ground and air attacks. Andrea refused to leave the town and he spent his time organising relief for soldiers, civilians, the wounded, the poor and the sick. He was imprisoned on the charge of defeatism and for refusing to join any one of the warring sides. On his release he resumed his pastoral duties and saw to the rebuilding of the some fifty parishes that had been destroyed. He was eventually awarded the Cross of Merit. In the aftermath of the First World War there was still no end to social upheaval, strikes and political unrest in Italy and in the early 1920s Mussolini's fascism was on the rise. Andrea saw the need to

maintain a Catholic ethos in the Catholic social movement, and to achieve this he insisted on social justice
and peace through a non-violent approach and on
loyalty to the Church. Recognising his peace-making
skills, Pope Pius XI made him the Apostolic Visitor
first in Padua and then in Udine to help heal the
divisions between priests and their bishop. In 1932 he
began to show the first signs of arteriosclerosis. Then
suddenly in 1935, at the end of a pastoral visit, Andrea
lost his sight and became paralysed. The official
Vatican biography notes that Andrea succumbed to
'an illness that deprived him progressively of his
mental faculties'. Andrea died in 1936 and he was
beatified by Pope John Paul II in 2002.

Saint Benedict Biscop (Biscop Baducing)

c.628–690

Confined to bed the last 3 years of his life

Feast Day 12 January

Biscop Baducing was born into a noble Northumbrian
family in about 628. He served as a warrior for King
Oswui until 653 when, with Saint Wilfrid, he made
several pilgrimages to Rome and decided to dedicate
himself to the service of God. In 665 on a return from
one of these pilgrimages, he stopped at the monastic
island of Lerins where he made his monastic vows and
he stayed there until 667. The Venerable Bede suggests
that it was at this stage that Biscop Baducing took the
name Benedict. After another expedition to Rome,
Pope Vitalian commissioned Benedict to accompany
Theodore, the new archbishop of Canterbury, and
Benedict was appointed abbot of Saint Augustine's in
Canterbury. In 674 Benedict persuaded King Egfrith
of Northumberland to grant him some land so that he

could build a monastery. Benedict brought back masons, glass makers and artisans from Italy to construct the monastery of St Peter's at Wearmouth, soon followed by a second foundation at Jarrow, St Paul's. Benedict also brought books to stock the new library, as well as pictures and relics, and scholars to advise on the liturgy. Benedict was suddenly struck with paralysis and he spent the last three years of his life confined to bed, though he frequently invited the monks to come and sing psalms and he joined in when he could. Benedict died in 690.

Saint Benedict Menni (Angelo Ercole Menni)

1841–1914

Stroke, senile dementia

Feast Day 24 April

Angelo was born on 11 March 1841 in Milan, the fifth of fifteen children, and his family were merchants. He started his working life as a bank clerk however he resigned his post when he was asked to falsify bank records. During the battle of Magenta in 1859 in the Second Italian War of Independence, Angelo volunteered to help the wounded. His job was to carry soldiers on stretchers from the trains to the waiting ambulances so that they could be transported to the hospital of the Brother Hospitallers of St John of God. Angelo was very impressed with the work of the Hospitallers and, at the age of nineteen he applied to enter their novitiate. Four years later in 1864 he made his solemn profession of vows taking the name Benedict. Benedict was ordained in 1866 and almost immediately Pope Pius IX sent him to Spain to restore the Hospitaller Order. Although founded in Spain in 1572, the Order had been banned in 1836 as a result of anti-clericalism. Benedict managed to open the first children's hospital and refuge in Barcelona in 1867.

In 1872 he was appointed the Superior of the Hospitallers in Spain but continuing persecution in the ongoing Carlist war forced him to leave the country. He and some of the Brothers joined the Red Cross in Marseilles and as neutral members they were able to return to help the wounded in the Basque Provinces. Benedict was also able to reorganise the children's hospital in Barcelona and then in 1877 he established a psychiatric hospital twenty miles outside Madrid. This represented the beginning of his most significant work, the revolutionising of care for mentally ill and disabled people. Benedict realised that women could have a particularly effective ministry with these patients, so he set up a female branch of the Order and his new congregation was formally recognised in 1892. He founded a further eleven hospitals for the mentally ill, and, in direct contrast to forms of treatment commonly used at the time, he forbade the use of all physical punishment.

The foundations were extended to Portugal and Mexico and the hospitals were recognised as being exemplars during outbreaks of cholera due to their hygienic approach to medical care. However there were difficulties and jealousies within the Order, especially from those who thought that Benedict favoured the female branch. Benedict moved to Rome but he was forced to move to Viterbo and then to France. He was left without even a secretary, so when he lost the use of his right hand after his first stroke he was unable to write or communicate by letter. In the last few years of his life Benedict lived with increasing senile dementia and he died of a second stroke in 1914.

Benedict was beatified by Pope John Paul II in 1985 and he was canonised in 1999.

Saint Francisco Coll y Guitart

1812–1875

Late onset blindness, stroke, mental frailty

Feast Day 2 April

Francisco was born on 18 May 1812 in Gombreny in the Catalan Pyrenees, the youngest of ten children. His father, who was a wool carder, died when Francisco was just four years old. In 1823 when Francisco was ten he joined the minor seminary in Vic and in 1830 he began his novitiate with the Dominicans in Gerona where he received minor orders and was ordained to the diaconate in 1831. Under a government decree of 1835 all religious orders in Spain were prohibited and the Dominicans were forced to leave their friary. However, Francisco was able to continue his studies at the major seminary in Vic and he was ordained to the priesthood in 1836. He received permission to devote himself to preaching and conducting retreats and parish missions. For the next thirty years he travelled throughout Catalonia fulfilling this task. Then in 1850 Francisco was appointed the director of the Third Order of Dominicans in Catalonia. He founded an order of nuns, the Dominican Sisters of the Annunciation, to teach girls and he wrote spiritual works for them.

From the end of 1869 Francisco began to have a series of severe strokes that finally left him blind and with limited mental abilities. Nevertheless, he continued to follow the Dominican rule as best he could while being cared for by the nuns of his congregation. Francisco died in 1875, he was beatified by Pope John Paul II in 1979 and canonised by Pope Benedict XVI in 2009.

Saint Francis Xavier Bianchi

1743–1815

Confined to bed with leg ulcers and swelling, difficulty breathing, near blindness, hernia, trembling, heart palpitations

Feast Day 31 January

Francis was born on 2 December 1743 in Arpino in central Italy. At an early age he had the opportunity to witness charity in action since his mother altered part of the house so that she could set up a small clinic where she nursed people in need. At the age of twelve Francis went to school with the Barnabites in Arpino where he was teased by the other children for being overweight. As he grew older, Francis felt called to the religious life and he decided to join the Society of Jesus, however his parents were opposed to him joining any religious order. Nonetheless, they did allow him to join the diocesan seminary in Nola, outside Naples in 1758, though they also insisted that he went to Naples University to study law. After a disastrous start, when even the money he had been given to buy books was stolen, he managed to complete his studies in 1762. By then his parents realised that he was sincere in his vocation and would not be persuaded so they relented and allowed him to join the novitiate for the Barnabites in Zagarolo. Francis made his vows in 1763 and went on to Macerata to study philosophy and science until 1765 before returning to Naples in 1766 to study theology. After his ordination in 1767 Francis began teaching in the Barnabite school in Arpino and then at the seminary in Naples. In 1773 he was elected superior of the College of St Mary in Cosmedin in Portanova and from 1778 he became a professor. However, Francis discerned a new path for his life. He decided that he would pursue a life of solitude, prayer and penance so he gave up his academic work. Living in the community in Naples, Francis spent long hours with penitents who came to his cell for advice and confession and among them were the poor as well as the rich and famous. The numbers coming to see Francis were so great that they caused difficulties for the local authorities.

In the early 1800s Francis began to suffer pains first in one leg then in both, and the pain developed into swelling and open wounds. He obediently underwent a series of painful attempts at a cure but to no avail. Now that the authorities saw him as a sick and suffering old man they thought that the crowds would abate, but in fact the number of people coming to Francis only increased. Despite having difficulty standing or even getting up, and even though he had trouble with his breathing, Francis celebrated Mass every day in his cell and recited the Rosary.

In 1809 the Barnabite monastery where he was living was suppressed along with other religious houses and Francis had to move into the city of Naples. Although in the last three years of his life Francis experienced trembling, heart palpitations and became confined to his bed, he still wrote letters of encouragement to those he could not visit and when his friends tried to restrict visitors to allow him to rest, he patiently listened to and advised those who managed to get past. Gradually the number of people visiting him began to lessen especially as he no longer had the strength to hear confessions or to speak at any great length. He spent many hours alone and in his last few months was left with just hired servants. He now had difficulty breathing, was nearly blind, had a twisted hernia and gangrene in his legs. Francis died in 1815 in the presence of a few friends after receiving Viaticum. He was beatified by Pope Leo XIII in 1893 and was canonised by Pope Pius XII in 1951.

Blessed Giovanni Maria Boccardo

1848–1913

Paralysis, stroke

Giovanni was born on 20 November 1848 in Moncalieri in Italy into a farming family and he was the eldest of ten children. After elementary school he attended school with the Barnabite fathers where he began to discern his vocation to the priesthood. He entered the seminary of Turin in 1864, his cassock bought from money he received from Princess Clothilde of Savoy in recompense for a dog bite he received from one of the guard dogs who had escaped from the castle at Moncalieri. He was ordained a priest in 1871 and was assigned to the seminary eventually becoming the spiritual director.

In 1882 he took over a parish in the countryside of Turin and he sought to ensure that Sunday Mass and religious instruction became the centre of the Christian life of his flock. Giovanni's community was particularly threatened when in 1884 the town was struck by cholera and Giovanni organised many young volunteers who wanted to help. After the cholera epidemic had passed he realised that there was still work to be done especially among those who had been orphaned and the elderly so he set up the Congregation of the Poor Sisters of St Cajetan. However, he became concerned that in his personal life he was growing indifferent and so he determined to grow more in holiness through self-denial and attention to the Eucharist and St Joseph. In 1911 on his way back from preaching a sermon he suffered hemiparesis, severe muscle weakness, possibly from a stroke, and remained paralysed until he died in his own hospice in 1913. Giovanni was beatified by Pope John Paul II in 1998.

Blessed Jacques Ghazir Haddad (Khalil Haddad)

1875–1954

A 'walking hospital' of ailments, leukaemia

Khalil was born on 1 February 1875 in Ghazir in the Lebanon into a Marionite Christian family. He was academically inclined and after studying at school in Ghazir he went to college in Beirut where he studied Arabic, French and Syriac. In 1892 he went to Alexandria to teach Arabic at the college of the Christian Brothers. By the time he was nineteen Khalil was sure that he was called to be a priest and he returned to the Lebanon to tell his father of his decision. Initially, his father was opposed but realising that his son was determined, he reluctantly agreed and Khalil joined the Capuchin Convent in Khashbau where he took the name Brother Jacques. Jacques made his final profession in 1898 and when he had completed his studies he was ordained priest in 1901 in Beirut. Jacques was appointed bursar for the Capuchin monasteries in Lebanon and this involved extensive travel by foot.

In 1905 he had overall responsibility for the schools established by the Capuchins in the mountainous areas, and his desire always was to strengthen the faith of young children. His travels allowed him to visit many schools and to preach retreats. Moreover, his experience in Lebanon in the First World War led him to see the need for a monument where people could come and pray for the thousands of forgotten Lebanese people who had died, but who had no one to place a cross on their grave. So in 1919 he bought land on a hill north of Beirut, built a chapel there to Our Lady of the Sea, and later marked the site with a huge cross. A hospital encounter with a sick priest gave him the impetus to found a new religious order affiliated with the Third Order of St Francis.

The Franciscan Sisters of the Holy Cross of Lebanon had the mission to help the sick and the poor but especially sick priests, disabled people and in particular people with mental disabilities. Jacques organised schools and hospitals and in 1933 he opened an orphanage for girls that later became a hospital for people with disabilities. In 1948 he opened a hospital for the paralysed and the chronically sick and he founded one of the few hospitals dedicated exclusively to people who had mental illnesses. By 1954 he declared himself to be like a 'walking hospital' since by then he was suffering from insomnia, cataracts and near blindness, prostate problems and eczema. He was further diagnosed with leukaemia. Having made preparations for his death he died later on in the year. Jacques was beatified by Pope Benedict XVI in 2008.

Saint Joaquina de Vedruna de Mas

1783–1854

Paralysis

Feast Day 22 May

Joaquina was born on 16 April 1783 in Barcelona in Spain into an aristocratic family and although she felt called to be a nun her parents saw her future in an advantageous marriage. In 1799 when she was sixteen years old, Joaquina married Teodoro de Mas, a young lawyer. They had nine children together and instilled in their children the practice of prayer and works of charity. In 1816, after a spell in the Spanish forces during the wars with Napoleon, Teodoro suddenly died leaving Joaquina a widow at thirty three years old. For ten further years Joaquina devoted herself to the children, relying on her inheritance to secure their futures. In 1826, when the children had left home, Joaquina established a congregation, the Carmelites of Charity, to teach the young and to care for the sick. Despite exile during the Carlist wars, the congregation began to expand beyond Spain. However, by 1850 Joaquina began to suffer from slow paralysis and she retired as head of the congregation. She eventually became almost immobile. Joaquina died in a cholera epidemic in 1854, she was beatified by Pope Pius XII in 1940 and canonised by Pope John XXIII in 1959.

Pope Saint John XXIII (Angelo Roncalli)

1881–1963

Stomach cancer

Feast Day 11 October

Angelo was born on 25 November 1881 at Sotto il Monte, Bergamo, in Italy and his family were relatively poor sharecroppers. He attended the local school where he was teased and called the 'little cleric' for being helpful in the parish church. Nevertheless, his priest saw potential in the small boy and he arranged for Angelo to receive Latin lessons. At the age of twelve Angelo entered the seminary at Bergamo and in 1901 he continued his studies at the Apollinare, the

major seminary in Rome, his seminary studies being
interrupted by a short spell on military service. After
completing his doctorate in theology, he was ordained
in 1904 just a few months short of the canonical age of
twenty three. He continued his studies in canon law
and he then went to teach history and patrology in the
seminary at Bergamo. During the First World War
Angelo worked as a chaplain despite the existence of
anti-clericalism, and he later said that this experience
gave him great insight into the human heart.

He returned to the seminary in 1918 where he was
appointed spiritual director and he took it upon
himself to organise retreats for the young people in the
locality and to advise them on Catholic Action. In the
1920s he helped reorganise the Society for the Propagation of the Faith in Rome and then in 1934 he became
the apostolic delegate to Turkey and Greece where,
during the Second World War, he set up an office to
locate prisoners of war. In 1944 he was appointed
nuncio to Paris and he became the first permanent
observer of the Holy See at UNESCO.

In 1953 he became the cardinal-patriarch of Venice.
Called to the conclave of cardinals in Rome on the
death of Pope Pius XII, Angelo was elected Pope in
1953 at the age of seventy six and he took the name
John because, he said it was the name of a long line of
popes whose pontificate had been short. He issued his
encyclical *Mater et Magistra* in 1961 to commemorate
Rerum novarum, the encyclical of Pope Leo XIII, and he
issued *Pacem in terris* on human dignity and freedom
as the basis for world order and peace, in 1963. He
convoked the Second Vatican Council in 1962 and set
up a commission to revise the Code of Canon Law in
1963. Pope John did not live to see the conclusion of

the Council. He had noticed as far back as November 1961 the beginning of an ailment that he put down to the effects of old age.

At the age of eighty he knew that restrictions and sacrifices mark the last phase of life and, reminding himself of the words of Jesus to Peter, he prayed 'O Jesus, I am ready to stretch out my hands, now weak and trembling, and allow others to dress me and support me along the way'. Stomach cancer in the elderly is slow to develop and painful. In the case of Pope John XXIII it was the disability of the family since some seven members, including his sisters and brothers, succumbed to the illness. Although the symptoms became more noticeable in July 1962, diagnosis of a gastric tumour and ulceration was only confirmed in October 1962. Pope John XXIII died from stomach cancer, bleeding and peritonitis in 1963. He was beatified by Pope John Paul II in 2000 and canonised by Pope Francis in 2014.

Pope Saint John Paul II (Karol Wojtyła)

1920–2005

Parkinson's Disease, deafness, osteoarthrosis, heart failure, circulatory problems,

Feast Day 22 October

Karol was born on 18 May 1920 in the small town of Wadowice near Krakow in Poland. His father was a tailor who later worked in the administration of the Austro-Hungarian and then the Polish army, Karol's elder brother was a medical student. When Karol was nine years old his mother died and Karol's father devoted himself to the care of his son. Karol's brother died a few years later and Karol and his father moved to Kracow. Karol later discovered that he had had a baby sister who died before he was born. Karol began his university studies in philosophy and Polish philology in 1938 and he was especially interested in literature and theatre. At the outbreak of the Second World War, the Nazis closed the university and faced the students with either enforced work or deportation to Germany. Karol went to work in a quarry and then a chemical factory.

Although Karol felt called to the priesthood he also was drawn to the theatre and he became a member of a clandestine theatre group that worked to keep the Polish language, culture, traditions and Catholic religion alive. Eventually, in 1942 he joined the underground seminary run by the Archbishop of Krakow. After the war Karol resumed his studies and he was ordained in 1946. He was sent to Rome where he completed his doctorate on *Faith according to St John of the Cross.* He also worked with Polish immigrants in France, Belgium and Holland. On his return to Poland in 1948, Karol served in Krakow in various parishes and he worked as a university chaplain.

He took up further studies in theology and philosophy in 1951 and in 1953 wrote a thesis on the possible integration of the philosophy of phenomenology and Christianity. He then became professor of moral theology and social ethics in the seminary in Krakow and in the Faculty of Theology at the University of Lublin. In 1958 Karol became auxiliary bishop of Krakow. He was made archbishop of Krakow in 1964 and a cardinal in 1967.

Karol took part in the Second Vatican Council, as far as he was able given the reluctance of the communist authorities in Poland, and he also attended all the assemblies of the Synod of Bishops. Karol was elected

Pope in 1978 after the sudden death of Pope John Paul I, and he took the name John Paul after his three predecessors. Known as the Pilgrim Pope, Pope John Paul II took the papacy to the people in their own countries. He welcomed pilgrims to Italy, he set up World Days for young people, for sick and disabled people, and organised meetings for families. He encouraged dialogue with the Jews, Muslims and with separated Christians by his messages calling for forgiveness. He apologised on behalf of the Church for the treatment of Galileo, for the Church's involvement in the slave trade, for burnings at the stake and religious wars, for injustice during colonial times, for injustice to women, for inactivity and silence during the holocaust, for the 'stolen generations' of Aboriginal children in Australia. He also apologised for the action of priests involved in sexual abuse.

Pope John Paul II was a prolific writer issuing encyclicals, exhortations, addresses and letters on a huge range of topics. However, his starting point was always Jesus Christ: as he explained 'we shall not be saved by a formula but by a Person, and the assurance which he gives us: I am with you!'.[2] He promoted spiritual renewal, and beatified and canonised more people than ever before with the conviction that holiness is the necessary measure of ordinary life. Pope John Paul II survived an assassination attempt in 1981 where he was critically wounded, another attempt in 1982, and a failed bomb plot in 1995. In late 1991 Pope John Paul II showed the first signs of Parkinson's disease and in 1992 he had an operation to remove a colon tumour. The Vatican confirmed the diagnosis of Parkinson's in 2003. The Pope's hearing became worse and he suffered from severe osteoarthrosis.

In 2005 he was hospitalised with influenza and breathing problems. He left hospital but a few months later developed a urinary tract infection, then septic shock, high fever and low blood pressure. After receiving the Anointing of the Sick lights were kept burning in the room in the Vatican where he lay dying. Tens of thousands of people lined the streets to keep vigil with him for the following two days. On hearing this, the Pope is reported to have said, 'I have searched for you, and now you have come to me, and I thank you'. Pope John Paul II died from heart failure and circulatory collapse in 2005. Upon his death he was acclaimed by many as the Great. Pope John Paul II was beatified by Pope Benedict XVI in 2011 and canonised by Pope Francis in 2014.

Blessed Josepha Hendrina Stenmanns

1852–1903

Severe illness, cough, violent asthma

Hendrina was born on 28 May 1852 in Issum in Germany, the eldest of seven brothers and sisters. She helped support the family by her work as a silk weaver and also took care of local people who were sick and dying. When she was nineteen years old, Hendrina joined the Third Order of St Francis and began to discern a vocation to the religious life. However, the political situation made religious life near impossible and furthermore she promised her dying mother that she would care for her younger brothers and sisters. After some years, at the age of nearly thirty two and when her promise was fulfilled, Hendrina made her way to Holland and applied for a job as a kitchen maid in the Mission House, a centre training priests for mission work. She hoped that in this small way she would contribute to the missions while waiting for a women's branch of the Mission House to be founded.

Eventually, in 1889 she and a few other women became postulants and they joined a novitiate. In 1894 Hendrina took her vows for the Missionary Sisters Servants of the Holy Spirit and she was given the name Josepha. By this time Josepha was well known for her practical manner, wisdom, understanding and empathy and soon she was given charge of the postulants. She led by example with a rich prayer life, devotion to the Blessed Sacrament and total devotion to God. In 1902 Josepha's health began to decline and in the final months of her life Josepha suffered from serious and painful illness, coughing fits and especially from violent attacks of asthma. She used this breathing problem to remind the sisters that every breath of a servant of the Holy Spirit should be 'come Holy Spirit'. She received the Sacrament of the Sick and was allowed daily communion. Josepha died in 1903 and was beatified by Pope Benedict XVI in 2008.

Saint Katharine Drexel (Catherine Drexel)

1858–1955

Heart problems, ailments of old age, wheelchair user then confined to bed

Feast Day 3 March

Catherine Drexel was born on 26 November 1858 in Philadelphia in the United States of America. Her father was a well-regarded banker and the family were wealthy philanthropists. Her mother died about a month after Catherine was born and her father married again some two years later. Catherine's step mother continued to instil the family ideal of wealth as something to be shared. Catherine was devoted to her step mother, and when her step mother fell ill with cancer she nursed her until she died in 1883. Two years later, her father also died leaving his three daughters extremely well off financially. Catherine had by this stage begun to think of becoming a nun but her spiritual advisor, anxious for her health under a religious regime, counselled her to wait and pray.

In 1885 Catherine and her three sisters travelled to the Western area of the United States and Catherine was particularly concerned with the plight of native American Indians who lived in poverty on reservations. She began to organise the building of schools and provided food and clothing as well as paying for teachers and finding priests to minister to the Indians. In 1887, the year she founded her first boarding school, she also visited Rome and was able to meet Pope Leo XIII. She asked the Pope to provide missionaries for the Indians and he suggested that she become a missionary herself.

In 1891 Catherine made her first profession of vows and, embracing personal poverty, she founded the Sisters of the Blessed Sacrament, an order dedicated to bringing the Gospel and the Eucharist to the American Indians and to Afro-Americans. She took the name Sister Mary Katharine, and as the congregation grew she became Mother Katharine. Oppression of native and African Americans and lack of education were rife. Mother Katharine spent much time fighting against injustice and discrimination and she made schooling her priority. In 1935 Mother Katharine suffered a serious heart attack and her doctor confined her to a wheelchair. She agreed, as long as it did not cost too much since, she believed, funds were better spent elsewhere and the convent workers made her a make-shift wheelchair from an old folding chair. Mother Katharine spent the last twenty years of her life in contemplation and prayer, the last five years she was confined to bed. Mother Katharine died in 1955. She was beatified by Pope John Paul II in 1988 and canonised in 2000.

Saint Louis and Saint Marie-Azelie (Zelie) Martin

Louis, 1823–1894

Stroke, paralysis, cerebral arteriosclerosis, mental frailty

Zelie, 1831–1877

Breast cancer

Feast Day 12 July

Louis was born on 22 August 1823 in Bordeaux, in France and Zelie was born on 23 December 1831 in Orne, France. Both Louis and Zelie came from military families. Louis had hoped to become a monk but he was not accepted into the Augustinian order because he did not know enough Latin. Zelie had wanted to become a nun with the Sisters of Charity of Saint Vincent de Paul but she had respiratory problems and recurrent headaches that made her unsuitable for the rigors of convent life. Louis became a watch maker and Zelie became a lace maker. They met and married in 1858 settling in Alençon. Although they had nine children, only five daughters survived. Zelie died of breast cancer in 1877 and for the sake of the children Louis moved to Lisieux to be nearer to the family of his brother-in-law. All five of their daughters became nuns, one of them being Saint Thérèse of Lisieux. In 1889 Louis suffered two severe and paralyzing strokes coupled with cerebral arteriosclerosis, a condition related to vascular dementia. He spent three years at the Bon Sauveur asylum, a psychiatric hospital, in Caen where in his own way he brought admiration and respect. He returned home to Lisieux in 1892 paralyzed and unable to speak and he was cared for by his daughters Celine and Leonie until his death in 1894. Louis and Zelie were beatified by Pope Benedict XVI in 2008 and canonised by Pope Francis in 2015.

Saint Maria Guadalupe Garcia Zavala (Anastasia 'Lupita' Guadalupe Garcia Zavala)

1878–1963

Heart disease, diabetes, extreme illness in the last two years of life

Feast Day 24 June

Maria was born on 27 April 1878 in Zapopan in Mexico where her father ran a shop near the basilica selling religious goods. The family was relatively well off and even as a child Maria showed particular concern for the poor. When Maria was in her early twenties and engaged to be married she found herself torn between marriage and the religious life. In the end she broke off her engagement and decided that her future life was to care for sick and poor people. After discussions with her spiritual director who also saw the need for a new congregation, Maria helped him found the Congregation of the Handmaids of St Margaret Mary Alacoque and the Poor. Maria worked as a nurse in their hospital and cared for the physical and spiritual needs of her patients regardless of their poverty. Maria became the superior general of the congregation, and she constantly reminded her sisters that it was only by loving and living poverty that they could truly be poor with the poor. At times the sisters had to beg for funds for the hospital. They also taught catechism and assisted in parishes. From 1911 to 1936 the Church in Mexico faced persecution. The convent was regarded as a hospital rather than a religious institution so it remained open and Maria risked her own life to hide priests and the archbishop from the authorities there. However, raids were common and soldiers were stationed at the doors of the hospital. Nevertheless, she also gave care, compassion and food to the oppressors wining them round to the ideals of the hospital. In the last two years of her life Maria suffered from serious heart disease and diabetes. She died in 1963, was beatified by Pope John Paul II in 2004 and canonised by Pope Francis in 2013.

Saint Mary MacKillop

1842–1909

Dysmenorrhea, rheumatism, stroke, paralysis, wheelchair user

Feast Day 8 August

Mary was born on 15 January 1842 in Fitzroy, Victoria in Australia to Scottish immigrants. Her father made various attempts to succeed in business, but he frequently failed, so the family lived in straightened circumstances. To support her family Mary began her working life at the age of fourteen as a clerk in Melbourne and then later as a teacher in Portland. In 1860 she went to Penola in southern Australia to become the governess to the children of her aunt and uncle. She was already interested in helping the poor and so she included other local farming children from the family estate. She later taught at a school in Portland and opened up her own school for young ladies in 1864. At the suggestion of Father Woods, a local priest from Penola who was concerned at the lack of opportunities for Catholic education, Mary returned to Penola with two of her sisters and in 1866 they opened a Catholic school there. Mary decided to dedicate her life to God and in 1867 she became the first sister and mother superior of the newly formed order, the Sisters of St Joseph of the Sacred Heart, the Josephites, taking the name Sister Mary of the Cross.

The sisters moved to a new convent in Adelaide where they founded a school dedicated to the education of the poor. The order expanded rapidly. It opened more and more schools and became involved with orphanages, neglected children, elderly people, and incurably ill people. Conflict between Father Woods and the clergy over educational matters and tensions with some lay people led to a campaign to discredit the Josephites. This included spreading the false rumour that Mary had an alcohol problem though in fact she was being treated for dysmenorrhea. Moreover, the Josephites became aware of allegations of sexual abuse against a priest and were instrumental in his eventual dismissal back to Ireland though publicly his disgrace was put down to alcohol abuse. This caused further tensions resulting in a clerical colleague of the priest demanding that the constitution of the Josephites be changed and when Mary refused, she was excommunicated by the bishop for insubordination. Mary was forbidden any contact with the church though she did take shelter with some Jesuit priests. Mary was later exonerated by an Episcopal Commission.

In 1873 Mary went to Rome for approval of the congregation; however the fine detail of the revised rule caused a rift between her and Father Woods though they were later personally reconciled. Further wrangling and internal dispute meant that Mary was removed as Mother General in 1883 though the work of the order expanded and Mary assisted the new Mother General as best she could. In 1889 Mary was once more elected Mother Superior General. However, her health had begun to deteriorate. She suffered from rheumatism and in 1902 had a stroke that paralysed her right side. This meant that she had to use a wheelchair to move around. Nevertheless, she was re-elected as Mother General in 1905. Mary died in 1909, she was beatified by Pope John Paul II in 1995 and canonised by Pope Benedict XVI in 2010.

Saint Robert Bellarmine

1542–1621

Poor health, swollen legs, deaf

Feast Day 17 September

Robert was born on 4 October 1542 in Montepulciano in Tuscany. He came from an impoverished noble family and he was the third of twelve children. Robert's maternal uncle became Pope Marcellus II in 1555. As a young child, Robert was frail, short in stature, and often in poor health. Nevertheless, he excelled at his studies. Initially, Robert's father hoped that his son's quick intelligence would help to revive the family fortunes through a career in either medicine or politics. However, Robert was drawn to the Jesuit order and he entered the novitiate in Rome in 1560, where he also took studies in philosophy. Robert was ordained in 1570 and he was sent to teach at the newly opened Jesuit theological college at Louvain. Religious controversies and eventually rebellion and religious war plagued the Low Countries. Throughout this turmoil, Robert defended traditional Catholic teaching that had been affirmed at the Council of Trent and he produced a Hebrew grammar and a guide to patristic writings for his students. Robert's health began to suffer and when the university itself was under threat from the war, Robert was recalled to Rome to take up a post in the new field of controversial theology at the Roman College.

In 1590 Robert was sent to Paris as a special legate to examine the situation of the French Church during the civil war. He wrote of the hardships endured by the townspeople during the siege of Paris, and the privations of the mission further undermined his health. Less than two years later he returned to Rome and then to Naples where he wrote a catechism and helped to compile the regulations for Jesuit colleges. Robert was made a cardinal in 1599, and, while working in the Congregations in the Roman Curia, he became involved in the case against Galileo.

In 1602 Robert was appointed archbishop of Capua and, in the spirit of the Catholic Reformation he visited and inspired the rural parishes and religious institutions in his diocese. In particular, he spoke of the need to alleviate the dire poverty of the area, especially around Naples and his own frugality and generosity became a model for clergy. Recalled to duties at the Vatican in 1605, Robert soon became embroiled in the plight of Catholics in Protestant England who had been forced to swear an oath that in effect rejected the papacy and Catholic doctrine. In the last few years of his life, Robert wrote spiritual books including *The Art of Dying Well or How to be a Saint Now and Forever*. In the *Art of Dying Well*, Robert counselled his readers to think about living and dying well by renouncing worldly attachments, by developing personal relationships and by attending to the sacraments of the Church.

By 1619 Robert was suffering from various illnesses and suffered considerably from swollen legs. He asked Pope Paul V for permission to retire but he was considered to be too necessary to the Vatican. In 1621 Gregory XV was elected pope but he too refused permission. However, by August 1621 Robert had become deaf and he was finally allowed to leave for the Jesuit novitiate in Rome. He contracted a fever that gradually grew worse and he died the following month. Robert was beatified in 1923 and canonised in 1930 by Pope Pius XI. He was declared a Doctor of the Church in 1931.

Blessed Rosalie Rendu (Jeanne Marie Rendu)

1786–1856

Increasing infirmity and blindness

Feast Day 7 February

Jeanne Marie Rendu was born on 9 September 1786 at Confort in the Jura Mountains into a family of small property owners. The family offered refuge to priests persecuted during the French Revolution and Jeanne attended Mass and made her First Communion in secret. When life returned to normal, Jeanne was sent to be educated with the Ursuline sisters in Gex. In the two years she was with the sisters she came into contact with the Daughters of Charity who worked in the local hospital. At just short of seventeen years old in 1802 Jeanne joined the Daughters of Charity in Paris taking the name Rosalie.

Although her health was weak she was sent to work with poor and destitute people. She opened a free clinic, a pharmacy, a school, an orphanage, a child care centre, a youth centre and a home for destitute elderly people. Given the volume of work, Rosalie often made her prayer be her action for people in need. She had particular talent working with sisters who found their vocation difficult. In the cholera epidemics, at great risk to themselves, she and her sisters nursed those who had contracted the disease. During the Parisian uprisings of 1830 and 1848 she looked after the wounded on both sides, at times climbing the barricades to rescue the fallen, and she intervened for victims of the fierce repression that followed. Her health had always been fragile and in the last two years she suffered from increasing infirmity and blindness. She died in 1856 after a brief and acute illness. Rosalie was beatified by Pope John Paul II in 2003.

Mother Teresa of Calcutta (Agnes Gonxha Bojaxhiu)

1910–1997

Frail health, club foot as a child, problems with heart, lungs and kidneys

Feast Day 5 September

Agnes Bojaxhiu, known as Gonxha, flower bud, was born on 26 August 1910 in the small town of Skopje in Albania. By all accounts she was a sickly child prone to whooping cough and malaria and she was born with a club foot. Her father, a building contractor, died when she was seven and the family of three children was supported by her mother who sold embroidered cloth. Gonxha was a self-disciplined, tidy and helpful child who loved books. Having decided that she would like to be a nun, at the age of twelve, Gonxha became actively involved in parish activities including the Sodality of the Blessed Virgin Mary, a group set up by the local priest to teach children about the lives of the saints and missionaries. Here Gonxha first found out about the Loreto nuns who worked in Bengal. At the age of eighteen Gonxha applied to the Loreto order and she was sent to an Irish convent near Dublin to learn English. After just two months in 1928 she set sail for India and she began her novitiate in Darjeeling. Alongside her theological studies, Gonxha perfected her English and studied Bengali and Hindi.

She took the white habit and black veil of the sisters in 1929 taking the name Mary Teresa. She was sent to Calcutta to teach in the convent school of St Mary's and she would go out of the convent every Sunday to visit the poor in the slums. In 1937 she made her final vows at the convent in Darjeeling taking the name Mother Teresa. She then returned to Calcutta to teach and by 1944 she had become the principal at St Mary's. At this stage the city of Calcutta was overflowing with people who had fled the famine in Bengal in 1943. By 1946 violence had erupted in Calcutta between Hindus and Muslims. Rioting interrupted food supplies and the students at St Mary's had nothing to eat. Sister Teresa went out into the streets and managed to persuade soldiers to bring rice to the convent. In 1946 Sister Teresa set off for her annual retreat at the Darjeeling convent. During the train journey she felt an intense call to leave the convent and to live among the poor. After two years of petition and discernment, Mother Teresa was given permission to leave the Loreto convent.

In 1948 she bought a cheap and simple white sari with a blue trim and she went to stay with the Little Sisters of the Poor at St Joseph's convent. After venturing out into the slums she set up a school in the open for poor children and their learning often involved scratching letters in the ground with a stick. She gave practical lessons in hygiene and gave her charges milk at midday. She was offered a place to live by a Catholic family and some of her former pupils came to join her. In 1950 the new congregation of the Missionaries of Charity was officially established in Calcutta. By 1952 there were twenty seven sisters living in cramped conditions however new premises were soon found for the congregation to continue its work with the dying, the poor, orphans and the sick.

In the 1960s and 1970s new foundations began to spring up all around the world and foundations for men and for lay co-workers were set up. Mother Teresa received numerous awards for her work, notably the Nobel Peace Prize which she accepted 'for the glory of God and in the name of the poor'. Despite her many smiling public appearances Mother Teresa experienced an intense and painful darkness of the soul. She also became increasingly frail. She had her first heart attack in 1989 and in 1992 suffered a severe bout of pneumonia. In 1996 she succumbed to malaria and had to use either a wheelchair or remain in bed. Suffering further from heart, lung and kidney problems she died in 1997 and was beatified by Pope John Paul II in 2003.

Blessed Teresa Mary of the Cross Manetti

1846–1910

Poor health, stomach ailment, tumour, depression

Teresa was born on 2 March 1846 in San Martino a Campi Bisenzio in the province of Florence in Italy. Teresa's father died when she was young and she stayed at home to help her mother. With a talent for organisation Teresa, got together other local girls to look after the local children and she was given the nickname Bettina reflecting the blessings she brought to everyone. In 1872 Teresa and two companions began a communal life in her family home and in 1874 the little community moved to a house near the local chapel. The work of the community was to pray, care for sick people, and offer religious education to other girls. Later in 1874 the community was admitted to the Teresian Third Order, a secular order of the Discalced Carmelites, and Bettina took the name Teresa Mary of the Cross.

In 1877 the house opened up to include the care of orphans and Teresa acquired more houses and the chapel to accommodate her growing convent and for space to continue their charitable works. She built a larger church and the convent joined with the Order of Discalced Carmelites. Teresa and twenty seven companions received the Carmelite habit in 1888. Teresa's institute gained papal recognition and became the Third Order Carmelite Sisters of St Teresa (of Avila). Further houses opened in Tuscany and missions were opened in Syria and at the foot of Mount Carmel. Teresa herself gained a following of people keen to see her and seek advice or consolation. Throughout her life Teresa had a great love of the Eucharist and she organised a house and had a church built in Florence dedicated to perpetual adoration. Teresa had always had poor health and, although at one point thought delusional, her life-long stomach ailments worsened after 1896. She was eventually diagnosed with a malignant tumour. For a time she fell into a dark night of despair and feeling of abandonment perhaps exacerbated by a month long stay in a nursing home in 1909. However, through grace she returned to God. She died in 1910. Teresa was beatified by Pope John Paul II in 1986.

Saint Thomas Aquinas

1225 or 1226–1274

Possible stroke

Feast Day 28 January

Thomas was born in either 1225 or 1226 at the family castle at Roccasecca which was midway between Rome and Naples. His father was descended from the counts of Aquino. Thomas began his schooling at Monte Cassino and then Naples. In Naples Thomas came across a new Order of Preachers, the Dominicans and he joined them in 1242. His family disapproved of his choice since the Dominicans were a mendicant (begging) order and they had hoped Thomas would one day become the abbot of Mont Cassino. So Thomas was captured by his brothers and imprisoned by the family in the hopes he would change his mind.

After a year, Thomas was allowed to study in Paris with Saint Albert the Great. He followed Albert to Cologne in 1248 and by 1252 Thomas and Albert were back in Paris where Thomas began teaching. Thomas wrote a commentary on the *Sentences* of Peter Lombard which was the standard university text consisting of a collection of extracts from the Church Fathers. Thomas also wrote his first major set of disputed questions called *De Veritate* after the topic of the first question, on truth. By 1259 Thomas had begun his *Summa contra Gentiles*, a handbook for preachers that sets out the reasons for the Christian faith. Thomas taught in Orvieto, Rome and Naples. In Naples he began his work the *Summa Theologiae* in 1266, intended for 'the little ones', however he did not finish it.

On 6 December, 1273 Thomas celebrated Mass as usual but, unusually he did not return to his writing. His friend and fellow friar Reginald urged him to continue his work, and Thomas said he could not. By all accounts Thomas was profoundly changed after this date. He took to his bed and was eventually sent to stay with his sister for rest. He made the journey with considerable difficulty and his sister was reported to be shocked at his appearance and near inability to speak. Reginald again tried to persuade Thomas to write and Thomas replied, 'All that I have written seems to me to be straw compared to what I have seen and what has been revealed to me.'[3]

Thomas returned to Naples at the end of December but by the end of January, summoned by the pope, he was travelling again on foot to attend the Council of Lyons (friars were not allowed to travel on horseback). It appears that on the journey Thomas either fell or hit his head on a tree branch hard enough to be stunned. However, he was able to dictate an interpretation of a disputed text for the monks at Monte Cassino. In February the party reached the castle where his niece lived but Thomas grew ill, could not eat, and required the services of a doctor.

After a few days the prior of the Cistercian monastery at Fossanova paid him a visit and Thomas returned with him to the monastery, travelling on horseback since he was too weak to walk. He stayed at Fossanova for a month during which he was often confused, nevertheless he was still able to receive the Eucharist and when the time came, to make the responses for the Last Rites. Thomas died on 7 March in 1274. He was canonised by Pope John XXII in 1323 and was declared Doctor of the Church by Pope Pius

V in 1567. His feast is kept on 28 January, the date when his body was translated to the Dominican church at Toulouse in 1369.

Notes

1   Pope Saint John Paul II, *Letter to the Elderly* (1 October 1999).
2   Pope Saint John Paul II, *Novo Millennio Ineunte*, 29.
3   This phrase is first recorded in the process for Thomas' canonization as a saint in 1319, when Bartholomew of Capua said he heard it from John del Guidice, who heard it from Reginald.

10

A Lived Theology of Disability and Suffering

Whoever remains in me, with me in him, bears fruit in plenty.

John 15:5

CCORDING TO POPE Francis, 'if we want to understand what faith is, we need to follow the route it has taken, the path trodden by believers',[1] and he encourages people to draw inspiration from the saints who witnessed to the faith in their own personal encounters with God. Certainly, each of us has a different story to tell and, like the flowers of the fields, each of us grows in a different way and each of us is called to produce our own particular fruit with the help of grace. However, Pope Francis added that people come to see themselves properly only through following Jesus: 'Christ is the mirror in which they find their own image fully realised'.[2]

This book contains stories, but they are stories of real and concrete people who lived real and concrete lives with a mix of joys and difficulties. Even if disability was not an issue for the saints themselves, and even if they did not see themselves as suffering from disability, the fact that they are all in one way or

another disabled suggests that they had to contend
with more difficulties than the average person,
whether it be difficulties from their disabilities or
difficulties caused by the attitudes of others. However,
if we think about the path to holiness, difficulties on
this path are not due to disability. After all what is a
barrier to holiness is not a missing limb, nor a chronic
condition, nor an apparently slow intellect, nor a
mental issue. What is crippling is sin, especially the sin
of pride in my own abilities, the sin of malice, the sins
of care-lessness. And people with disabilities are no
less immune than any other human being from these
spiritual sins.

In one of his beatification homilies, Pope John Paul
II described very powerfully one aspect of holiness that
is especially relevant to saints and the blessed with
disabilities. The Pope explained that holiness is the
awareness of being 'watched over', watched over by
God. In a very real sense, all of the saints and blessed
in this book have grown in their awareness of God's
loving concern for them, even when the circumstances
of their lives have seemed to indicate that they are
powerless and alone. In the same homily Pope John
Paul II added, 'the saint knows very well his frailty, the
precariousness of his existence, of his capacities. Yet he
is not frightened. He feels secure in spite of all this'.[3]
People with disabilities and people who are sick are
perhaps more aware of the fragility and limits of human
existence. In contrast, people who are strong, autonomous and abled often do not think that they live in any
way a diminished life. Those who think that what
counts in life are strength, autonomy and power often
marginalise or pity people with disabilities. Those who
live with what Pope John Paul II called a Promethean

attitude may indeed baulk at the idea that they are being watched over, that they require loving concern. However, the saints and the blessed with disabilities witness to the truth that all people are interdependent, we all rely on each other. By entrusting themselves to the care of others, as well as by exercising their own care for others, the saints and blessed witness to this truth in their lives and, according to Pope John Paul II, one of the fundamental needs of our time is for solicitude by each person for the other.[4]

It is perhaps more to the point, that the saints and the blessed with disabilities witness to the greater truth that all human beings are dependent on God. This is shown time and again in their stories as they give themselves over to Christ though often not without spiritual struggle.

Pope John Paul II commented that the single end the Church serves is that each person may be able to find Christ who is the way to the Father.[5] For those who choose their own path to what they consider to be their own fulfilment, the many cases of the varied and usually unsought paths of the saints and blessed with disabilities gives an important insight into the nature of vocation. Vocation and the call to discipleship are not merely a matter of our desires or choices, though our co-operation plays a significant part. Every human being has a part to play in God's plan of salvation. As Blessed John Henry Newman explained, 'God has created me to do Him some definite service; He has committed some work to me which He has not committed to another. I have my mission—I never may know it in this life, but I shall be told it in the next.....I am a link in a chain, a bond of connexion between persons'.[6] Saints and the blessed with disabilities have often been

called upon to discern their vocations and to turn their
desires towards the will of God in ways that require the
strength of virtue especially when an aspect of that
vocation involves the acceptance of suffering. The
heroism they demonstrate is not so much living a life
with disability. Rather it is living a life heroic in virtues.

The saints and blessed have a strong desire to be
near to God. This desire, even if it is expressed in
monastic solitude, is a communal desire: it is a desire
to join the company of saints in the Kingdom. The
common feelings of loneliness, marginalisation and
sometimes isolation often experienced by people with
disabilities are overcome by grateful acceptance of
assistance from others but more significantly by holding onto Christ. Inevitably, a life centred on Christ in
this way has a profound effect on those around the
saint. They too begin to perceive a way out of their
own often unacknowledged loneliness caused by
selfishness and self-absorption. For many people
watching those who are suffering and ill there is the
temptation to doubt the goodness of God. However,
by actively taking hold of the grace offered by Christ
who also suffered, the saints and the blessed show in
their lives the hope of future glory.

Nevertheless, the path taken by the saints and
blessed is not an easy one. In the battle for holiness sin
does not want to die. This is why the saints and blessed
with disabilities insist on receiving the sacraments and
why many clearly and deliberately join their sufferings
with the sufferings of Christ. It is understandable that
some people think that those with disabilities and
those who suffer are passive victims of a grave injustice or an evil, the 'why me' scenario. In this scenario
it is easy to think that Jesus joins them on the Cross out

of pity. However, this is to miss some of the deeper messages of the Passion. It is true that, as a theological mystery, the depths of the Passion can never be fully plummeted. Still, the lives of the saints help at least partially to explore this mystery.

To begin with, suffering is an inevitable part of earthly life. Moreover, the suffering experienced in the stories of the saints and blessed, as with all people, is not simply the suffering associated with illness or disability. Suffering can also be spiritual soul pain. And this suffering cannot be cured or alleviated with medicines or therapies. Of course as Pope John Paul II pointed out, the definitive suffering is the loss of eternal life and the Son was given to the world 'primarily to protect man against this definitive evil and against definitive suffering'.[7] Traditionally suffering is associated with sin, though not personal sin, because we live in a fallen world, fallen due to the original disobedience of human beings. However, the good news is that God has not simply discarded this fallen world as broken and beyond repair. Rather, God loved the world so much that God sent his Son to redeem it.

There are times when a person feels despised and rejected or abandoned by friends, and there is some comfort that Jesus can walk that path with them. For some, Jesus is with them in their Gethsemane or on their cross or even in the tomb. Nevertheless, the suffering of Jesus the Son of God is unique and of incomparable depth and intensity to any other human suffering precisely because it is the suffering of the God-man; it is suffering which is estrangement from God.[8] Yet, Pope John Paul II explained that through the Passion of Christ 'all human suffering has found itself in a new situation': suffering has been redeemed.[9] So the inevitable suffer-

ing that earthly life brings need not make us despair or
feel abandoned. Now we can take suffering and join it
to Christ's redemptive suffering.[10] We live in hope and
this hope is not a vague optimism but a true hope.
Specifically, because Christ's redemption is profoundly
beyond our understanding it remains open to all love
and so while the work of Christ was accomplished once
and for all on the Cross, we can still share in that
suffering and in our own way. As Saint Paul puts it, we
complete the suffering through which Christ accomplished the Redemption.[11] Just as the Cross reveals both
the great love of the Father and the glory of the Son in
overcoming sin and death, so too does a union of
suffering with Christ reveal a gift of grace. Indeed, the
only place that can deal with the abyss that is soul pain
is the profound depth of the Paschal Mystery that leads
to the glory of the resurrection.

Many of the saints and the blessed with disabilities
showed a deep devotion to the Eucharist and the
sacraments. The Eucharist is where believers most
fully experience the reality of the Body of Christ as a
reality for the whole Church. At every Mass this is a
present reality and not simply a reminder of a past
event. By sharing in the Eucharist believers become
fully one with Christ and one with each other. This
means that the person is no longer isolated but is
joined to the living body of Christ, the Church. The
sacrament of the Anointing of the Sick is a sign of hope,
comfort and support. It gives the grace of the Holy
Spirit and strengthens against temptations to despair
or to anxiety. As an action of the Church, as with the
Eucharist, the person is united sacramentally with the
community. The giving of the Eucharist as Viaticum,
in Latin the term refers to food for the journey, is the

last sacrament for the dying Christian. It signifies that the person is following Christ to eternal glory.

The saints and the blessed give us graced human insights into our faith. The message of a lived theology of disability and suffering as demonstrated by the stories of saints and the blessed with disabilities is a call to become Christ centred. Being Christ centred is to see the face of Christ in ourselves and in all human beings because whatever our situation or condition all human beings are made in the image of God and we never lose that image. Being Christ centred is to trust in God's providence and to realise that, while there is work to be done here on earth in building up the Kingdom, our future lies in becoming friends of God for eternity.

Prayer from Pope John Paul's Letter to the Elderly (1999)

> *Iube me venire ad te!*, bid me come to you: this is the deepest yearning of the human heart, even in those who are not conscious of it. Grant, O Lord of life, that we may be ever vividly aware of this and that we may savour every season of our lives as a gift filled with promise for the future. Grant that we may lovingly accept your will, and place ourselves each day in your merciful hands. And when the moment of our definitive passage comes, grant that we may face it with serenity, without regret for what we shall leave behind. For in meeting you, after having sought you for so long, we shall find once more every authentic good which we have known here on earth, in the company of all who have gone before us marked with the sign of faith and hope.

And Carers

Let us love, then, because he first loved us.

1 John 4:19

Saint Cuthman of Steyning

c.681

Carer

Feast Day 8 February

Cuthman was a shepherd and he lived possibly at Chidham near Bosham in West Sussex, in England. Even as a young boy Cuthman was known for his love of God and legend has it that whenever he had to leave his flock, he simply drew a circle round them and commanded them to stay. When his father died he became the sole carer for his crippled or possibly paralysed mother and as they became poorer, Cuthman had to go begging from door to door. Cuthman felt called by God to build a church among the pagans and so he decided to leave Chidham and travel eastwards, bringing his mother with him in a one-wheeled cart he had made. Part of the weight of the cart was taken by ropes through the handles which looped over his shoulders. Along the journey the ropes broke and Cuthman had to improvise with makeshift ropes using withies, willow sticks. Some haymakers, seeing Cuthman's trials, began to laugh at him but a sudden rainstorm ruined their hay. Cuthman decided that the next time the ropes broke would be a sign for him from God to stop at that place and build a church. The ropes finally broke at Steyning close to a pagan site marked by a stone. Cuthman built a hut for his mother and himself and began to build a wooden church incorporating the old pagan stone. Soon some local people also came to help. However, as the church was nearing completion Cuthman found he could not fix up the roof beam. Fortunately, he was helped by a stranger. On asking the name of the stranger, the stranger replied, 'I am he in whose name you are building this church.' The stranger appears to have been Saint Andrew. Cuthman was venerated as a saint and man of prayer before the Norman Conquest. His church became an important place and the father of Alfred the Great, King Ethelwulf of Wessex was buried there in 857. After the Norman Conquest the church was given over to the authority of the Abbey at Fécamp in Normandy and Cuthman's relics were transferred there. The church at Steyning was rebuilt in stone and dedicated to St Andrew. Cuthman's prayer before he began his building project is recorded by his anonymous biographer:

> Father Almighty, you have brought my wanderings to an end; now enable me to begin this work. For who am I, Lord, that I should build a house to name? If I rely on myself, it will be of no avail, but it is you who will assist me. You have given me the desire to be a builder; make up for my lack of skill, and bring the work of building this holy house to its completion.

Notes

1   Pope Francis, *Lumen fidei,* 8.

2   *Ibid.,* 22.

3   Pope Saint John Paul II, *Homily on the Beatification of Sister Teresa Maria of the Cross* (19 October 1986).

4   Pope Saint John Paul, *Redemptor Hominis,* 15.

5   *Ibid.,* 13.

6   Blessed John Henry Newman 'Part One: Meditations on Christian Doctrine' [1893] in Ian Ker (ed.), *Meditations and Devotions* (London: Darton, Longman and Todd, 2010), p. 11.

7   Pope Saint John Paul II, *Salvifici Dolores*, 14.

8   *Ibid.,* 18.

9   *Ibid.,* 19.

10   *Ibid.,* 20.

11   Col 1:24; Pope Saint John Paul II, *Salvifici Dolores*, 24.

INDICES

Patron saints

Saint Albert the Great
Philosophers, natural scientists, medical technicians, students

Saint Alberto Hurtado Cruchaga
Chile, the poor, street children, social workers

Saint Aleydis
Blind, paralysed

Saint Benedict Biscop
English Benedictines, musicians, painters

Saint Benedict Joseph Labre
Homeless, tramps, bachelors, people suffering from mental illness, the marginalised

Saint Drogo
Shepherds, coffee house keepers, coffee house owners

Saint Charles Borromeo
Cardinals, bishops, seminarians, catechists, catechumens, spiritual directors, apple orchards, starch makers, against ulcers and stomach diseases

Saint Camillus de Lellis
Sick, hospitals, nurses, physicians

Saint Catherine of Sienna
Nurses, people who have suffered miscarriages, against fire, people mocked for their piety

Saint Cuthman
Shepherds

Saint Gabriel of Our Lady of Sorrows
Students, seminarians, clerics

Saint Germaine
Shepherdesses

Saint Joaquina de Vedruna de Mas
Survivors and victims of abuse, death of children, exiles, widows

Saint John Dukla
Poland, Lithuania

Saint John of God
Hospitals, sick, nurses, firefighters, alcoholics, book sellers, people suffering from mental illness, heart patients, the dying

Saint John Vianney
Priests

Pope Saint John XXIII
Papal delegates

Pope Saint John Paul II
Youth, families

Saint Joseph Cafasso
Prisoners, people condemned to death

Saint Joseph of Cupertino
Air travellers, aviators, astronauts, test takers, people with intellectual disability

Saint Katharine Drexel
Philanthropists, racial justice

Saint Laura Montoya Upegui
Orphans, people suffering from racial discrimination

Saint Lydwine
Skaters

Blessed Mary Bartholomea Bagnesi (Marietta Bagnesi)
Abuse victims

Saint Maximilian Kolbe
Drug addicts, political prisoners, journalists

Saint Nicholas Owen
Illusionists, escapologists

Padre Pio da Pietrelcina
Civil defence volunteers, stress/worry relief

Saint Peter of St Joseph Betancur
Canary Islands, Guatemala, the homeless

Saint Rafael Arnáiz Barón
Diabetics

Saint René Goupil
Anesthesiologists

Saint Robert Bellarmine
Canon lawyers, catechists, catechumens

Saint Seraphina
Spinners, people with physical disabilities

Saint Servulus
People suffering from cerebral palsy, people with disabilities

Saint Teresa of Avila
People suffering from headaches and physical ailments, orphans, people who are ridiculed, chess players, lace makers

Mother Teresa of Calcutta
World Youth Day

Saint Thérèse of Lisieux
Florists, aviators, missionaries, HIV/AIDS sufferers, France

Saint Thomas Aquinas
Academics, schools and universities, philosophers, against lightning, against sudden death

Feast Days

January 1 Saint Zygmunt Gorazdowski
January 5 Saint Genoveva Torres Morales
January 6 Saint Andre Bessette
January 7 Saint Aidric
January 12 Saint Benedict Biscop
January 18 Saint Jaime Hilario Barbel
January 20 Saint Maria Cristina Brando
January 22 Saint Caterina Volpicelli
January 28 Saint Thomas Aquinas
January 31 Saint Francis Xavier Bianchi
February 3 Blessed Marie Rivier
February 4 Saint Jeanne de Valois
February 7 Blessed Rosalie Rendu
February 8 Saint Cuthman of Steyning
February 9 Blessed Anna Katharina Emmerick
February 10 Blessed Alojzije Stepinac
February 10 Blessed Eusebia Palomino Yenes
February 11 Saint Gilbert of Sempringham
February 13 Blessed Eustochium of Padua
February 19 Saint Lucy Yi Zhenmei
February 28 Saint Gabriel of Our Lady of Sorrows
March 2 Saint Angela of the Cross
March 3 Saint Katharine Drexel
March 8 Saint John of God
March 10 Blessed Elias del Socorro Nieves
March 12 Blessed Angela Salawa
March 19 Blessed Marcel Callo
March 22 Saint Nicholas Owen

March 23 Saint Rafqa

March 30 Blessed Amadeus IX of Savoy

April 2 Saint Francisco Coll y Guitart

April 5 Saint Albert of Montecorvino

April 6 Saint Notker the Stammerer (Notcerus Balbulus)

April 9 Blessed Ralph Ashley

April 13 Blessed Margaret of Castello

April 14 Saint Lydwine

April 16 Saint Drogo

April 17 Saint Benedict Joseph Labre

April 18 Saint Peter of St Joseph Betancur

April 24 Saint Benedict Menni

April 26 Saint Rafael Arnáiz Barón

April 29 Saint Catherine of Siena

May 1 Saint Richard Pampuri

May 4 Blessed Michael Giedroyc

May 5 Blessed Nunzio Sulprizio

May 20 Saint Arcangelo Tadini

May 21 Blessed Hyacinthe Marie Cormier

May 22 Saint Joaquina de Vedruna de Mas

May 27 Blessed Mary Bartholomea Bagnesi

June 4 Saint Filippo Smaldone

June 9 Saint José de Anchieta

June 9 Blessed Luigi Boccardo

June 12 Venerable Nicola D'Onofrio

June 15 Saint Aleydis

June 15 Saint Germaine Cousin

June 17 Saint Albert Chmielowski

June 17 Blessed Joseph Marie Cassant

June 23 Saint Joseph Cafasso

June 24 Saint Maria Guadalupe Garcia Zavala

June 26 Blessed Andrea Giacinto Longhin

June 26 Blessed Sister Maria Giusepinna of Jesus Crucified

June 27 Blessed Louise Therese de Montaignac de Chauvance

July 1 Blessed Antonio Rosmini

July 1 Saint Junípero Serra (Miguel José Serra)

July 8 (September 28) Saint Marie de Saint Just

July 9 Saint Paulina of the Agonizing Heart of Jesus

July 12 Saint Louis and Saint Marie-Azelie (Zelie) Martin

July 13 Blessed Carlos Manuel Rodriguez

July 14 Saint Camillus de Lellis

July 15 Saint Pompilio Maria Pirrotti

July 30 Saint Leopold Mandic

August 2 Blessed Augustus Czartoryski

August 4 Saint John Vianney

August 7 Blessed Edmund Bojanowski

August 8 Saint Mary MacKillop

August 13 Blessed Otto Neururer

August 14 Saint Maximilian Kolbe

August 18 Saint Alberto Hurtado Cruchaga

August 25 Blessed María del Transito de Jesus Sacramentado

August 26 Blessed Zepherin Namuncura

September 5 Mother Teresa of Calcutta

September 7 Blessed Anna Eugenia Picco

September 9 Blessed Frederic Ozanam
September 9 Blessed Maria Euthymia Uffing
September 15 Blessed Paolo Manna
September 17 Saint Robert Bellarmine
September 18 Saint Joseph of Cupertino
September 19 Saint Alonso de Orozco
September 23 Padre Pio da Pietrelcina
September 24 Saint Pacificus of San Severino
September 25 Saint Herman the Cripple
September 26 Saint René Goupil
September 29 Saint John Dukla
October 3 Saint Thérèse of Lisieux
October 5 Saint Anna Schaffer
October 5 Saint Flora
October 6 Blessed Isidore of St Joseph de Loor
October 9 Saint Marciano José (Filomeno López y López)
October 10 Blessed Angela Truszkowska
October 11 Pope Saint John XXIII
October 12 Blessed Maria Teresa of Cascia
October 13 Blessed Alexandrina Maria da Costa
October 15 Saint Teresa of Avila
October 17 Saint John the Dwarf
October 20 Saint Bertilla Boscardin
October 21 Saint Laura Montoya Upegui
October 22 Pope Saint John Paul II
October 29 Blessed Chiara Badano
November 4 Saint Charles Borromeo
November 9 Blessed Elizabeth of the Trinity

November 15 Saint Albert the Great
November 23 Blessed Miguel Pro
November 24 Blessed Mary Anna Sala
December 17 Saint Josep Manyanet y Vives
December 23 Saint Servulus
December 31 Blessed Giuseppina Nicoli

Conditions

Addison's Disease
Blessed Elizabeth of the Trinity

Amyotropic lateral sclerosis (Lou Gehrig's disease, motor neuron disease)
Venerable Aloysius Schwartz

Amputee, born without a limb
Saint Albert Chmielowski
Blessed Anna Eugenia Picco
Venerable Brother Anthony Kowalczyk
Venerable Mother Carmen Martinez Rendiles
Saint Genoveva Torres Morales
Blessed Nunzio Sulprizio
Saint Paulina of the Agonizing Heart of Jesus

Apoplexy
Saint Genoveva Torres Morales

Arteriosclerosis
Blessed Andrea Giacinto Longhin

Arthritis, osteoarthrosis

Saint Alonso de Orozco
Venerable Giunio Tinarelli
Pope Saint John Paul II
Saint Leopold Mandic
Blessed Manuel Lozano Garrido
Blessed Pina Suriano

Asthma

Blessed Eusebia Palomino Yenes
Blessed Isidore Ngei Ko Lat
Blessed Josepha Hendrina Stenmanns
Saint Junípero Serra (Miguel José Serra)
Blessed Maria Teresa of Cascia
Blessed Mary Bartholomea Bagnesi
Padre Pio da Pietrelcina

Bed bound

Blessed Alexandrina Maria da Costa
Saint Aleydis
Blessed Anna Katharina Emmerick
Saint Benedict Biscop
Blessed Edward Poppe
Saint Francis Xavier Bianchi
Saint Katharine Drexel
Saint Lydwine
Blessed Margaret Ebner
Venerable Marthe Robin
Blessed Mary Bartholomea Bagnesi

Bone condition (degenerative)

Blessed Anna Eugenia Picco
Blessed Nunzio Sulprizio

Bronchitis

Blessed Marcel Callo
Saint Maria Cristina Brando

Bronchial catarrah

Blessed Alojzije Stepinac

Bronco-pneumonia

Saint Richard Pampuri

Cancer

Saint Alberto Hurtado Cruchaga
Blessed Angela Truszkowska
Blessed Carlos Manuel Rodriguez
Blessed Chiara Badano
Blessed Isidore of St Joseph de Loor
Pope Saint John XXIII
Saint Leopold Mandic
Blessed Maria Euthymia Uffing
Blessed Maria Teresa of Cascia
Blessed Mary Anna Sala
Venerable Nicola D'Onofrio
Blessed Nunzio Sulprizio
Saint Zelie Martin

Cerebral arteriosclerosis

Saint Louis Martin

Cerebral palsy

Blessed Herman the Cripple
Saint Servulus

Circulatory problems

Blessed Maria Teresa of Cascia
Pope Saint John Paul II

Convulsions

Saint Pompilio Maria Pirrotti

Coping difficulties, mental illness

Saint Benedict Joseph Labre
Blessed Eustochium of Padua
Saint Heimrad
Saint John of God

Dementia, age related mental frailty

Saint Albert the Great
Blessed Andrea Giacinto Longhin
Venerable Brother Anthony Kowalczyk
Saint Benedict Menni
Saint Francisco Coll y Guitart
Saint Louis Martin

Depression

Venerable Giunio Tinarelli
Saint Flora
Saint Lydwine
Blessed Marcel Callo
Blessed Margaret Ebner
Saint Marie de Saint Just
Blessed Otto Neururer
Saint Pompilio Maria Pirrotti
Blessed Teresa Mary of the Cross Manetti

Despair
Venerable Marthe Robin
Blessed Pina Suriano

Diabetes
Saint Filippo Smaldone
Saint Maria Guadalupe Garcia Zavala
Blessed Maria Teresa of Cascia
Saint Paulina of the Agonizing Heart of Jesus
Saint Rafael Arnáiz Barón

Diphtheria
Venerable Solanus Casey

Dysmenorrhea
Saint Mary MacKillop

Eating and swallowing problems
Saint Catherine of Siena
Venerable Marthe Robin

Eczema
Blessed Jacques Ghazir Haddad
Venerable Solanus Casey

Epilepsy
Blessed Amadeus IX of Savoy

Erysipelas
Venerable Solanus Casey

Eyesight problems, blindness
Saint Albert of Montecorvino

Saint Aleydis
Blessed Andrea Giacinto Longhin
Saint Anna Schaffer
Blessed Dolores Rodriguez Sopena
Blessed Elias del Socorro Nieves
Saint Francisco Coll y Guitart
Saint Francis Xavier Bianchi
Saint Gilbert of Sempringham
Blessed Herman the Cripple
Saint John Dukla
Blessed Jacques Ghazir Haddad
Saint Leopold Mandic
Blessed Manuel Lozano Garrido
Blessed Sister Maria Giusepinna of Jesus Crucified
Venerable Marthe Robin
Saint Pacificus of San Severino
Saint Paulina of the Agonizing Heart of Jesus
Saint Rafqa
Blessed Rosalie Rendu

Fevers

Blessed Anita Cantieri
Saint Charles Borromeo
Blessed Marcel Callo
Padre Pio da Pietrelcina
Saint Pompilio Maria Pirrotti

Haemoptysis (coughing blood)

Saint Thérèse of Lisieux

Haemorrhages

Blessed Hyacinthe Marie Cormier

Headache

Blessed Angela Truszkowska
Blessed Marcel Callo
Venerable Marthe Robin
Padre Pio da Pietrelcina
Saint Teresa of Avila

Hearing problems, deafness, labyrinthitis

Blessed Angela Truszkowska
Saint Jaime Hilario Barbel
Saint Marciano José (Filomeno López y López)
Pope Saint John Paul II
Blessed Sister Maria Giuseppinna of Jesus Crucified
Saint Pacificus of San Severino
Saint René Goupil
Saint Robert Bellarmine

Heart problems, chest pains

Blessed Anita Cantieri
Blessed Edward Poppe
Pope Saint John Paul II
Saint Junípero Serra (Miguel José Serra)
Saint Katharine Drexel
Venerable Manuel Aparici Navarro
Saint Maria Cristina Brando
Saint Maria Guadalupe Garcia Zavala
Blessed Maria Teresa of Cascia
Blessed Pina Suriano
Padre Pio da Pietrelcina
Saint Teresa of Avila
Mother Teresa of Calcutta
Saint Thomas Aquinas

Hepatitis
Venerable Aloysius Schwartz

Hernia
Saint Francis Xavier Bianchi
Saint Nicholas Owen

Infection
Blessed Alexandrina Maria da Costa
Saint Junípero Serra (Miguel José Serra)
Blessed Marcel Callo
Blessed Ulrika Nisch

Intellectual disability
Rather than seeing 'learning disability' and 'slow learning' as conditions, it may be more worthwhile seeing them as simply other aspects of being human that challenge a perceived intellectual 'norm'.

Insomnia
Blessed Jacques Ghazir Haddad

Kidney disease
Blessed Frederic Ozanam
Blessed Mario Vergara
Blessed Mary Bartholomea Bagnesi
Mother Teresa of Calcutta

Lame, crippled, walking difficulties
Saint Arcangelo Tadini
Blessed Eusebia Palomino Yenes
Blessed Herman the Cripple
Saint Jeanne de Valois

Saint Junípero Serra (Miguel José Serra)
Blessed Margaret of Castello
Blessed Maria Teresa of Cascia
Blessed Michael Giedroyc
Saint Nicholas Owen
Blessed Nunzio Sulprizio
Saint Pacificus of San Severino

Leprosy

Saint Aleydis

Leukemia

Blessed Jacques Ghazir Haddad

Liver disease

Blessed Antonio Rosmini

Lymphatic system inflamation

Saint Laura Montoya Upegui

Multiple sclerosis

Blessed Angela Salawa
Saint Lydwine?
Blessed Sister Maria Giuseppinna of Jesus Crucified

Nervous complaints

Saint Pompilio Maria Pirrotti

Organ failure

Venerable Manuel Aparici Navarro

Parkinson's Disease

Pope Saint John Paul II

Paralysis

Saint Aidric
Saint Aleydis
Blessed Alexandrina Maria da Costa
Blessed Anna Katharina Emmerick
Saint Anna Schaffer
Venerable Brother Anthony Kowalczyk
Saint Catherine of Siena
Blessed Giovani Maria Boccardo
Venerable Giunio Tinarelli
Saint Joaquina de Vedruna de Mas
Blessed Louis Martin
Saint Lydwine
Blessed Manuel Lozano Garrido
Saint Mary MacKillop
Venerable Marthe Robin
Saint Rafqa
Saint Seraphina
Saint Servulus

Physical deformity

Saint Drogo
Saint Germaine Cousin
Saint Gilbert of Sempringham
Blessed Herman the Cripple
Saint Jeanne de Valois
Saint Leopold Mandic
Blessed Margaret of Castello
Blessed Michael Giedroyc
Saint Seraphina
Mother Teresa of Calcutta

Polycythemia rubra vera

Blessed Alojzije Stepinac

Poor health (general)

Saint Andre Bessette
Saint Angela of the Cross
Saint Arcangelo Tadini
Saint Benedict Joseph Labre
Blessed Carlos Manuel Rodriguez
Saint Caterina Volpicelli
Blessed Elias del Socorro Nieves
Blessed Frederic Ozanam
Saint Germaine Cousin
Saint Lucy Yi Zhenmei
Saint Marciano José (Filomeno López y López)
Saint Maria Cristina Brando
Blessed María del Transito de Jesus Sacramentado
Blessed Maria Euthymia Uffing
Blessed Marie Rivier
Blessed Mario Vergara
Padre Pio da Pietrelcina
Saint Rafael Arnáiz Barón
Saint René Goupil
Saint Richard Pampuri
Saint Robert Bellarmine
Venerable Solanus Casey
Saint Teresa of Avila
Mother Teresa of Calcutta
Blessed Teresa Mary of the Cross Manetti

Prolonged, chronic or incurable illness

Blessed Anna Katharina Emmerick
Saint Camillus de Lellis
Saint Josep Manyanet y Vives
Blessed Josepha Hendrina Stenmanns
Saint Laura Montoya Upegui
Saint Maria Guadalupe Garcia Zavala

Venerable Marthe Robin

Prostate problems

Blessed Jacques Ghazir Haddad

Respiratory disease and problems, pleurisy

Blessed Angela Truszkowska
Saint Francis Xavier Bianchi
Blessed Isidore of St Joseph de Loor
Blessed Josepha Hendrina Stenmanns
Blessed Mary Bartholomea Bagnesi
Padre Pio da Pietrelcina
Saint Richard Pampuri
Mother Teresa of Calcutta
Saint Zygmund Gorazdowski

Restricted growth, dwarfism

Saint Nicholas Owen?
Saint Jeanne de Valois
Saint John the Dwarf?
Saint Leopold Mandic
Blessed Margaret of Castello
Blessed Maria Euthymia Uffing
Blessed Michael Giedroyc

Rheumatism

Blessed Anita Cantieri
Venerable Brother Anthony Kowalczyk
Saint Mary MacKillop
Padre Pio da Pietrelcina

Rickets

Blessed Maria Euthymia Uffing
Blessed Marie Rivier

Sores, open wounds, ulcers, boils,

Saint Camillus de Lellis
Saint Charles Borromeo
Saint Genoveva Torres Morales
Saint Josep Manyanet y Vives
Saint Junípero Serra (Miguel José Serra)
Blessed Marcel Callo

Speech problems

Saint Anna Schaffer
Venerable Brother Anthony Kowalczyk
Saint Charles Borromeo
Blessed Herman the Cripple
Saint Leopold Mandic
Blessed Margaret Ebner
Saint Notker the Stammerer (Notcerus Balbulus)

Spinal problems, scoliosis, hunchback

Saint Filippo Smaldone
Blessed Herman the Cripple
Blessed James Alberione
Saint Jeanne de Valois
Saint José de Anchieta
Saint Joseph Cafasso
Blessed Luigi Boccardo
Blessed Margaret of Castello

Stomach and digestive ailments, peritonitis, ulcerative colitis

Saint Andre Bessette
Blessed Angela Salawa
Blessed Angela Truszkowska
Blessed Anita Cantieri

Blessed Carlos Manuel Rodriguez
Pope Saint John XXIII
Saint Leopold Mandic
Blessed Marcel Callo
Blessed Miguel Pro
Padre Pio da Pietrelcina
Saint Pompilio Maria Pirrotti
Blessed Teresa Mary of the Cross Manetti

Stroke

Saint Catherine of Siena
Saint Benedict Menni
Saint Francisco Coll y Guitart
Blessed Giovani Maria Boccardo
Saint Louis Martin
Saint Mary MacKillop
Saint Teresa of Avila
Saint Thomas Aquinas

Swollen legs

Saint Junípero Serra (Miguel José Serra)
Saint Robert Bellarmine

Thrombosis

Blessed Alojzije Stepinac

Tuberculosis

Blessed Angela Truszkowska
Blessed Augustus Czartoryski
Blessed Edmund Bojanowski
Blessed Elias del Socorro Nieves
Saint Gabriel of Our Lady of Sorrows
Blessed Giuseppina Nicoli
Blessed Joseph Marie Cassant

Blessed Louise Therese de Montaignac de Chauvance
Saint Maximilian Kolbe
Blessed Paolo Manna
Saint Rafqa
Saint Thérèse of Lisieux
Blessed Ulrika Nisch
Blessed Zepherin Namuncura

Tumour

Blessed Anita Cantieri
Saint Bertilla Boscardin
Blessed Teresa Mary of the Cross Manetti

Unspecified illness, severe pain

Saint Catherine of Siena
Blessed Eusebia Palomino Yenes
Blessed Ralph Ashley
Blessed Rosalie Rendu
Saint Teresa of Avila

Wheelchair user

Saint Katharine Drexel
Saint Laura Montoya Upegui
Venerable Manuel Aparici Navarro
Blessed Manuel Lozano Garrido
Blessed Sister Maria Giusepinna of Jesus Crucified
Saint Mary MacKillop
Mother Teresa of Calcutta

Resources

Benedictine saints and blessed

http://www.osb.org/gen/saints/bss1.html

Butler's Lives of the Saints

Arranged by feast days in months, London: Continuum.

Catholic Online

http://www.catholic.org/saints/

Carmelite saints and blessed

http://www.catholic-church.org/apcarmel/saints.htm

Dominican saints and blessed

http://communio.stblogs.org/index.php/category/dominican-saints-blesseds/

Ignatian saints and blessed

http://www.ignatianspirituality.com/ignatian-voices/all-saints-day/

New Advent, the Catholic Encyclopedia

http://www.newadvent.org/cathen/

Vatican Congregation for the Causes of Saints

http://www.vatican.va/roman_curia/congregations/csaints/index.htm

Lightning Source UK Ltd.
Milton Keynes UK
UKOW02f1636280616

277276UK00001B/6/P